Bombshells

UNITED

Volume 2
WAR BONDS

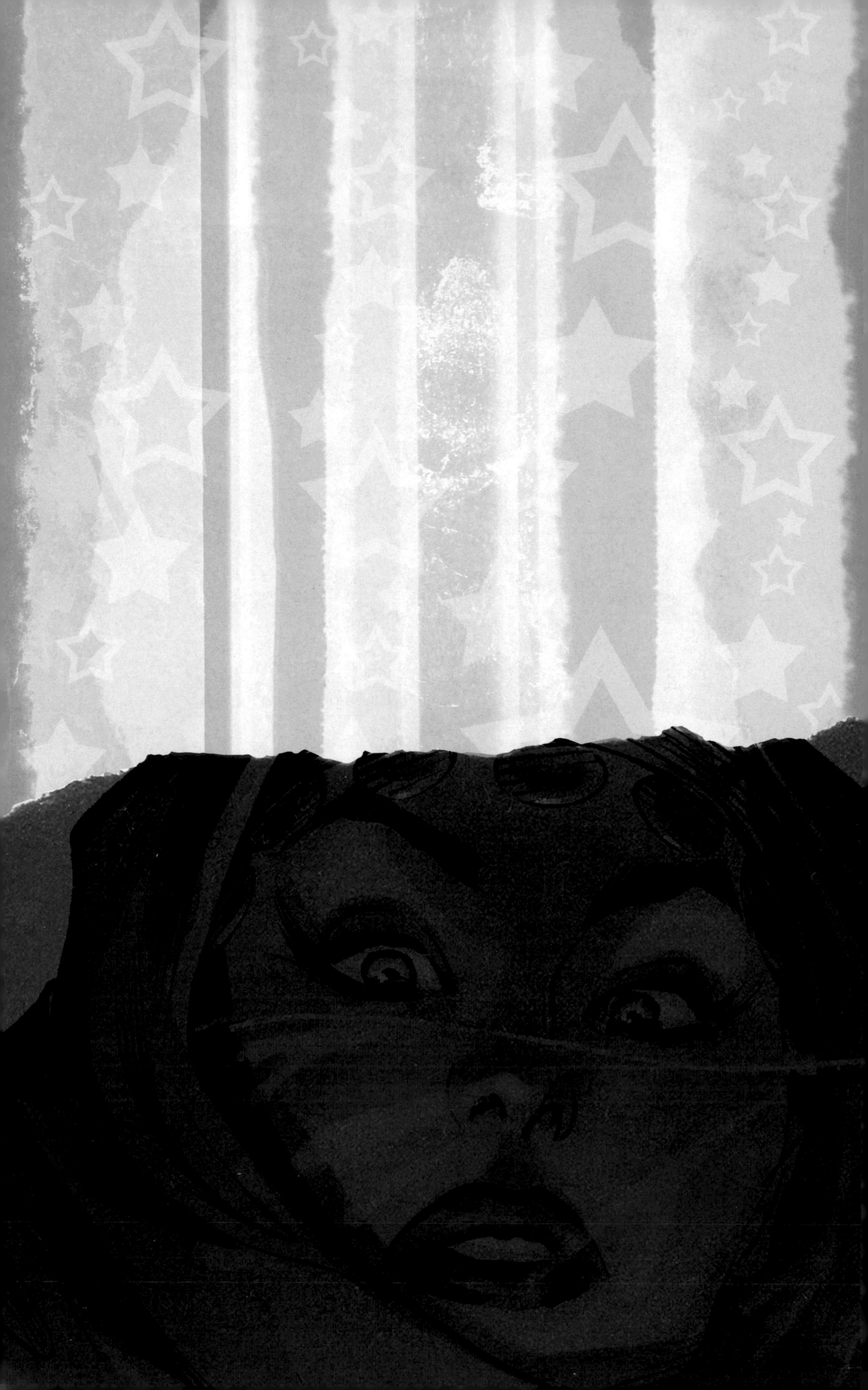

Bombshells

UNITED

Volume 2
WAR BONDS

MARGUERITE BENNETT
writer

MIRKA ANDOLFO
SIYA OUM
STEPHEN BYRNE
SANDY JARRELL
DAVID HAHN
RICHARD ORTIZ
artists

J. NANJAN
STEPHEN BYRNE
KELLY FITZPATRICK
colorists

WES ABBOTT
letterer

TERRY and RACHEL DODSON
collection cover artists

SUPERGIRL based on the characters created by JERRY SIEGEL and JOE SHUSTER.
By special arrangement with the Jerry Siegel family.

KRISTY QUINN JESSICA CHEN Editors – Original Series
JEB WOODARD Group Editor – Collected Editions
ERIKA ROTHBERG Editor – Collected Edition
STEVE COOK Design Director – Books
SHANNON STEWART Publication Design

BOB HARRAS Senior VP – Editor-in-Chief, DC Comics
PAT McCALLUM Executive Editor, DC Comics

DAN DiDIO Publisher * JIM LEE Publisher & Chief Creative Officer
AMIT DESAI Executive VP – Business & Marketing Strategy, Direct to Consumer & Global Franchise Management
BOBBIE CHASE VP & Executive Editor, Young Reader & Talent Development * MARK CHIARELLO Senior VP – Art, Design & Collected Editions
JOHN CUNNINGHAM Senior VP – Sales & Trade Marketing * BRIAR DARDEN VP – Business Affairs
ANNE DePIES Senior VP – Business Strategy, Finance & Administration * DON FALLETTI VP – Manufacturing Operations
LAWRENCE GANEM VP – Editorial Administration & Talent Relations * ALISON GILL Senior VP – Manufacturing & Operations
JASON GREENBERG VP – Business Strategy & Finance * HANK KANALZ Senior VP – Editorial Strategy & Administration
JAY KOGAN Senior VP – Legal Affairs * NICK J. NAPOLITANO VP – Manufacturing Administration
LISETTE OSTERLOH VP – Digital Marketing & Events * EDDIE SCANNELL VP – Consumer Marketing
COURTNEY SIMMONS Senior VP – Publicity & Communications * JIM (SKI) SOKOLOWSKI VP – Comic Book Specialty Sales & Trade Marketing
NANCY SPEARS VP – Mass, Book, Digital Sales & Trade Marketing * MICHELE R. WELLS VP – Content Strategy

BOMBSHELLS: UNITED VOL. 2: WAR BONDS

DC Comics, 2900 West Alameda Ave., Burbank, CA 91505
Printed by LSC Communications, Kendallville, IN, USA. 9/14/18. First Printing.
ISBN: 978-1-4012-8472-5

Library of Congress Cataloging-in-Publication Data is available.

PEFC Certified

Printed on paper from
sustainably managed
forests, controlled
sources

PEFC/29-31-337   www.pefc.org

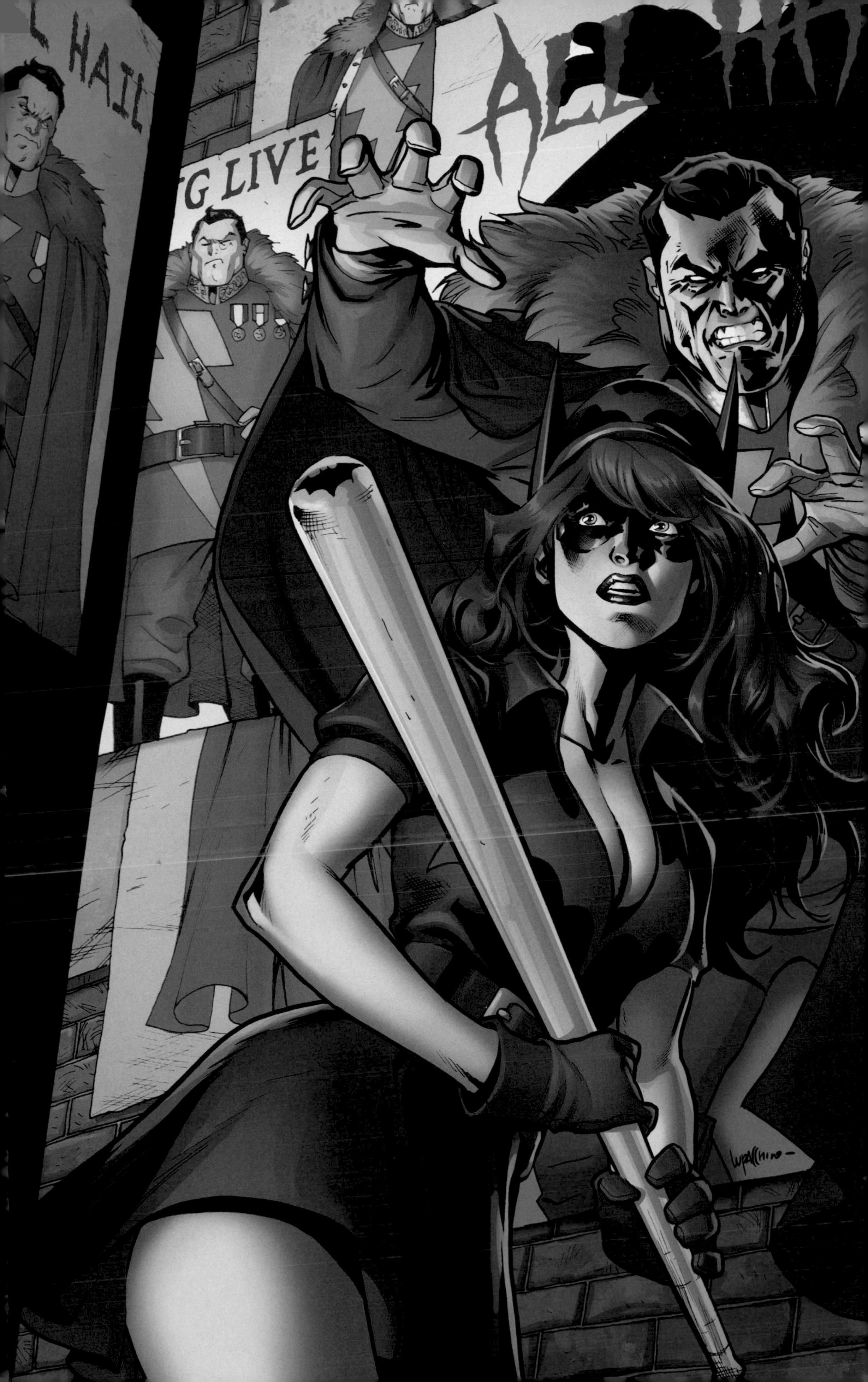

HAIL
G LIVE

WAR BONDS

PARTS ONE *and* TWO

Written by
MARGUERITE BENNETT

Art by
RICHARD ORTIZ

Colors by
J. NANJAN

Cover by
EMANUELA LUPACCHINO *and*
LAURA MARTIN

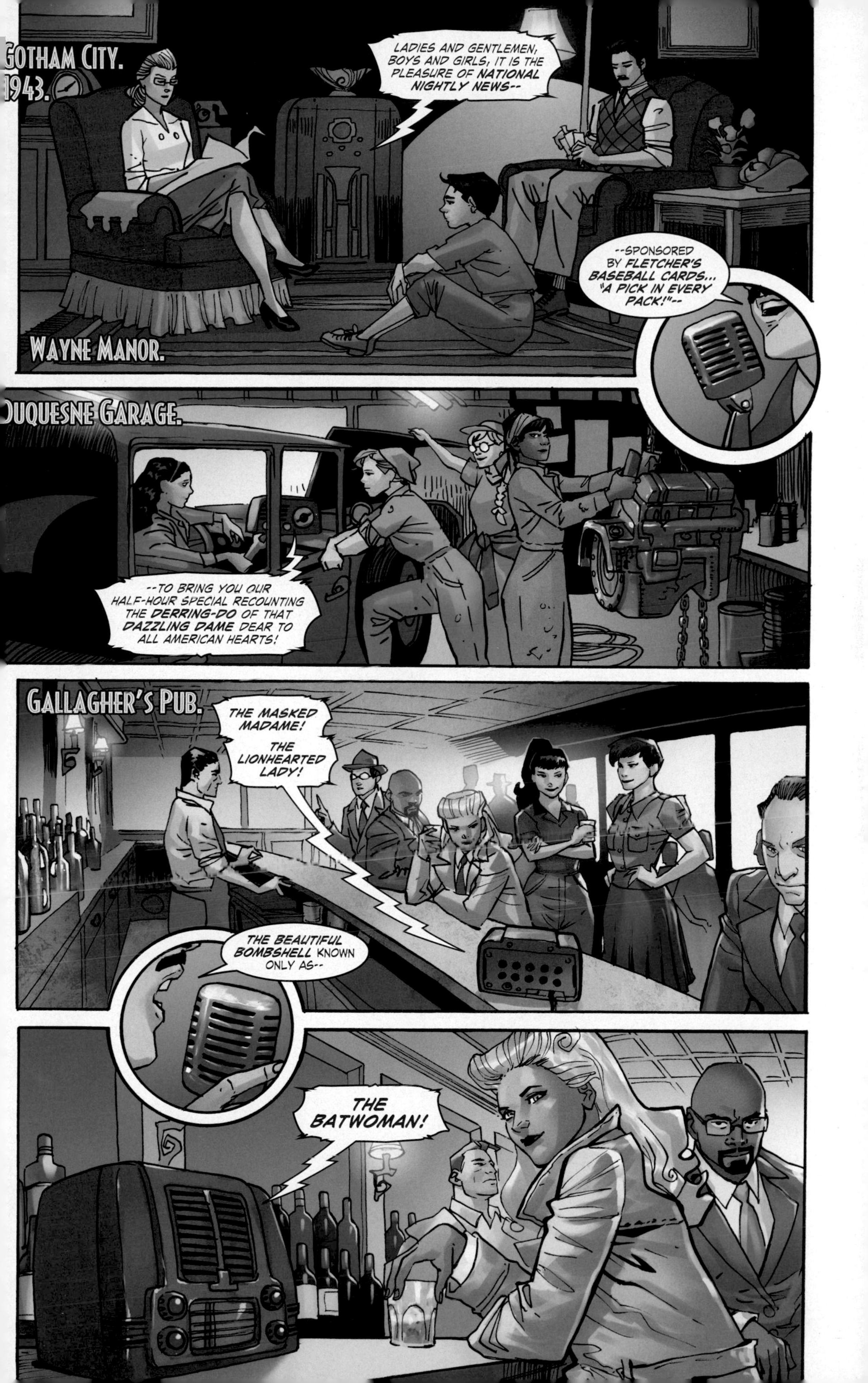
GOTHAM CITY. 1943.
LADIES AND GENTLEMEN, BOYS AND GIRLS, IT IS THE PLEASURE OF NATIONAL NIGHTLY NEWS--
WAYNE MANOR.
--SPONSORED BY FLETCHER'S BASEBALL CARDS... "A PICK IN EVERY PACK!"--
DUQUESNE GARAGE.
--TO BRING YOU OUR HALF-HOUR SPECIAL RECOUNTING THE DERRING-DO OF THAT DAZZLING DAME DEAR TO ALL AMERICAN HEARTS!
GALLAGHER'S PUB.
THE MASKED MADAME!
THE LIONHEARTED LADY!
THE BEAUTIFUL BOMBSHELL KNOWN ONLY AS--
THE BATWOMAN!

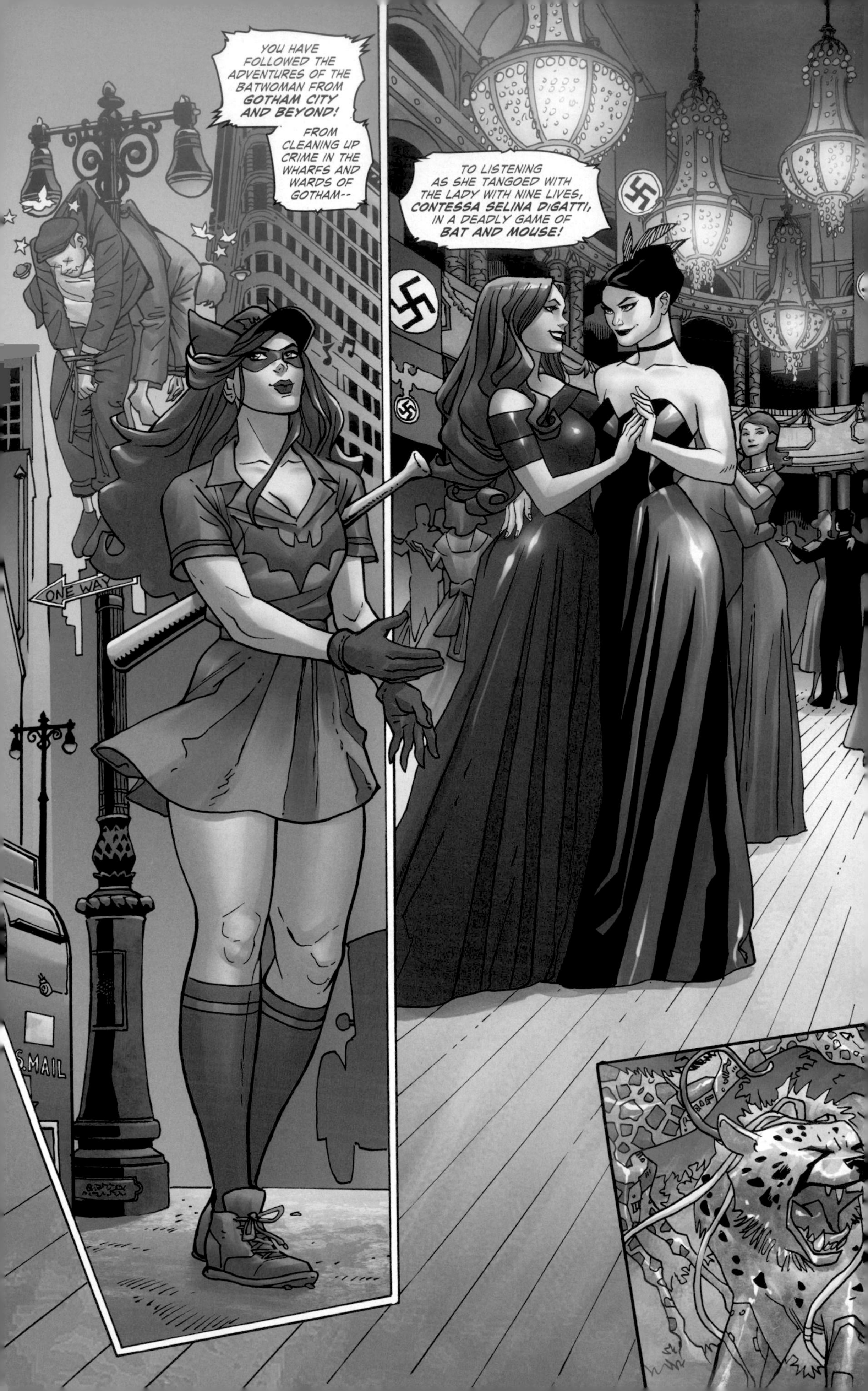
YOU HAVE FOLLOWED THE ADVENTURES OF THE BATWOMAN FROM GOTHAM CITY AND BEYOND!
FROM CLEANING UP CRIME IN THE WHARFS AND WARDS OF GOTHAM--
TO LISTENING AS SHE TANGOED WITH THE LADY WITH NINE LIVES, CONTESSA SELINA DIGATTI, IN A DEADLY GAME OF BAT AND MOUSE!
ONE WAY
S. MAIL

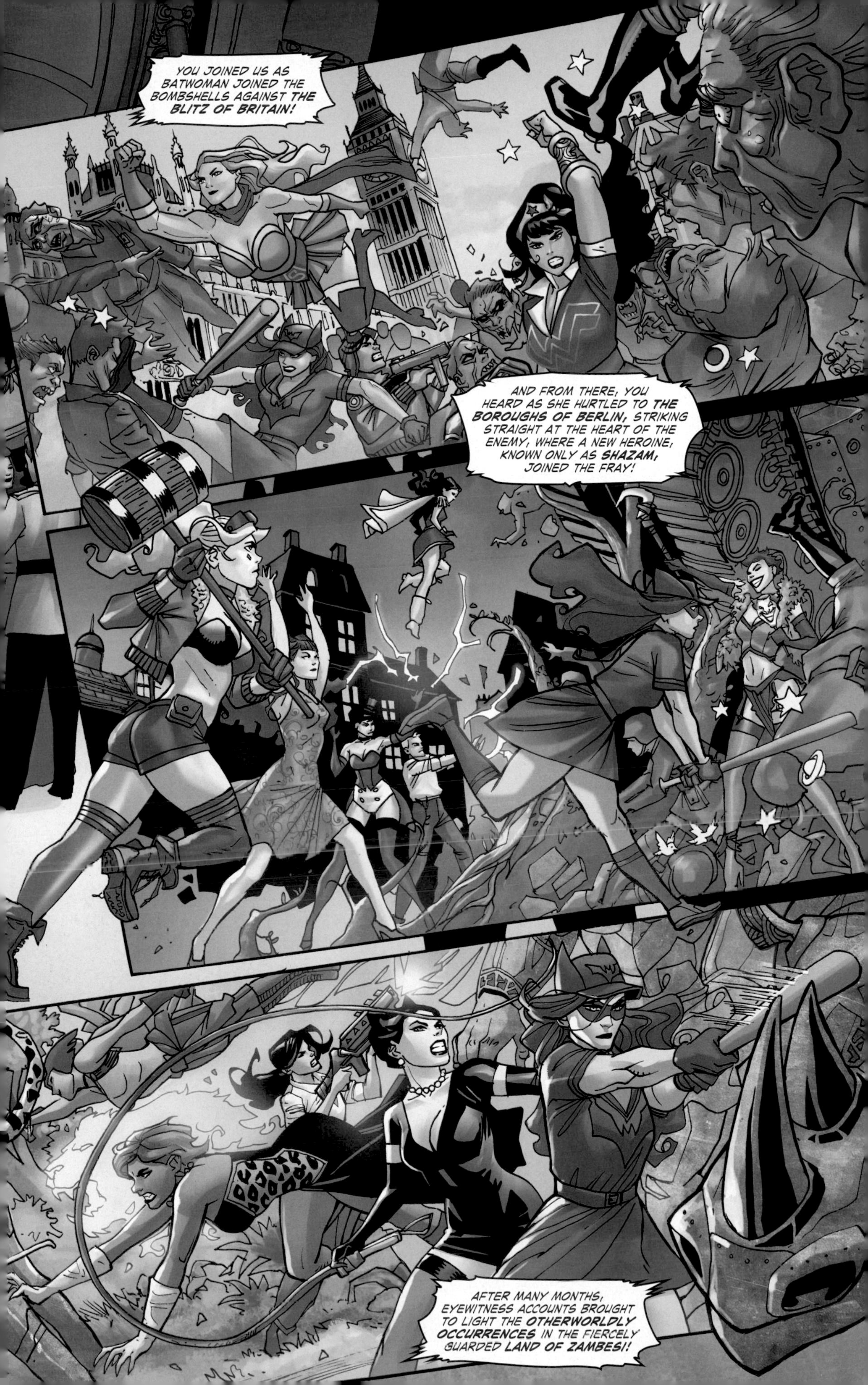
YOU JOINED US AS BATWOMAN JOINED THE BOMBSHELLS AGAINST **THE BLITZ OF BRITAIN!**
AND FROM THERE, YOU HEARD AS SHE HURTLED TO **THE BOROUGHS OF BERLIN,** STRIKING STRAIGHT AT THE HEART OF THE ENEMY, WHERE A NEW HEROINE, KNOWN ONLY AS **SHAZAM,** JOINED THE FRAY!
AFTER MANY MONTHS, EYEWITNESS ACCOUNTS BROUGHT TO LIGHT THE **OTHERWORLDLY OCCURRENCES** IN THE FIERCELY GUARDED **LAND OF ZAMBESI!**

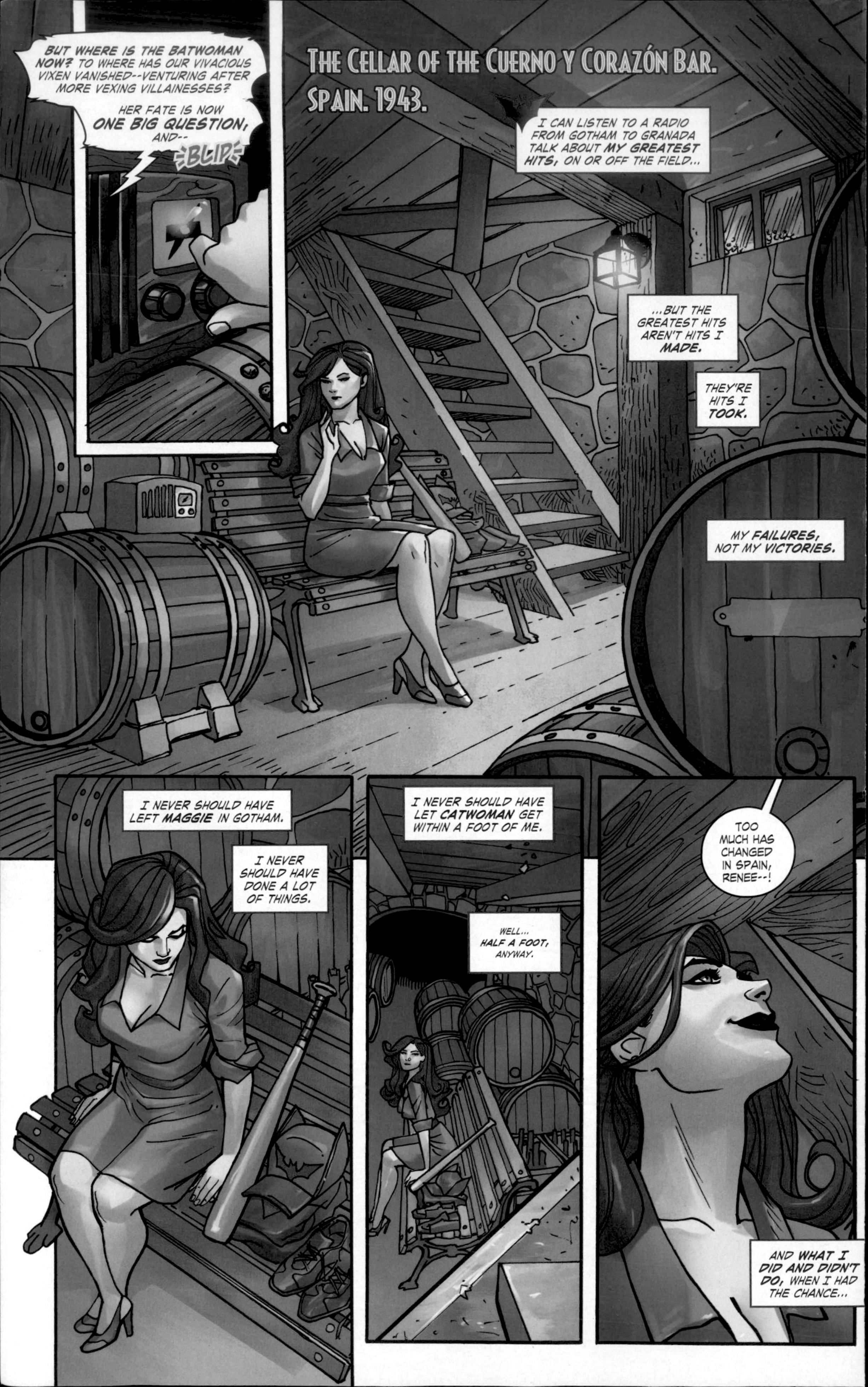
BUT WHERE IS THE BATWOMAN NOW? TO WHERE HAS OUR VIVACIOUS VIXEN VANISHED--VENTURING AFTER MORE VEXING VILLAINESSES?
HER FATE IS NOW ONE BIG QUESTION, AND--
BLIP
The Cellar of the Cuerno y Corazón Bar.
Spain. 1943.
I CAN LISTEN TO A RADIO FROM GOTHAM TO GRANADA TALK ABOUT MY GREATEST HITS, ON OR OFF THE FIELD...
...BUT THE GREATEST HITS AREN'T HITS I MADE.
THEY'RE HITS I TOOK.
MY FAILURES, NOT MY VICTORIES.
I NEVER SHOULD HAVE LEFT MAGGIE IN GOTHAM.
I NEVER SHOULD HAVE DONE A LOT OF THINGS.
I NEVER SHOULD HAVE LET CATWOMAN GET WITHIN A FOOT OF ME.
WELL... HALF A FOOT, ANYWAY.
TOO MUCH HAS CHANGED IN SPAIN, RENEE--!
AND WHAT I DID AND DIDN'T DO, WHEN I HAD THE CHANCE...

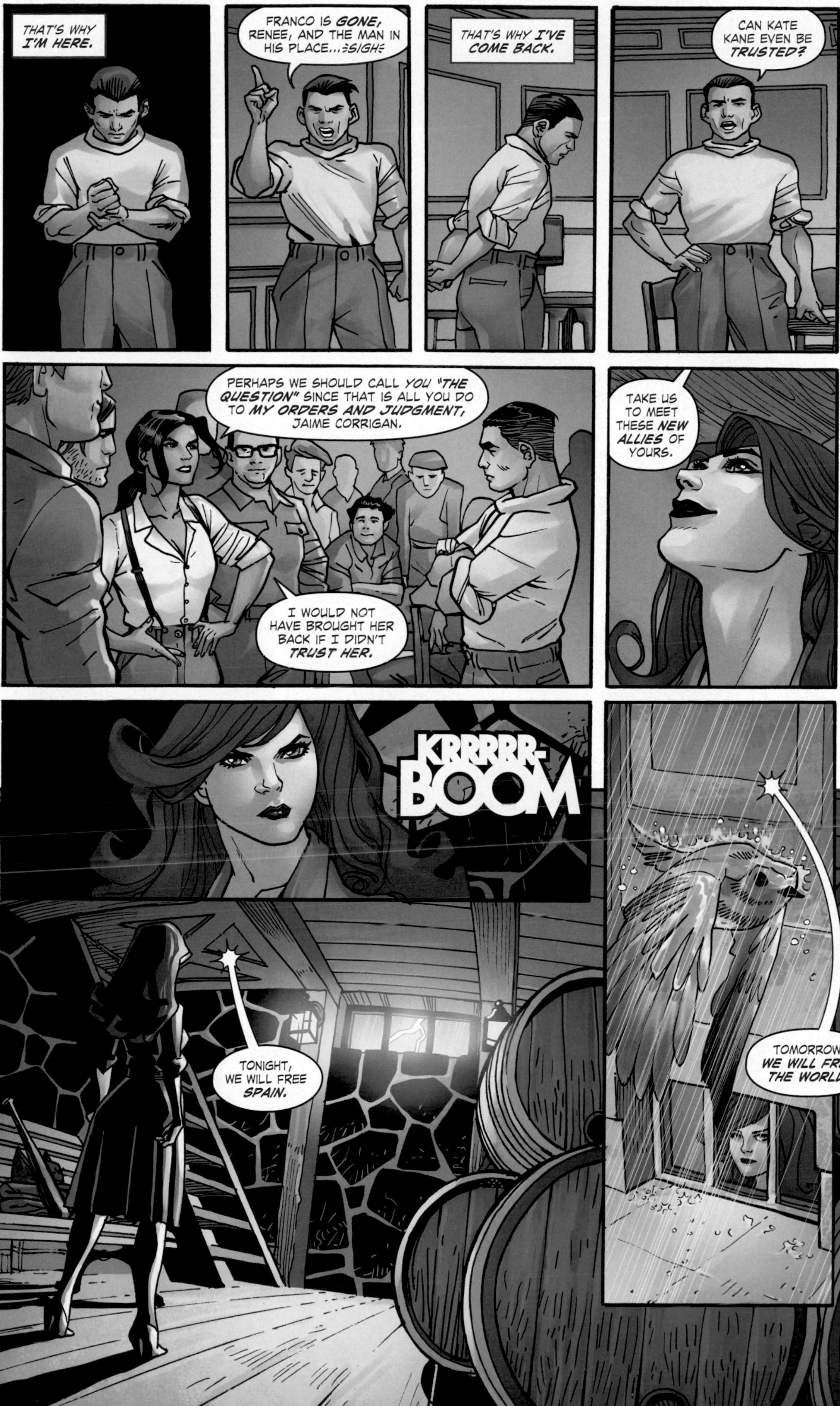
THAT'S WHY I'M HERE.
FRANCO IS GONE, RENEE, AND THE MAN IN HIS PLACE... *SIGH*
THAT'S WHY I'VE COME BACK.
CAN KATE KANE EVEN BE TRUSTED?
PERHAPS WE SHOULD CALL YOU "THE QUESTION" SINCE THAT IS ALL YOU DO TO MY ORDERS AND JUDGMENT, JAIME CORRIGAN.
I WOULD NOT HAVE BROUGHT HER BACK IF I DIDN'T TRUST HER.
TAKE US TO MEET THESE NEW ALLIES OF YOURS.
KRRRRR-BOOM
TONIGHT, WE WILL FREE SPAIN.
TOMORROW, WE WILL FREE THE WORLD.

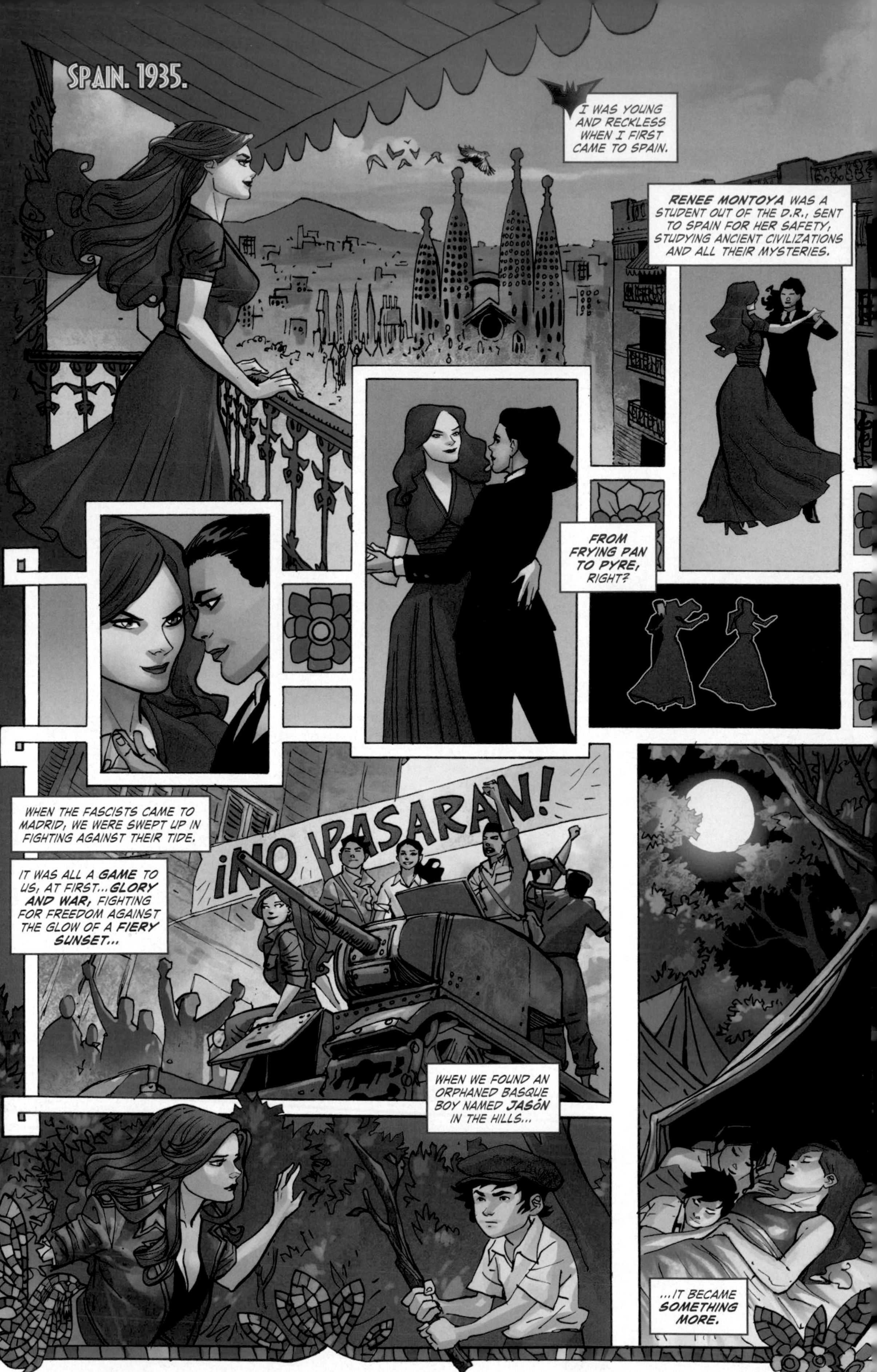
SPAIN. 1935.
I WAS YOUNG AND RECKLESS WHEN I FIRST CAME TO SPAIN.
RENEE MONTOYA WAS A STUDENT OUT OF THE D.R., SENT TO SPAIN FOR HER SAFETY, STUDYING ANCIENT CIVILIZATIONS AND ALL THEIR MYSTERIES.
FROM FRYING PAN TO PYRE, RIGHT?
WHEN THE FASCISTS CAME TO MADRID, WE WERE SWEPT UP IN FIGHTING AGAINST THEIR TIDE.
¡NO PASARAN!
IT WAS ALL A GAME TO US, AT FIRST...GLORY AND WAR, FIGHTING FOR FREEDOM AGAINST THE GLOW OF A FIERY SUNSET...
WHEN WE FOUND AN ORPHANED BASQUE BOY NAMED JASÓN IN THE HILLS...
...IT BECAME SOMETHING MORE.

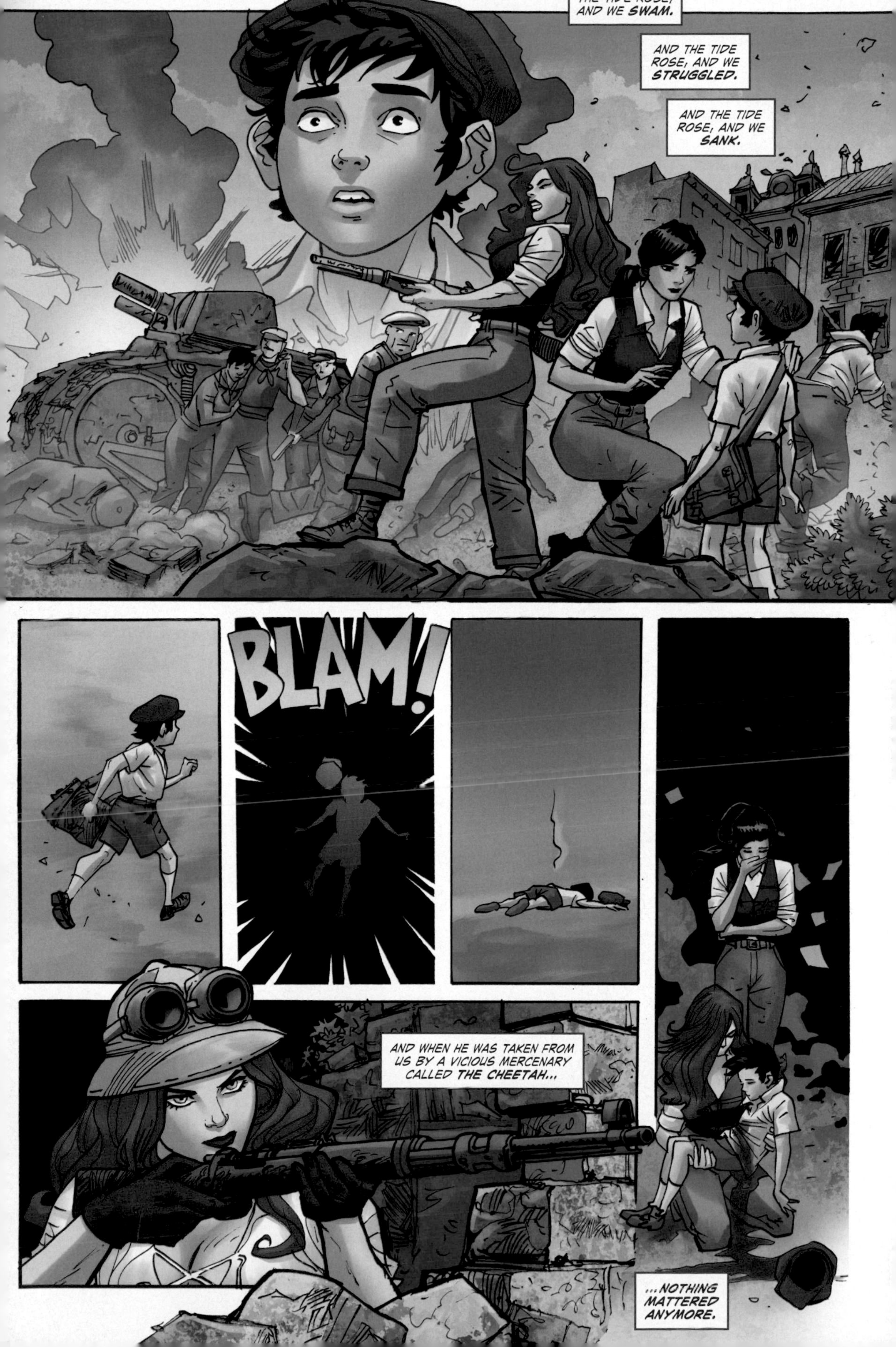
THE TIDE ROSE, AND WE SWAM.
AND THE TIDE ROSE, AND WE STRUGGLED.
AND THE TIDE ROSE, AND WE SANK.
BLAM!
AND WHEN HE WAS TAKEN FROM US BY A VICIOUS MERCENARY CALLED THE CHEETAH...
...NOTHING MATTERED ANYMORE.

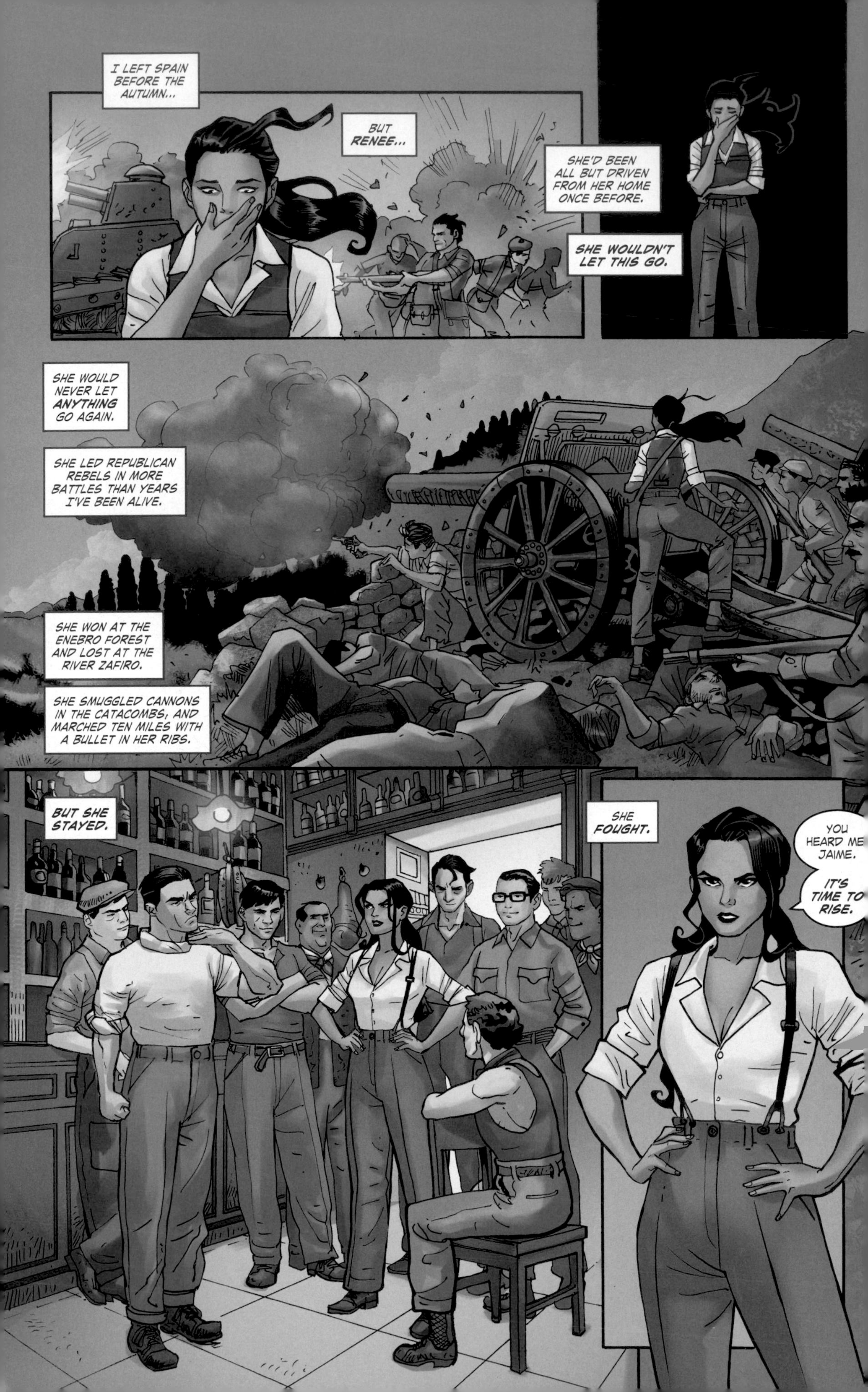
I LEFT SPAIN BEFORE THE AUTUMN...
BUT RENEE...
SHE'D BEEN ALL BUT DRIVEN FROM HER HOME ONCE BEFORE.
SHE WOULDN'T LET THIS GO.
SHE WOULD NEVER LET ANYTHING GO AGAIN.
SHE LED REPUBLICAN REBELS IN MORE BATTLES THAN YEARS I'VE BEEN ALIVE.
SHE WON AT THE ENEBRO FOREST AND LOST AT THE RIVER ZAFIRO.
SHE SMUGGLED CANNONS IN THE CATACOMBS, AND MARCHED TEN MILES WITH A BULLET IN HER RIBS.
BUT SHE STAYED.
SHE FOUGHT.
YOU HEARD ME JAIME.
IT'S TIME TO RISE.

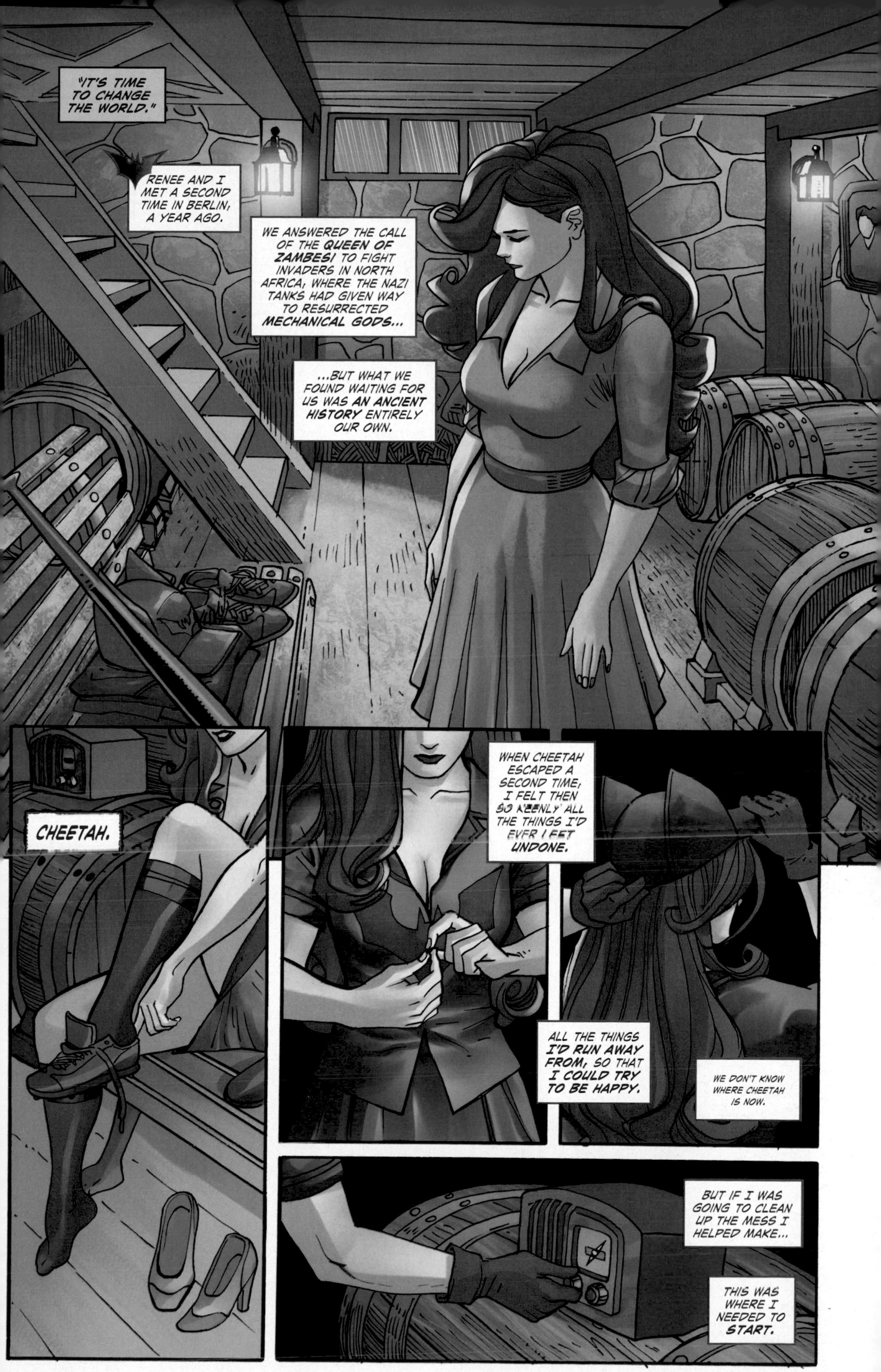
"IT'S TIME TO CHANGE THE WORLD."
RENEE AND I MET A SECOND TIME IN BERLIN, A YEAR AGO.
WE ANSWERED THE CALL OF THE QUEEN OF ZAMBESI TO FIGHT INVADERS IN NORTH AFRICA, WHERE THE NAZI TANKS HAD GIVEN WAY TO RESURRECTED MECHANICAL GODS...
...BUT WHAT WE FOUND WAITING FOR US WAS AN ANCIENT HISTORY ENTIRELY OUR OWN.
CHEETAH.
WHEN CHEETAH ESCAPED A SECOND TIME, I FELT THEN SO KEENLY ALL THE THINGS I'D EVER LEFT UNDONE.
ALL THE THINGS I'D RUN AWAY FROM, SO THAT I COULD TRY TO BE HAPPY.
WE DON'T KNOW WHERE CHEETAH IS NOW.
BUT IF I WAS GOING TO CLEAN UP THE MESS I HELPED MAKE...
THIS WAS WHERE I NEEDED TO START.

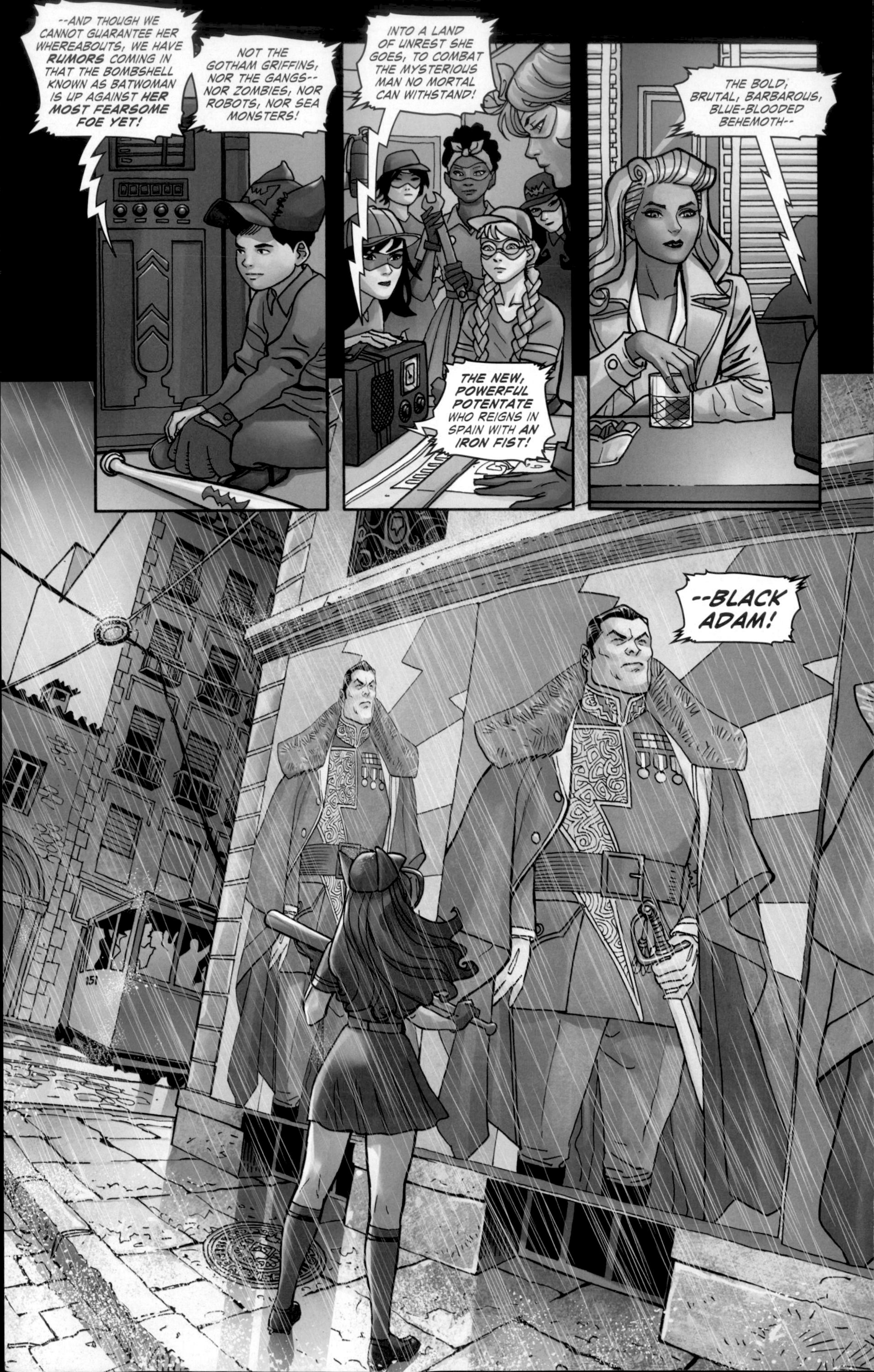
--AND THOUGH WE CANNOT GUARANTEE HER WHEREABOUTS, WE HAVE RUMORS COMING IN THAT THE BOMBSHELL KNOWN AS BATWOMAN IS UP AGAINST HER MOST FEARSOME FOE YET!
NOT THE GOTHAM GRIFFINS, NOR THE GANGS-- NOR ZOMBIES, NOR ROBOTS, NOR SEA MONSTERS!
INTO A LAND OF UNREST SHE GOES, TO COMBAT THE MYSTERIOUS MAN NO MORTAL CAN WITHSTAND!
THE NEW, POWERFUL POTENTATE WHO REIGNS IN SPAIN WITH AN IRON FIST!
THE BOLD, BRUTAL, BARBAROUS, BLUE-BLOODED BEHEMOTH--
--BLACK ADAM!

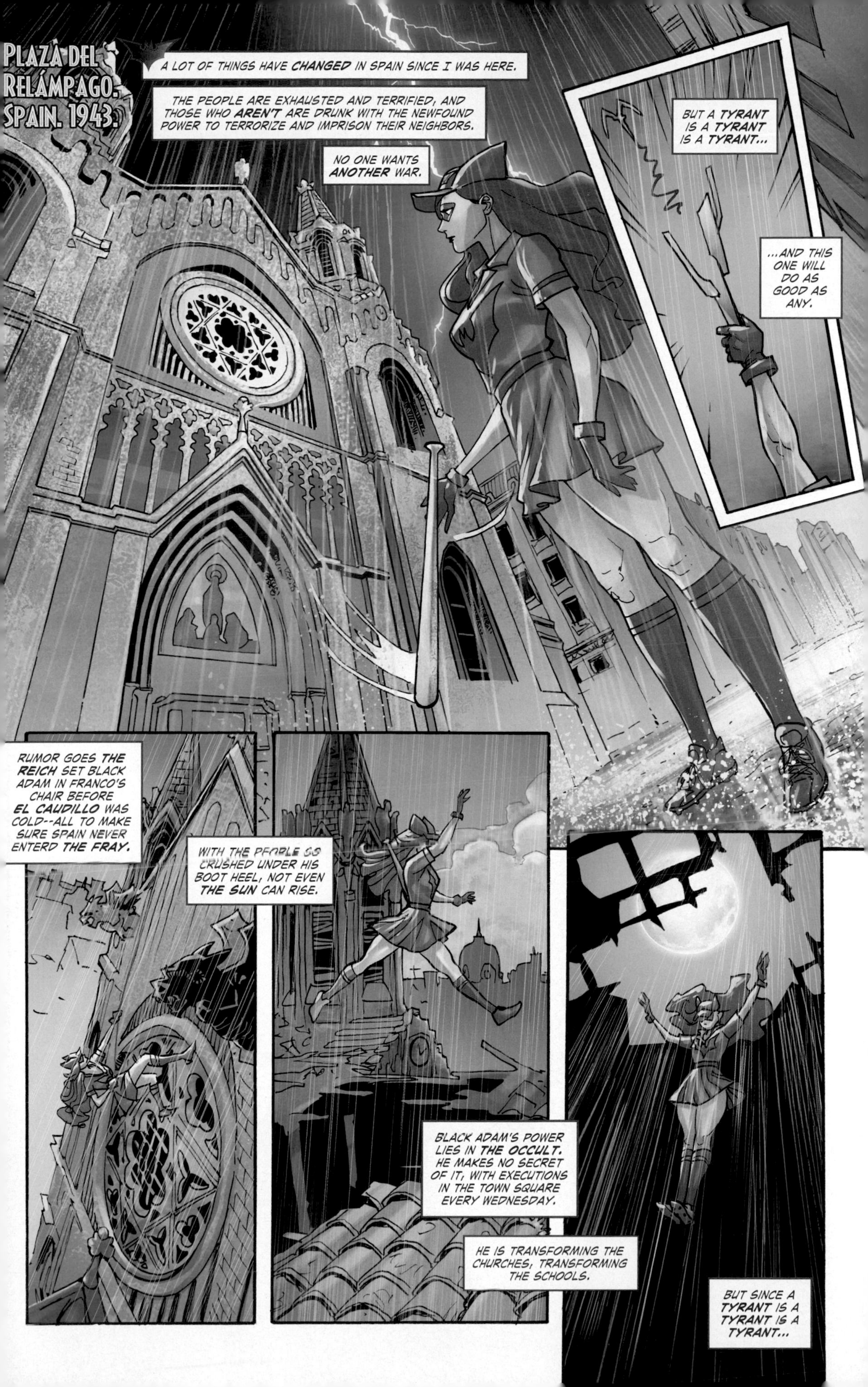
PLAZA DEL RELÁMPAGO. SPAIN. 1943.
A LOT OF THINGS HAVE CHANGED IN SPAIN SINCE I WAS HERE.
THE PEOPLE ARE EXHAUSTED AND TERRIFIED, AND THOSE WHO AREN'T ARE DRUNK WITH THE NEWFOUND POWER TO TERRORIZE AND IMPRISON THEIR NEIGHBORS.
NO ONE WANTS ANOTHER WAR.
BUT A TYRANT IS A TYRANT IS A TYRANT...
...AND THIS ONE WILL DO AS GOOD AS ANY.
RUMOR GOES THE REICH SET BLACK ADAM IN FRANCO'S CHAIR BEFORE EL CAUDILLO WAS COLD--ALL TO MAKE SURE SPAIN NEVER ENTERD THE FRAY.
WITH THE PEOPLE SO CRUSHED UNDER HIS BOOT HEEL, NOT EVEN THE SUN CAN RISE.
BLACK ADAM'S POWER LIES IN THE OCCULT. HE MAKES NO SECRET OF IT, WITH EXECUTIONS IN THE TOWN SQUARE EVERY WEDNESDAY.
HE IS TRANSFORMING THE CHURCHES, TRANSFORMING THE SCHOOLS.
BUT SINCE A TYRANT IS A TYRANT IS A TYRANT...

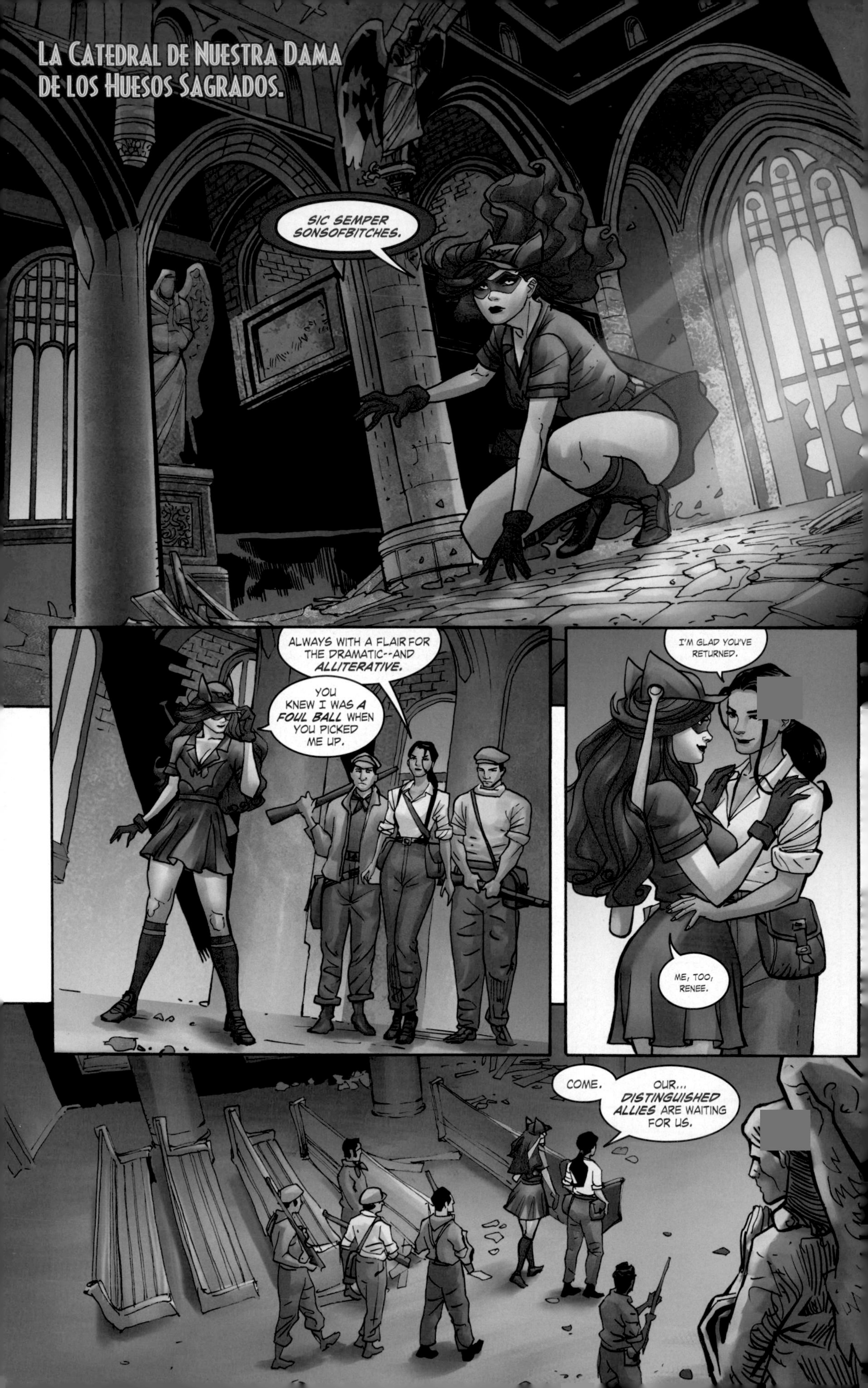
La Catedral de Nuestra Dama de los Huesos Sagrados.
SIC SEMPER SONSOFBITCHES.
ALWAYS WITH A FLAIR FOR THE DRAMATIC--AND ALLITERATIVE.
YOU KNEW I WAS A FOUL BALL WHEN YOU PICKED ME UP.
I'M GLAD YOU'VE RETURNED.
ME, TOO, RENEE.
COME.
OUR... DISTINGUISHED ALLIES ARE WAITING FOR US.

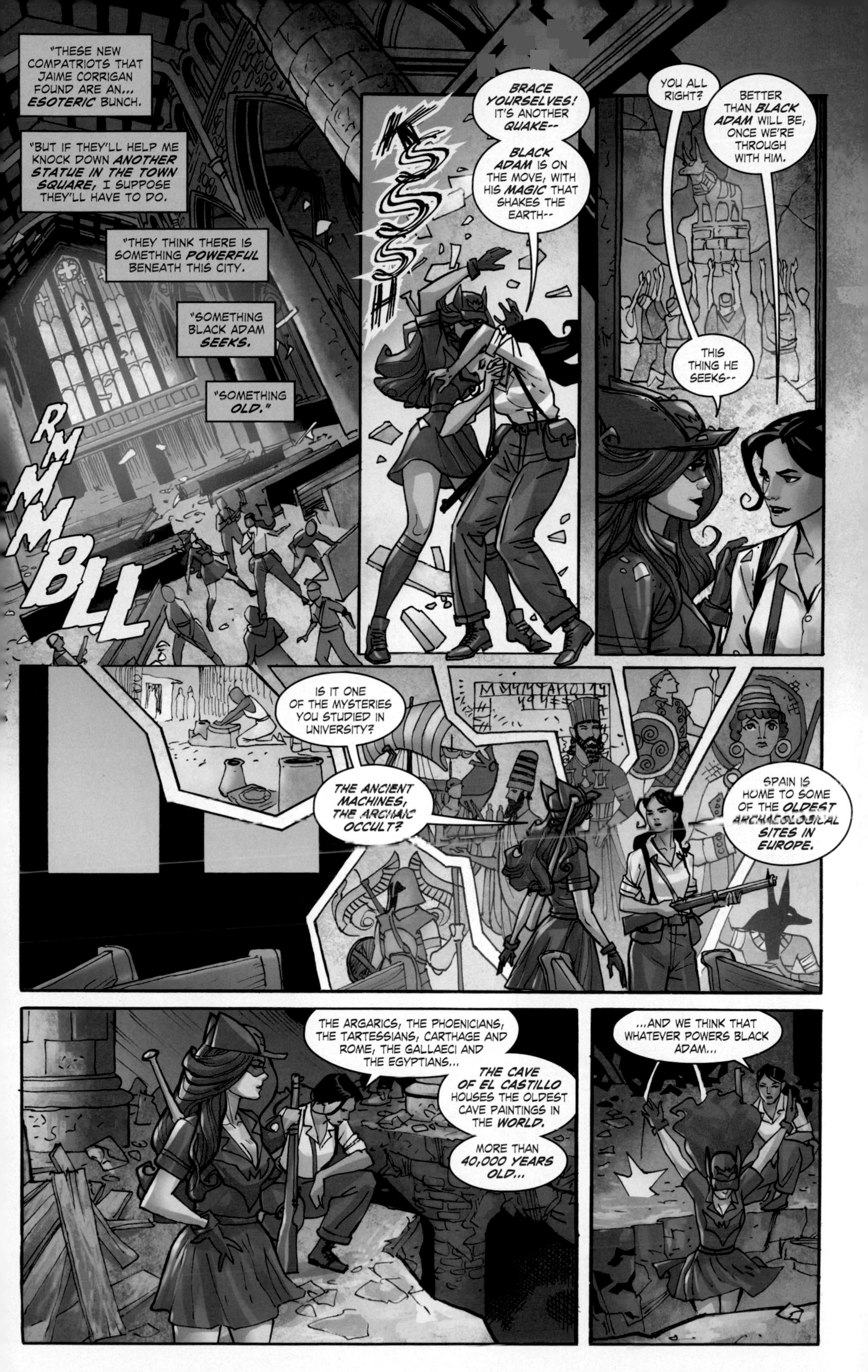
"THESE NEW COMPATRIOTS THAT JAIME CORRIGAN FOUND ARE AN... ESOTERIC BUNCH.
"BUT IF THEY'LL HELP ME KNOCK DOWN ANOTHER STATUE IN THE TOWN SQUARE, I SUPPOSE THEY'LL HAVE TO DO.
"THEY THINK THERE IS SOMETHING POWERFUL BENEATH THIS CITY.
"SOMETHING BLACK ADAM SEEKS.
"SOMETHING OLD."
RMMMBLL
KSSSH
BRACE YOURSELVES! IT'S ANOTHER QUAKE--
BLACK ADAM IS ON THE MOVE, WITH HIS MAGIC THAT SHAKES THE EARTH--
YOU ALL RIGHT?
BETTER THAN BLACK ADAM WILL BE, ONCE WE'RE THROUGH WITH HIM.
THIS THING HE SEEKS--
IS IT ONE OF THE MYSTERIES YOU STUDIED IN UNIVERSITY?
THE ANCIENT MACHINES, THE ARCHAIC OCCULT?
SPAIN IS HOME TO SOME OF THE OLDEST ARCHAEOLOGICAL SITES IN EUROPE.
THE ARGARICS, THE PHOENICIANS, THE TARTESSIANS, CARTHAGE AND ROME, THE GALLAECI AND THE EGYPTIANS...
THE CAVE OF EL CASTILLO HOUSES THE OLDEST CAVE PAINTINGS IN THE WORLD.
MORE THAN 40,000 YEARS OLD...
...AND WE THINK THAT WHATEVER POWERS BLACK ADAM...

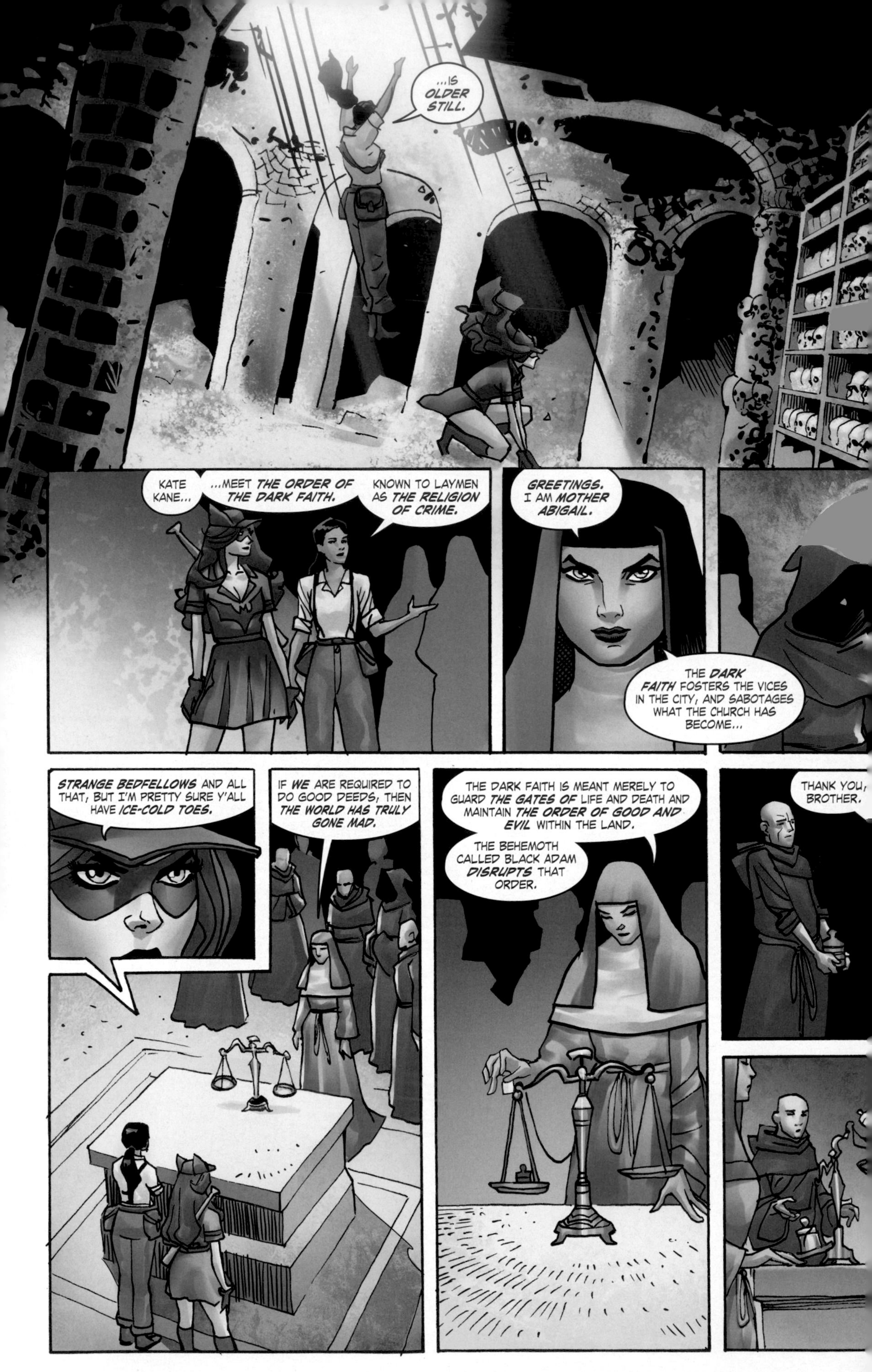
...IS OLDER STILL.
KATE KANE...
...MEET THE ORDER OF THE DARK FAITH.
KNOWN TO LAYMEN AS THE RELIGION OF CRIME.
GREETINGS. I AM MOTHER ABIGAIL.
THE DARK FAITH FOSTERS THE VICES IN THE CITY, AND SABOTAGES WHAT THE CHURCH HAS BECOME...
STRANGE BEDFELLOWS AND ALL THAT, BUT I'M PRETTY SURE Y'ALL HAVE ICE-COLD TOES.
IF WE ARE REQUIRED TO DO GOOD DEEDS, THEN THE WORLD HAS TRULY GONE MAD.
THE DARK FAITH IS MEANT MERELY TO GUARD THE GATES OF LIFE AND DEATH AND MAINTAIN THE ORDER OF GOOD AND EVIL WITHIN THE LAND.
THE BEHEMOTH CALLED BLACK ADAM DISRUPTS THAT ORDER.
THANK YOU, BROTHER.

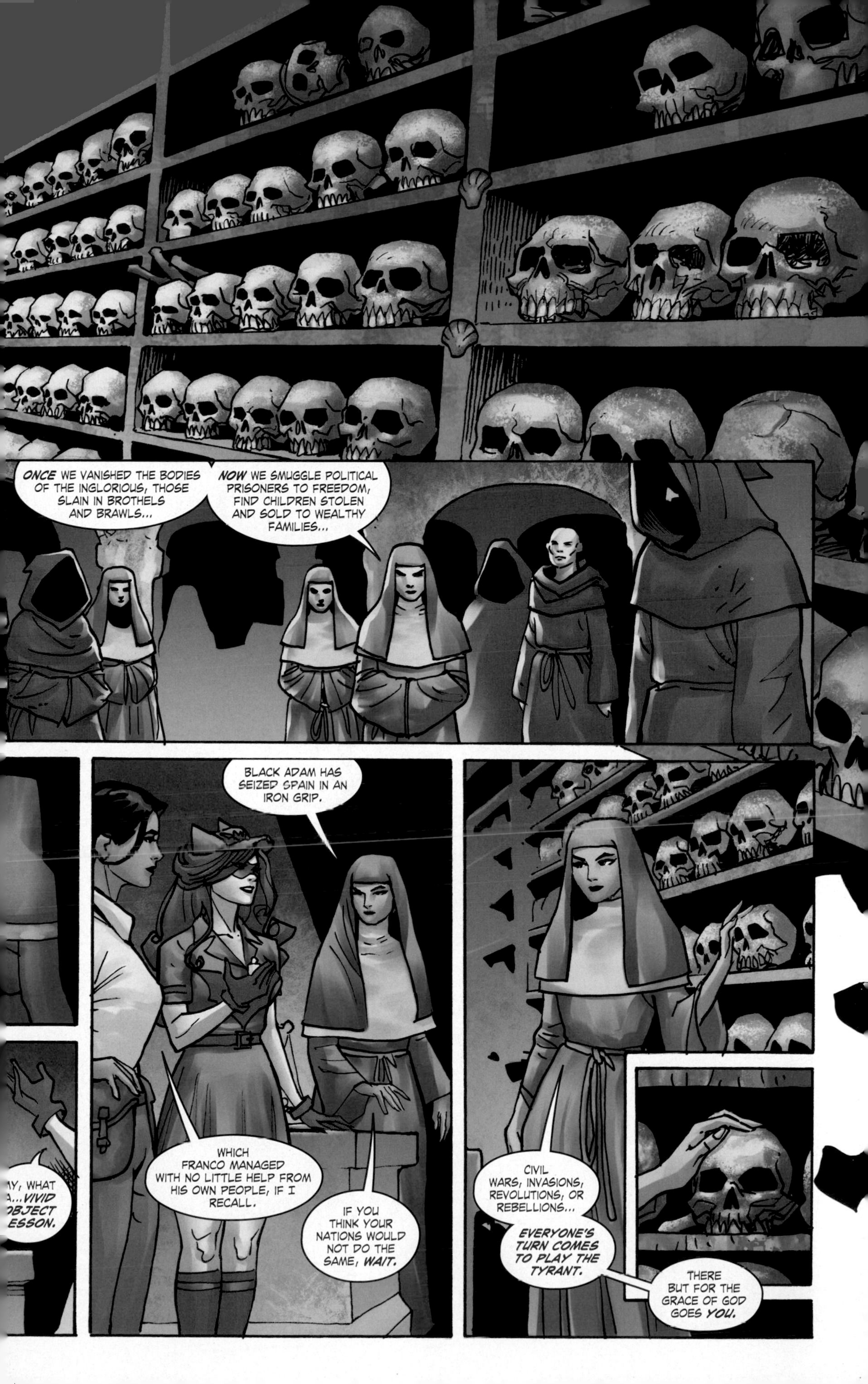
ONCE WE VANISHED THE BODIES OF THE INGLORIOUS, THOSE SLAIN IN BROTHELS AND BRAWLS...
NOW WE SMUGGLE POLITICAL PRISONERS TO FREEDOM, FIND CHILDREN STOLEN AND SOLD TO WEALTHY FAMILIES...
AY, WHAT A...VIVID OBJECT ESSON.
BLACK ADAM HAS SEIZED SPAIN IN AN IRON GRIP.
WHICH FRANCO MANAGED WITH NO LITTLE HELP FROM HIS OWN PEOPLE, IF I RECALL.
IF YOU THINK YOUR NATIONS WOULD NOT DO THE SAME, WAIT.
CIVIL WARS, INVASIONS, REVOLUTIONS, OR REBELLIONS...
EVERYONE'S TURN COMES TO PLAY THE TYRANT.
THERE BUT FOR THE GRACE OF GOD GOES YOU.

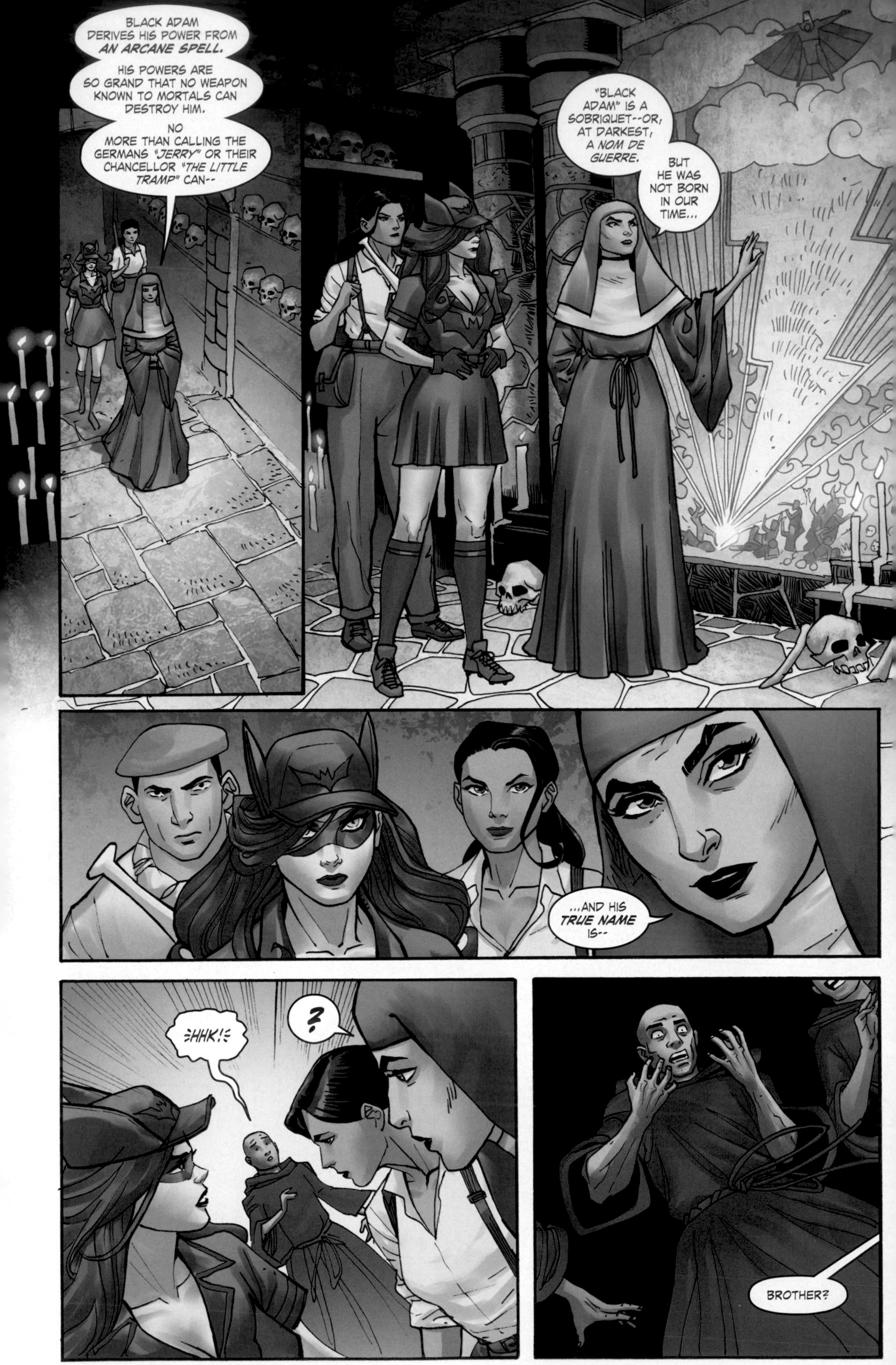
BLACK ADAM DERIVES HIS POWER FROM *AN ARCANE SPELL.*
HIS POWERS ARE SO GRAND THAT NO WEAPON KNOWN TO MORTALS CAN DESTROY HIM.
NO MORE THAN CALLING THE GERMANS *"JERRY"* OR THEIR CHANCELLOR *"THE LITTLE TRAMP"* CAN--
"BLACK ADAM" IS A SOBRIQUET--OR, AT DARKEST, A *NOM DE GUERRE.*
BUT HE WAS NOT BORN IN OUR TIME...
...AND HIS *TRUE NAME* IS--
HHK!
?
BROTHER?

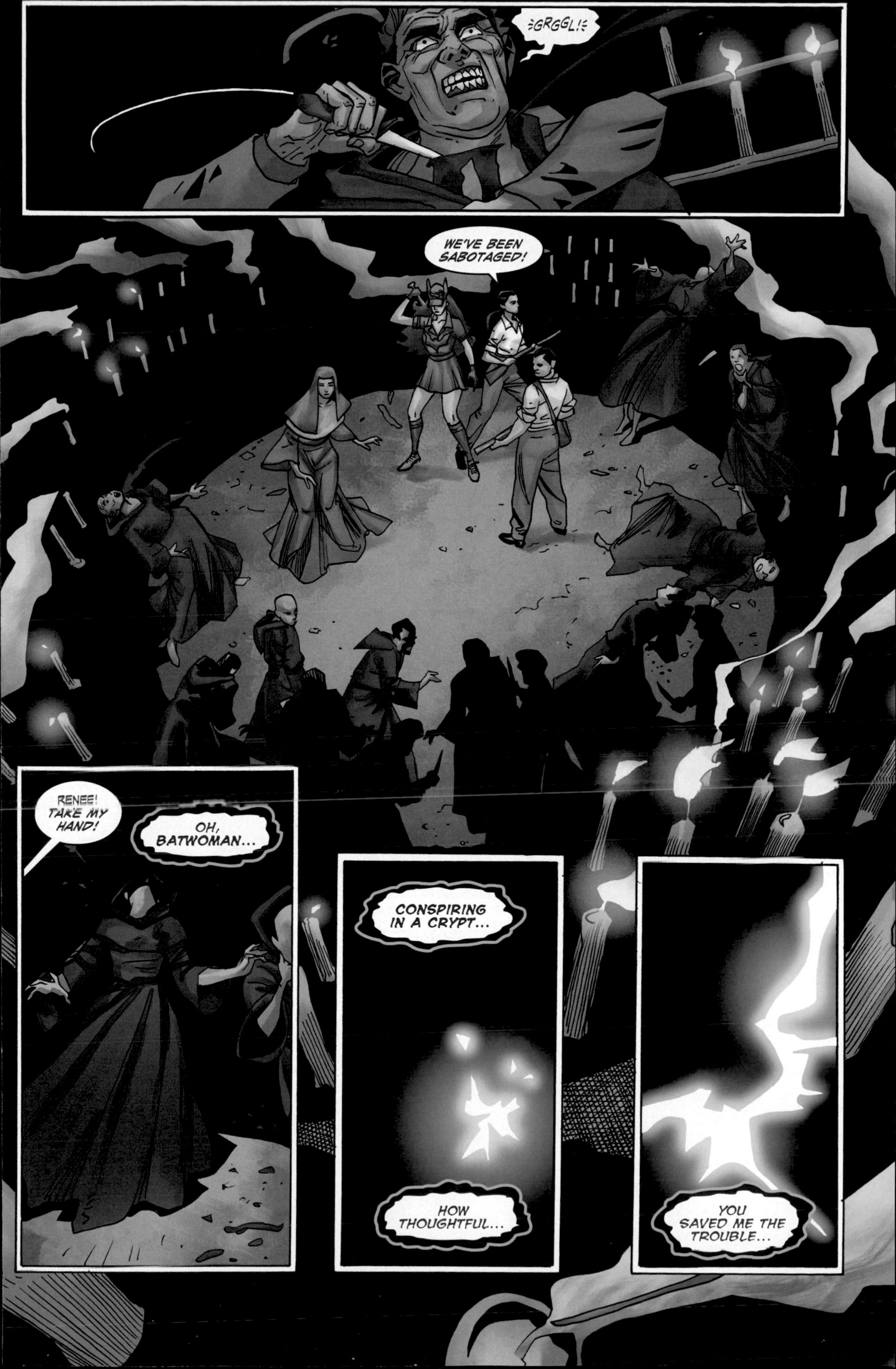
GRGGL!
WE'VE BEEN SABOTAGED!
RENEE! TAKE MY HAND!
OH, BATWOMAN...
CONSPIRING IN A CRYPT...
HOW THOUGHTFUL...
YOU SAVED ME THE TROUBLE...

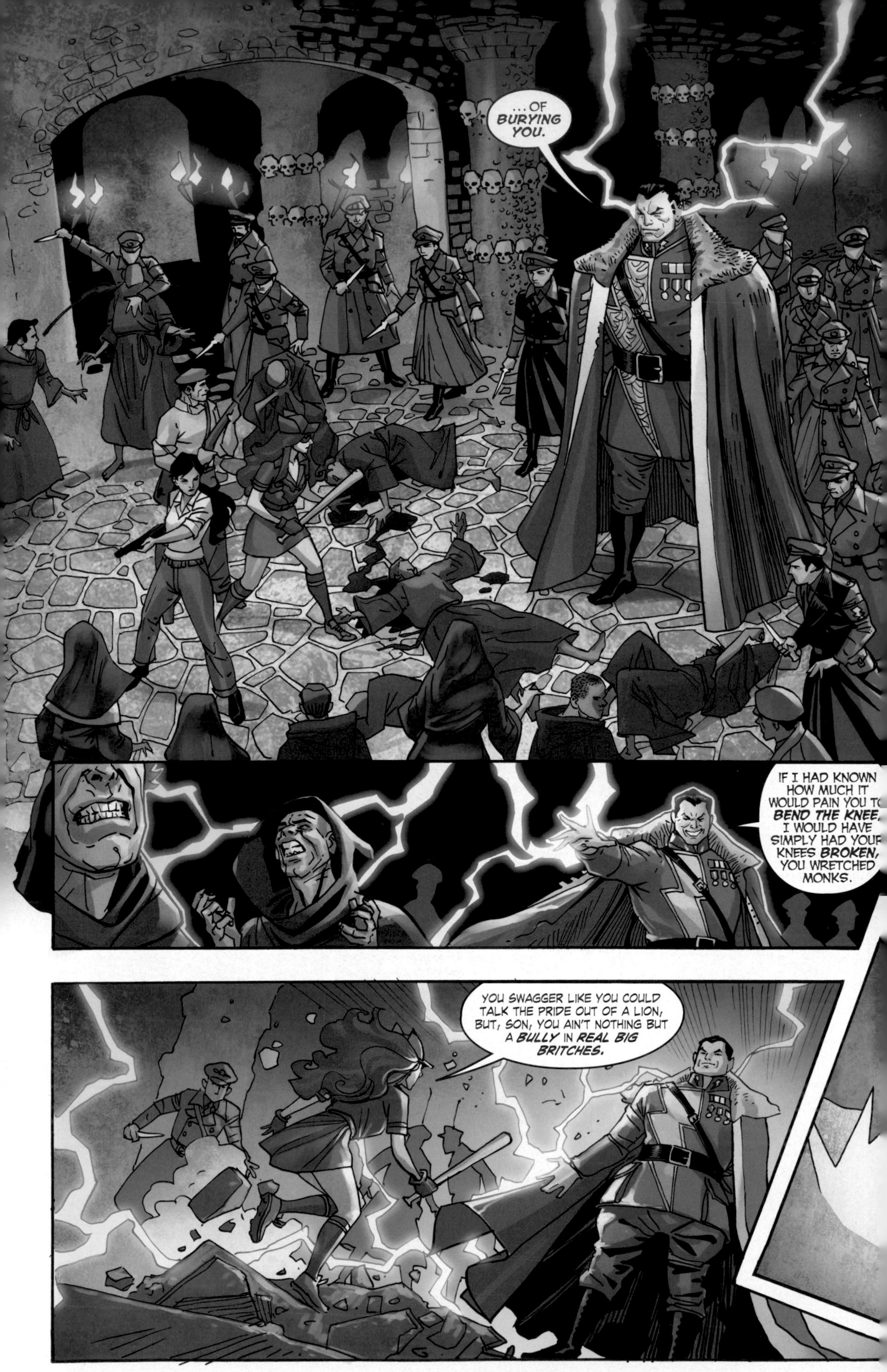

...OF BURYING YOU.
IF I HAD KNOWN HOW MUCH IT WOULD PAIN YOU TO BEND THE KNEE, I WOULD HAVE SIMPLY HAD YOUR KNEES BROKEN, YOU WRETCHED MONKS.
YOU SWAGGER LIKE YOU COULD TALK THE PRIDE OUT OF A LION, BUT, SON, YOU AIN'T NOTHING BUT A BULLY IN REAL BIG BRITCHES.

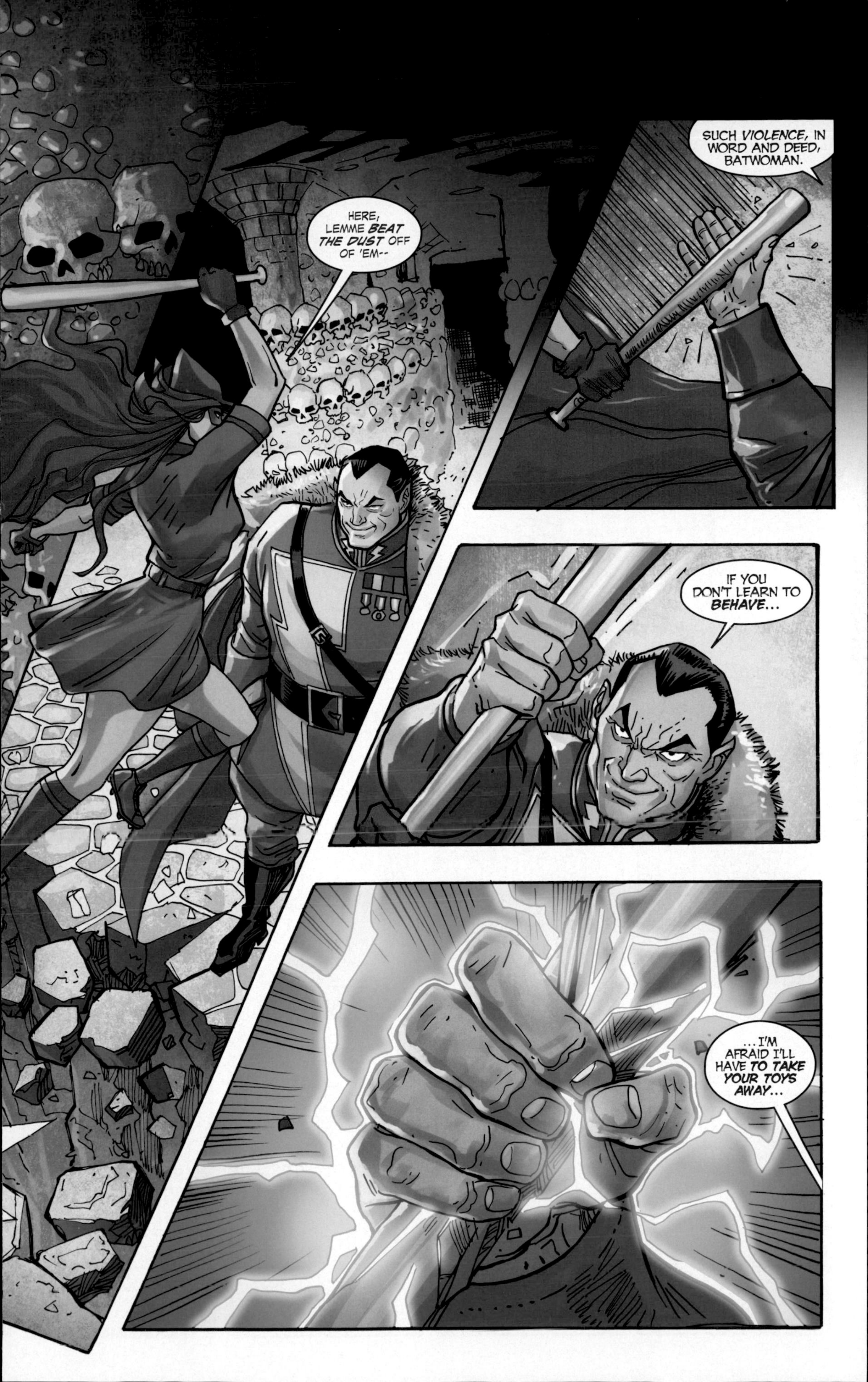
HERE, LEMME BEAT THE DUST OFF OF 'EM--
SUCH VIOLENCE, IN WORD AND DEED, BATWOMAN.
IF YOU DON'T LEARN TO BEHAVE...
...I'M AFRAID I'LL HAVE TO TAKE YOUR TOYS AWAY...

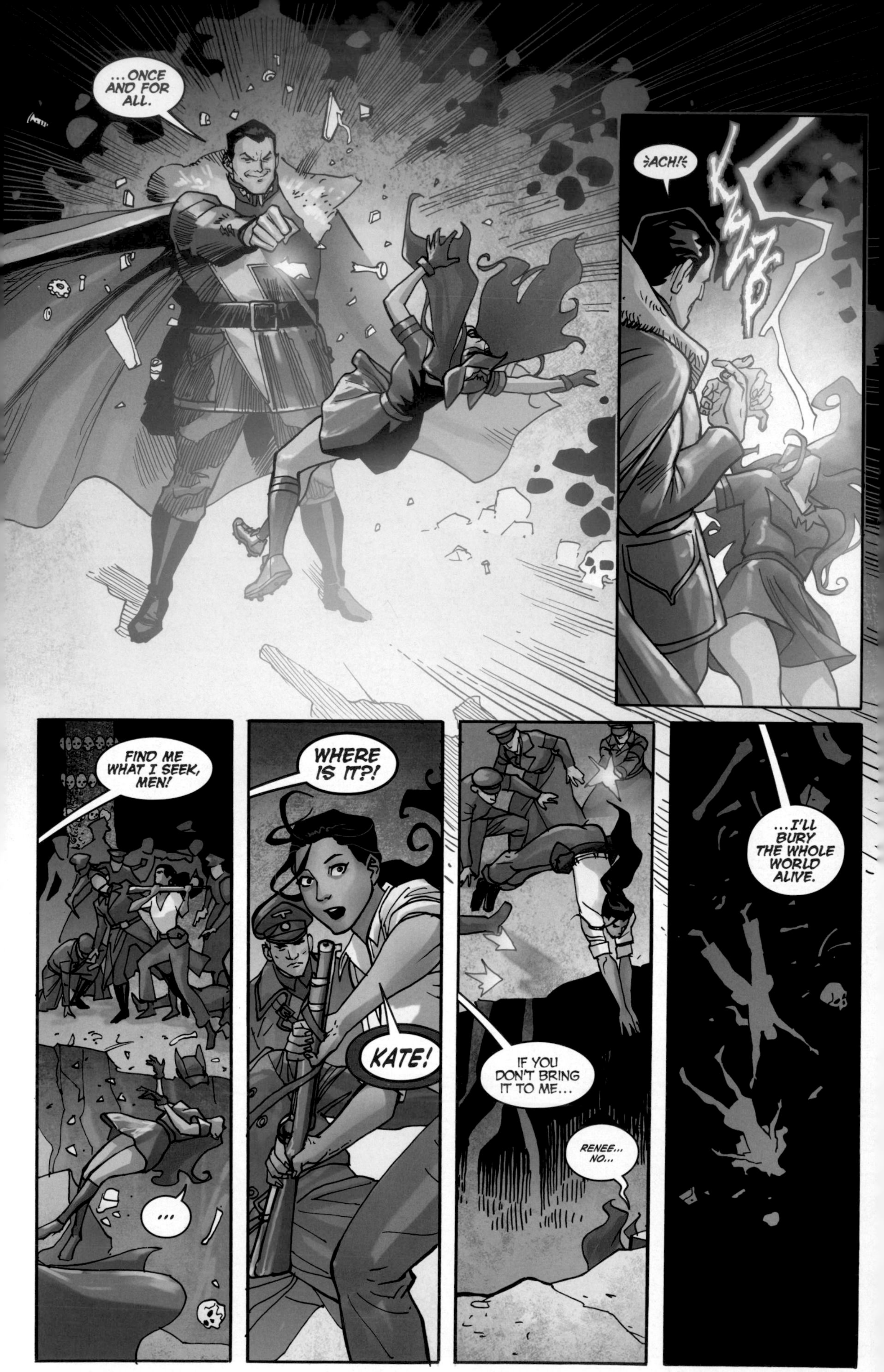
...ONCE AND FOR ALL.
¡ACH!¡
KZZZB
FIND ME WHAT I SEEK, MEN!
...
WHERE IS IT?!
KATE!
IF YOU DON'T BRING IT TO ME...
RENEE... NO...
...I'LL BURY THE WHOLE WORLD ALIVE.

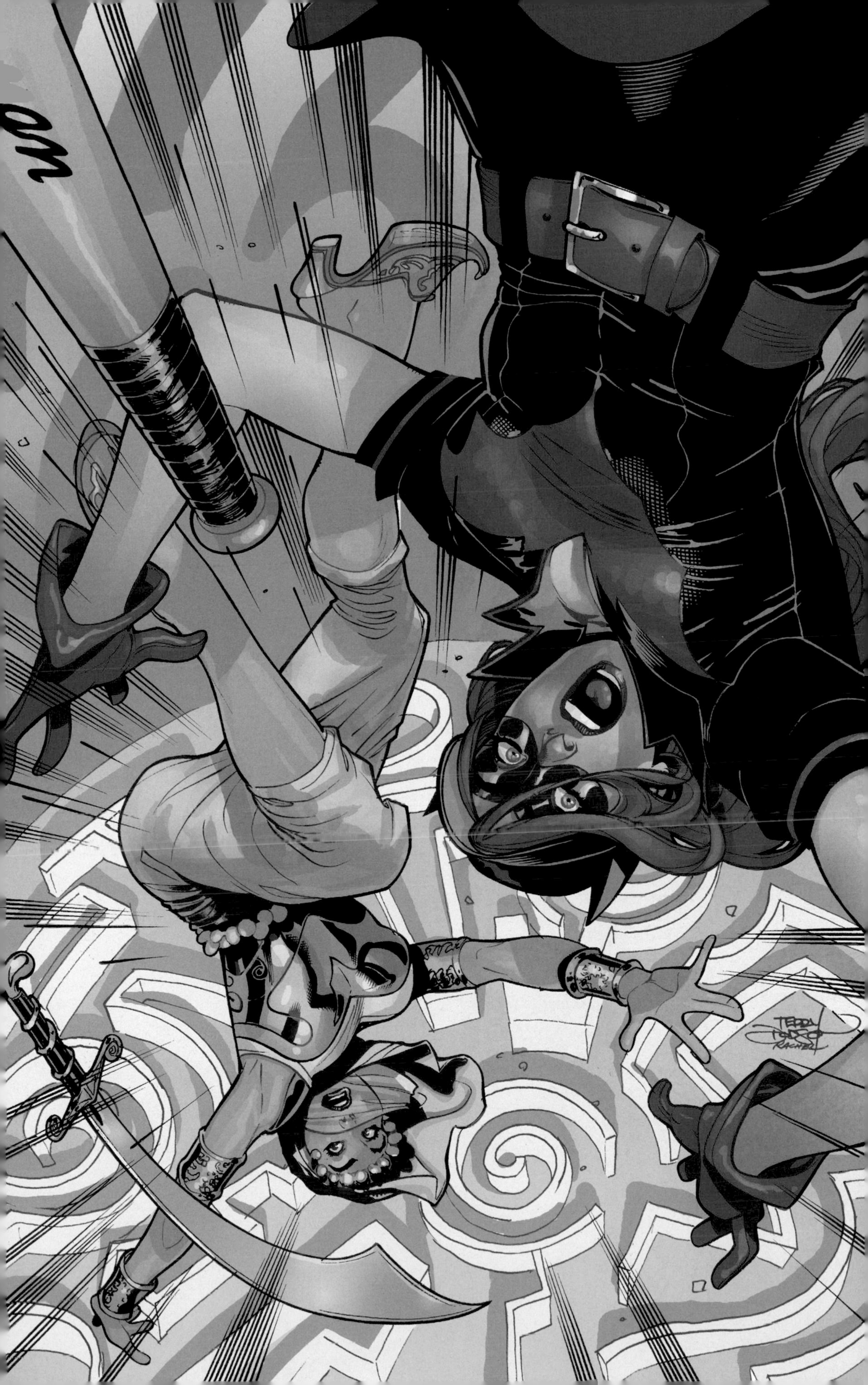

WAR BONDS

PARTS THREE *and* FOUR

Written by
MARGUERITE BENNETT

Art by
MIRKA ANDOLFO

Colors by
J. NANJAN

Cover by
TERRY *and* **RACHEL DODSON**

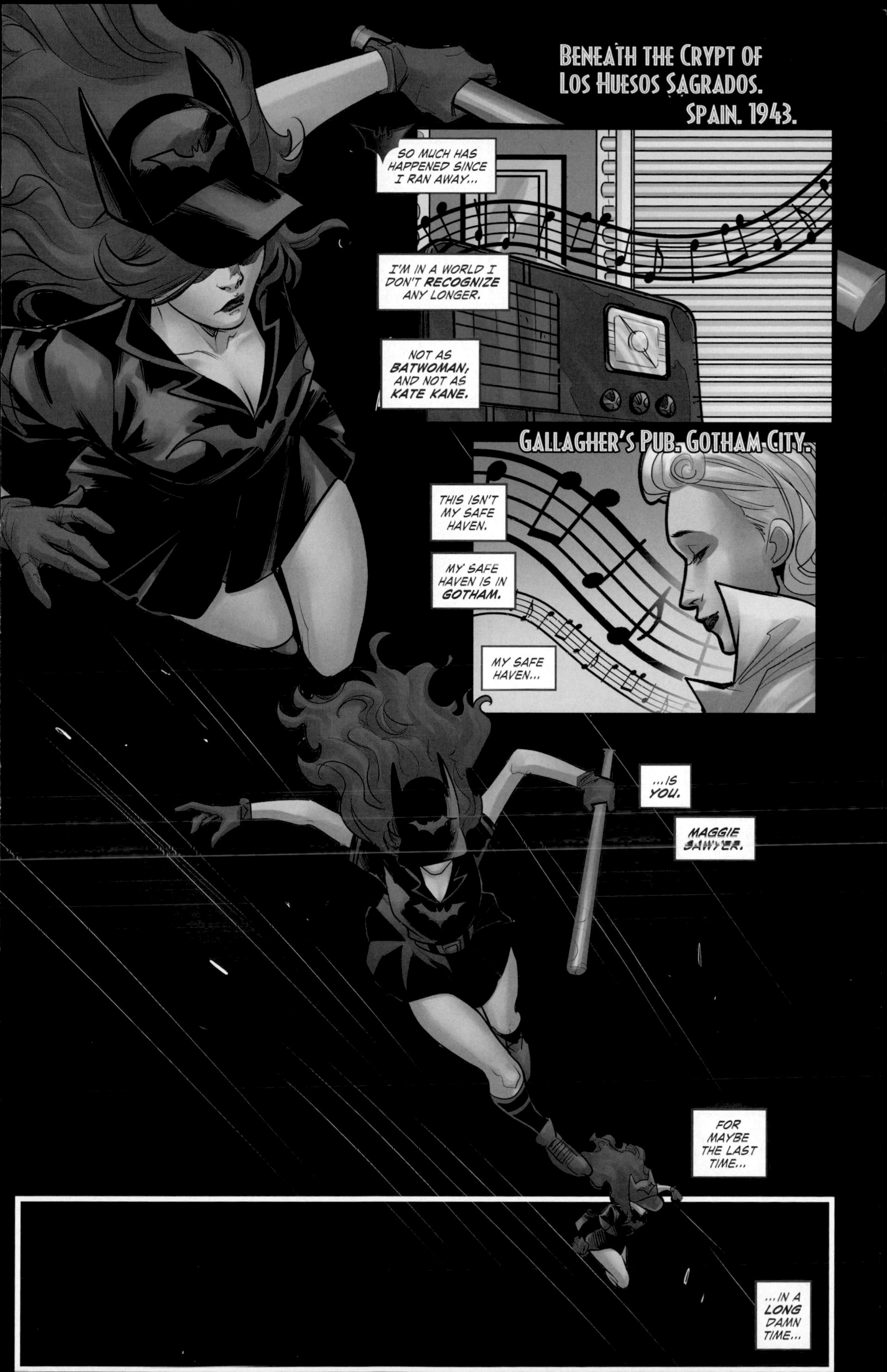
BENEATH THE CRYPT OF LOS HUESOS SAGRADOS. SPAIN. 1943.
SO MUCH HAS HAPPENED SINCE I RAN AWAY...
I'M IN A WORLD I DON'T RECOGNIZE ANY LONGER.
NOT AS BATWOMAN, AND NOT AS KATE KANE.
GALLAGHER'S PUB. GOTHAM CITY.
THIS ISN'T MY SAFE HAVEN.
MY SAFE HAVEN IS IN GOTHAM.
MY SAFE HAVEN...
...IS YOU.
MAGGIE SAWYER.
FOR MAYBE THE LAST TIME...
...IN A LONG DAMN TIME...

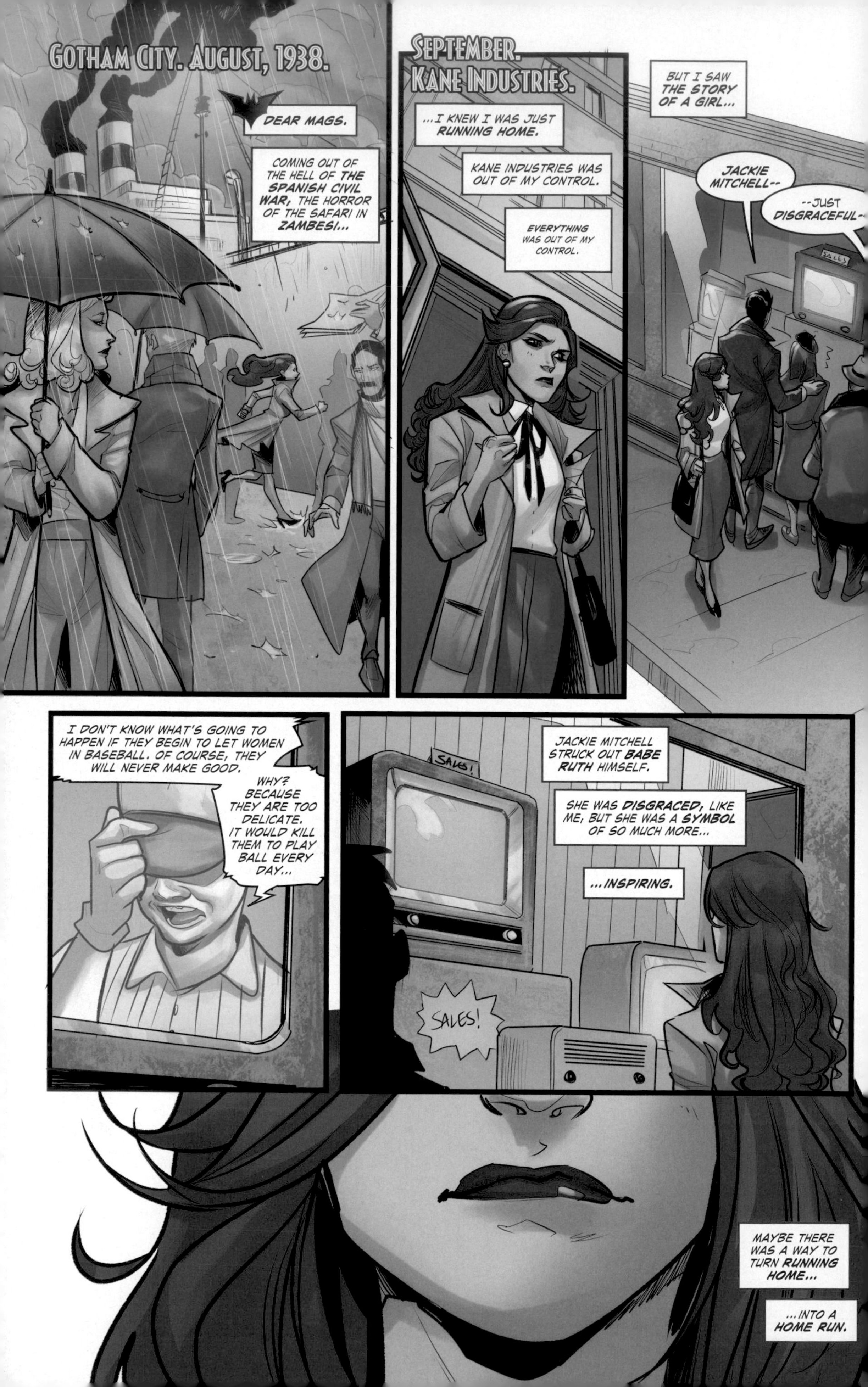
GOTHAM CITY. AUGUST, 1938.
DEAR MAGS.
COMING OUT OF THE HELL OF THE SPANISH CIVIL WAR, THE HORROR OF THE SAFARI IN ZAMBESI...
SEPTEMBER. KANE INDUSTRIES.
...I KNEW I WAS JUST RUNNING HOME.
KANE INDUSTRIES WAS OUT OF MY CONTROL.
EVERYTHING WAS OUT OF MY CONTROL.
BUT I SAW THE STORY OF A GIRL...
JACKIE MITCHELL--
--JUST DISGRACEFUL--
I DON'T KNOW WHAT'S GOING TO HAPPEN IF THEY BEGIN TO LET WOMEN IN BASEBALL. OF COURSE, THEY WILL NEVER MAKE GOOD.
WHY? BECAUSE THEY ARE TOO DELICATE. IT WOULD KILL THEM TO PLAY BALL EVERY DAY...
SALES!
JACKIE MITCHELL STRUCK OUT BABE RUTH HIMSELF.
SHE WAS DISGRACED, LIKE ME, BUT SHE WAS A SYMBOL OF SO MUCH MORE...
...INSPIRING.
SALES!
MAYBE THERE WAS A WAY TO TURN RUNNING HOME...
...INTO A HOME RUN.

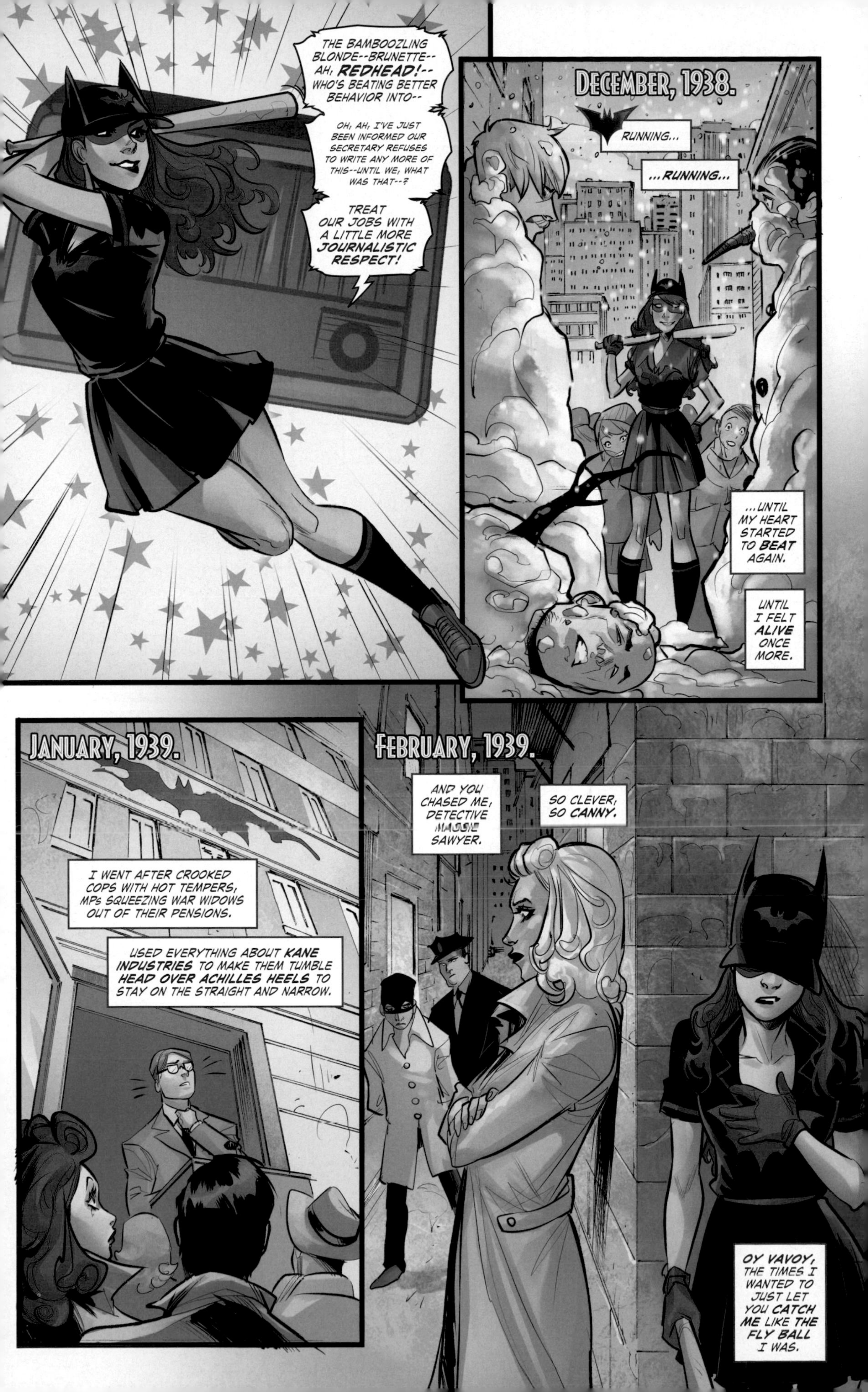

THE BAMBOOZLING BLONDE--BRUNETTE--AH, REDHEAD!--WHO'S BEATING BETTER BEHAVIOR INTO--
OH, AH, I'VE JUST BEEN INFORMED OUR SECRETARY REFUSES TO WRITE ANY MORE OF THIS--UNTIL WE, WHAT WAS THAT--?
TREAT OUR JOBS WITH A LITTLE MORE JOURNALISTIC RESPECT!
DECEMBER, 1938.
RUNNING...
...RUNNING...
...UNTIL MY HEART STARTED TO BEAT AGAIN.
UNTIL I FELT ALIVE ONCE MORE.
JANUARY, 1939.
I WENT AFTER CROOKED COPS WITH HOT TEMPERS, MPs SQUEEZING WAR WIDOWS OUT OF THEIR PENSIONS.
USED EVERYTHING ABOUT KANE INDUSTRIES TO MAKE THEM TUMBLE HEAD OVER ACHILLES HEELS TO STAY ON THE STRAIGHT AND NARROW.
FEBRUARY, 1939.
AND YOU CHASED ME, DETECTIVE MAGGIE SAWYER.
SO CLEVER, SO CANNY.
OY VAVOY, THE TIMES I WANTED TO JUST LET YOU CATCH ME LIKE THE FLY BALL I WAS.

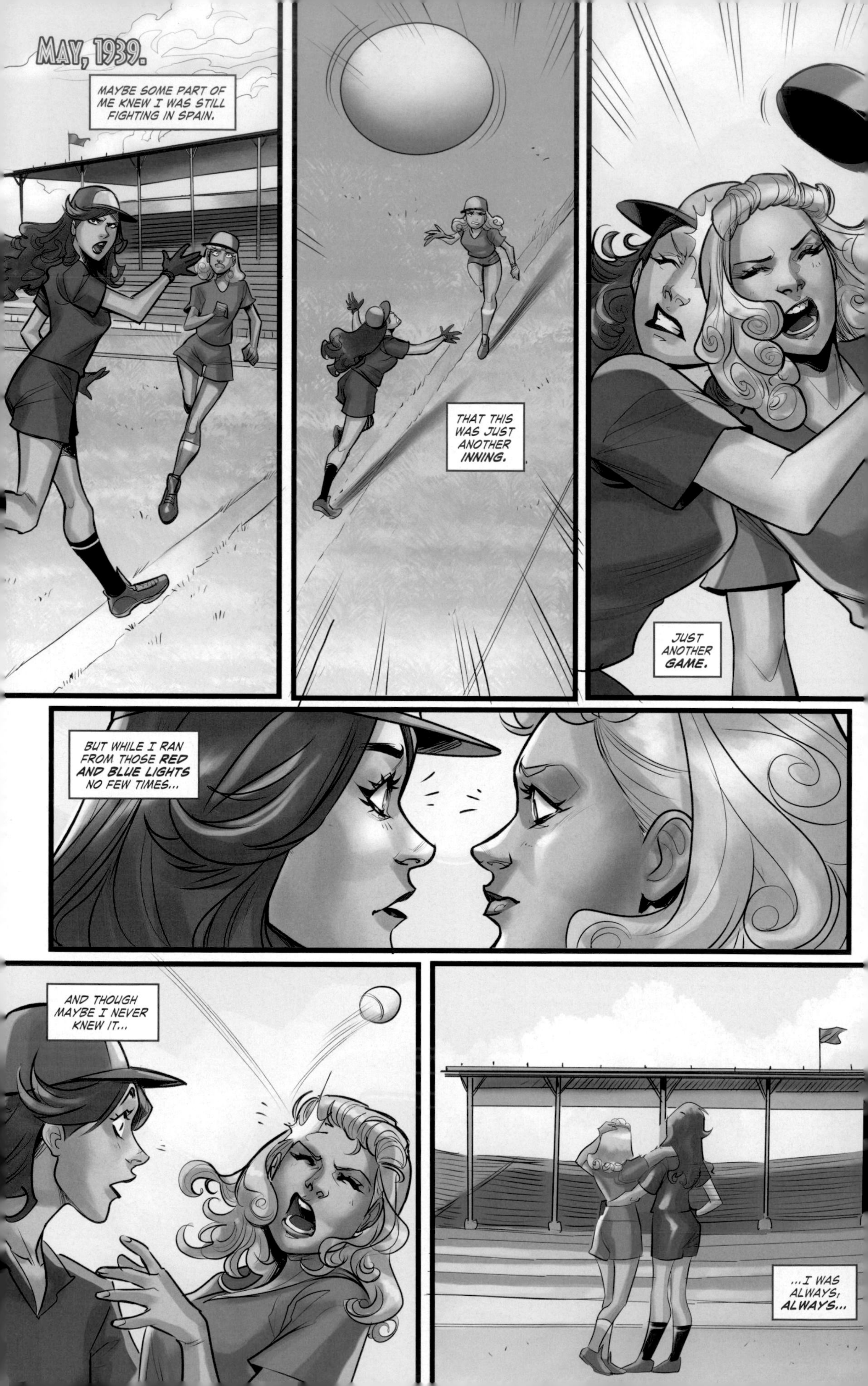
MAY, 1939.
MAYBE SOME PART OF ME KNEW I WAS STILL FIGHTING IN SPAIN.
THAT THIS WAS JUST ANOTHER INNING.
JUST ANOTHER GAME.
BUT WHILE I RAN FROM THOSE RED AND BLUE LIGHTS NO FEW TIMES...
AND THOUGH MAYBE I NEVER KNEW IT...
...I WAS ALWAYS, ALWAYS...

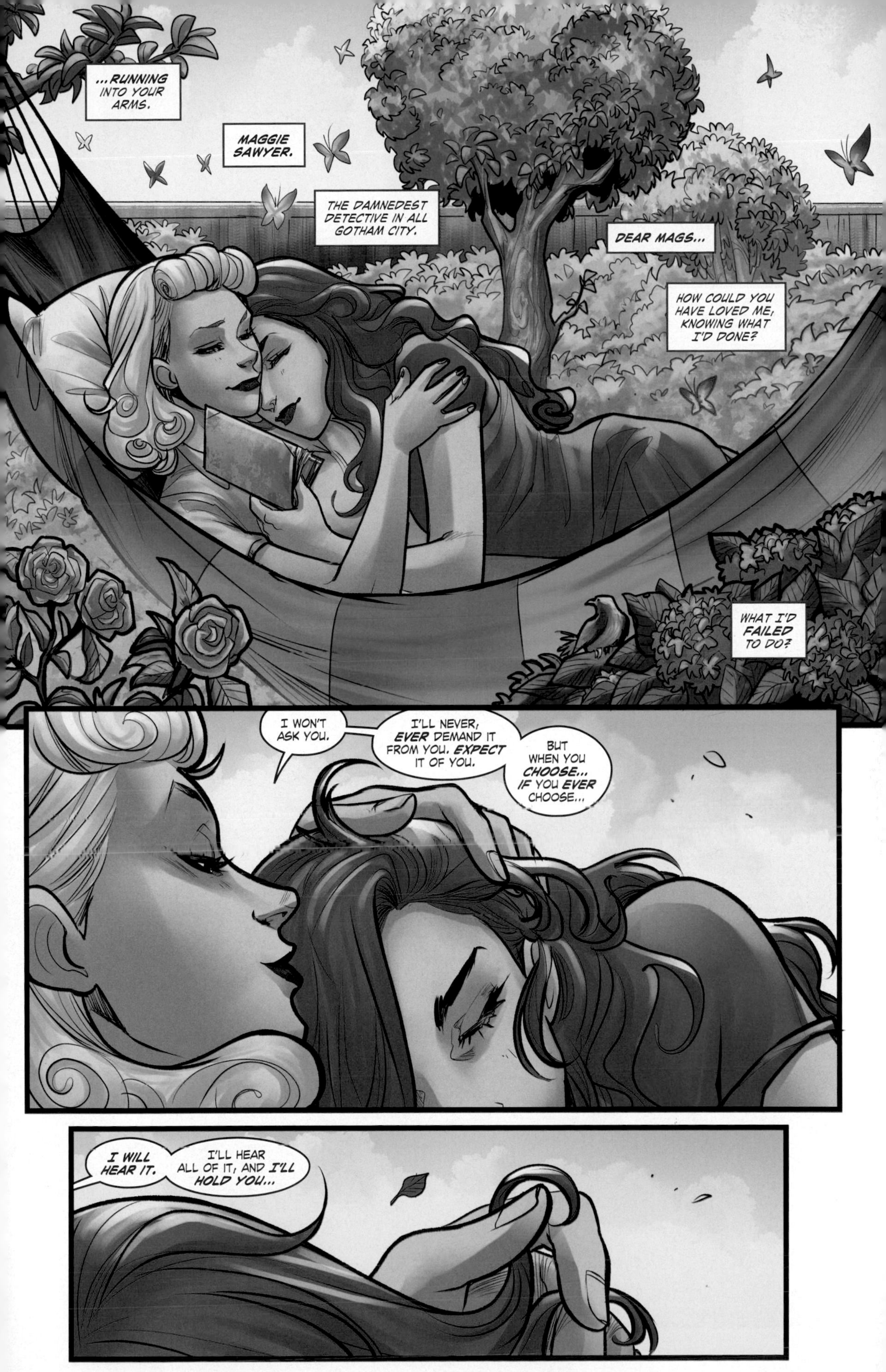

...RUNNING INTO YOUR ARMS.
MAGGIE SAWYER.
THE DAMNEDEST DETECTIVE IN ALL GOTHAM CITY.
DEAR MAGS...
HOW COULD YOU HAVE LOVED ME, KNOWING WHAT I'D DONE?
WHAT I'D FAILED TO DO?
I WON'T ASK YOU.
I'LL NEVER, EVER DEMAND IT FROM YOU. EXPECT IT OF YOU.
BUT WHEN YOU CHOOSE... IF YOU EVER CHOOSE...
I WILL HEAR IT.
I'LL HEAR ALL OF IT, AND I'LL HOLD YOU...

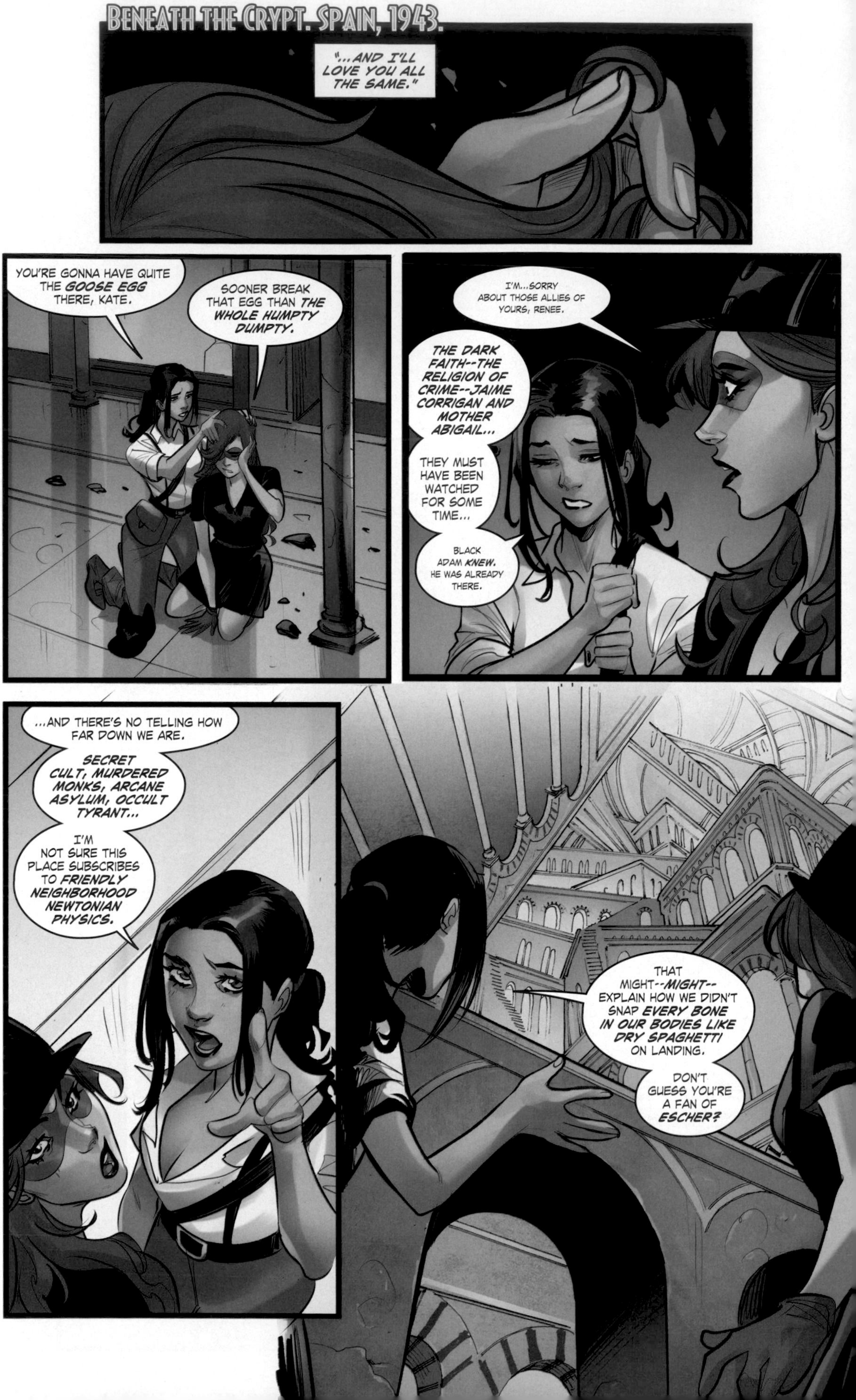
Beneath the Crypt. Spain, 1943.
"...AND I'LL LOVE YOU ALL THE SAME."
YOU'RE GONNA HAVE QUITE THE GOOSE EGG THERE, KATE.
SOONER BREAK THAT EGG THAN THE WHOLE HUMPTY DUMPTY.
I'M...SORRY ABOUT THOSE ALLIES OF YOURS, RENEE.
THE DARK FAITH--THE RELIGION OF CRIME--JAIME CORRIGAN AND MOTHER ABIGAIL...
THEY MUST HAVE BEEN WATCHED FOR SOME TIME...
BLACK ADAM KNEW. HE WAS ALREADY THERE.
...AND THERE'S NO TELLING HOW FAR DOWN WE ARE.
SECRET CULT, MURDERED MONKS, ARCANE ASYLUM, OCCULT TYRANT...
I'M NOT SURE THIS PLACE SUBSCRIBES TO FRIENDLY NEIGHBORHOOD NEWTONIAN PHYSICS.
THAT MIGHT--MIGHT--EXPLAIN HOW WE DIDN'T SNAP EVERY BONE IN OUR BODIES LIKE DRY SPAGHETTI ON LANDING.
DON'T GUESS YOU'RE A FAN OF ESCHER?

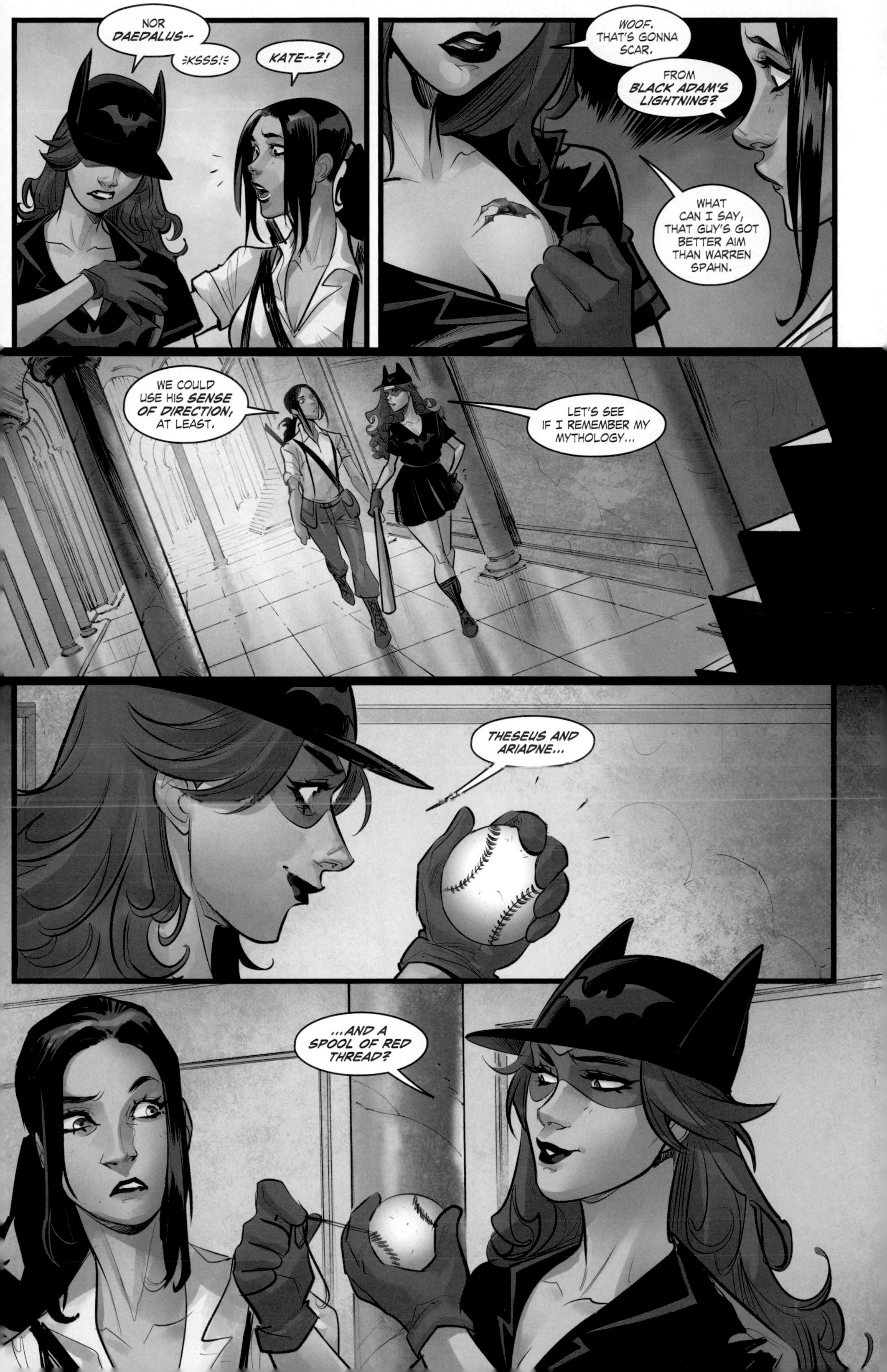

NOR DAEDALUS--
KSSS!
KATE--?!
WOOF. THAT'S GONNA SCAR.
FROM BLACK ADAM'S LIGHTNING?
WHAT CAN I SAY, THAT GUY'S GOT BETTER AIM THAN WARREN SPAHN.
WE COULD USE HIS SENSE OF DIRECTION, AT LEAST.
LET'S SEE IF I REMEMBER MY MYTHOLOGY...
THESEUS AND ARIADNE...
...AND A SPOOL OF RED THREAD?

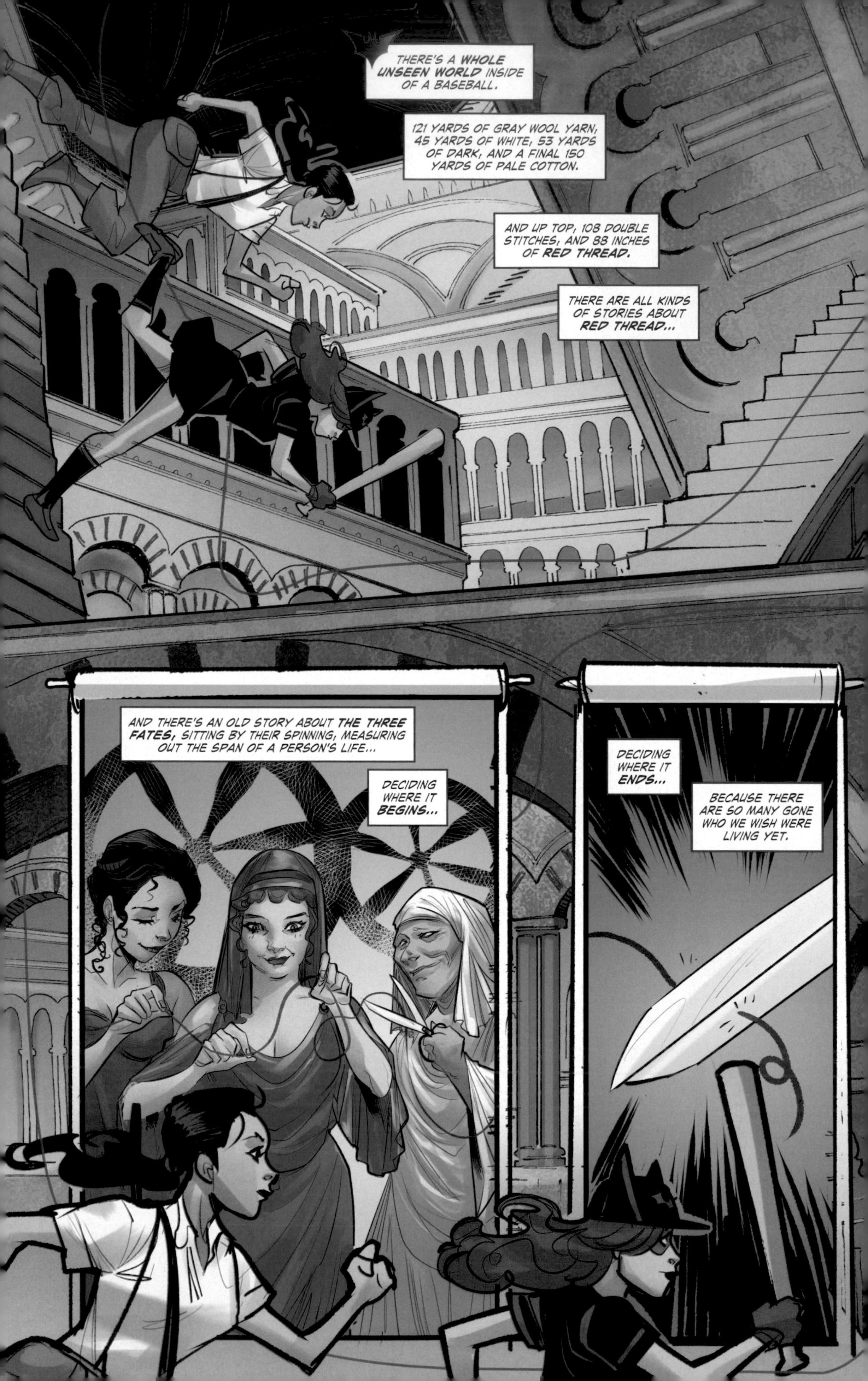

THERE'S A WHOLE UNSEEN WORLD INSIDE OF A BASEBALL.
121 YARDS OF GRAY WOOL YARN, 45 YARDS OF WHITE, 53 YARDS OF DARK, AND A FINAL 150 YARDS OF PALE COTTON.
AND UP TOP, 108 DOUBLE STITCHES, AND 88 INCHES OF RED THREAD.
THERE ARE ALL KINDS OF STORIES ABOUT RED THREAD...
AND THERE'S AN OLD STORY ABOUT THE THREE FATES, SITTING BY THEIR SPINNING, MEASURING OUT THE SPAN OF A PERSON'S LIFE...
DECIDING WHERE IT BEGINS...
DECIDING WHERE IT ENDS...
BECAUSE THERE ARE SO MANY GONE WHO WE WISH WERE LIVING YET.

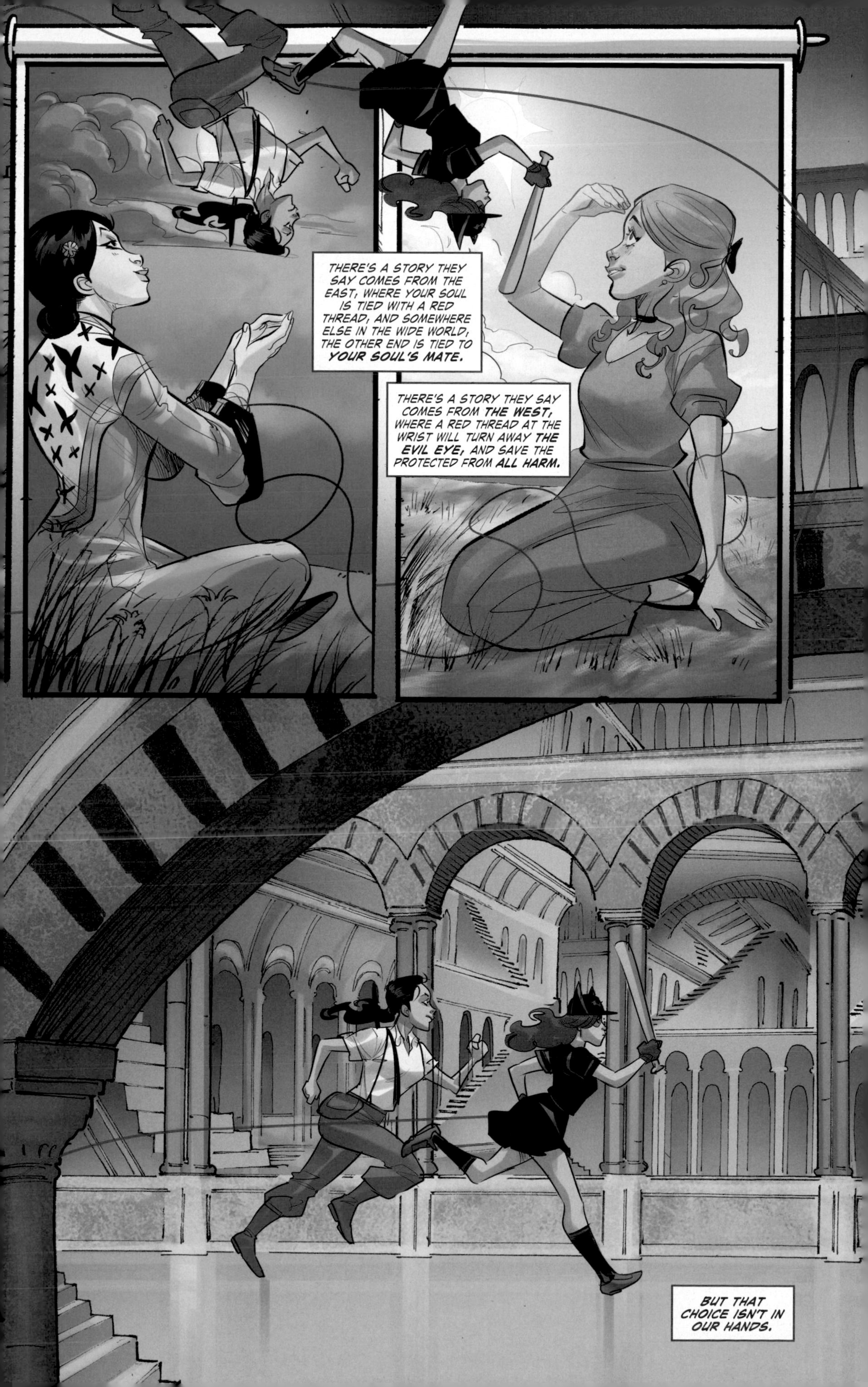
THERE'S A STORY THEY SAY COMES FROM THE EAST, WHERE YOUR SOUL IS TIED WITH A RED THREAD, AND SOMEWHERE ELSE IN THE WIDE WORLD, THE OTHER END IS TIED TO YOUR SOUL'S MATE.
THERE'S A STORY THEY SAY COMES FROM THE WEST, WHERE A RED THREAD AT THE WRIST WILL TURN AWAY THE EVIL EYE, AND SAVE THE PROTECTED FROM ALL HARM.
BUT THAT CHOICE ISN'T IN OUR HANDS.

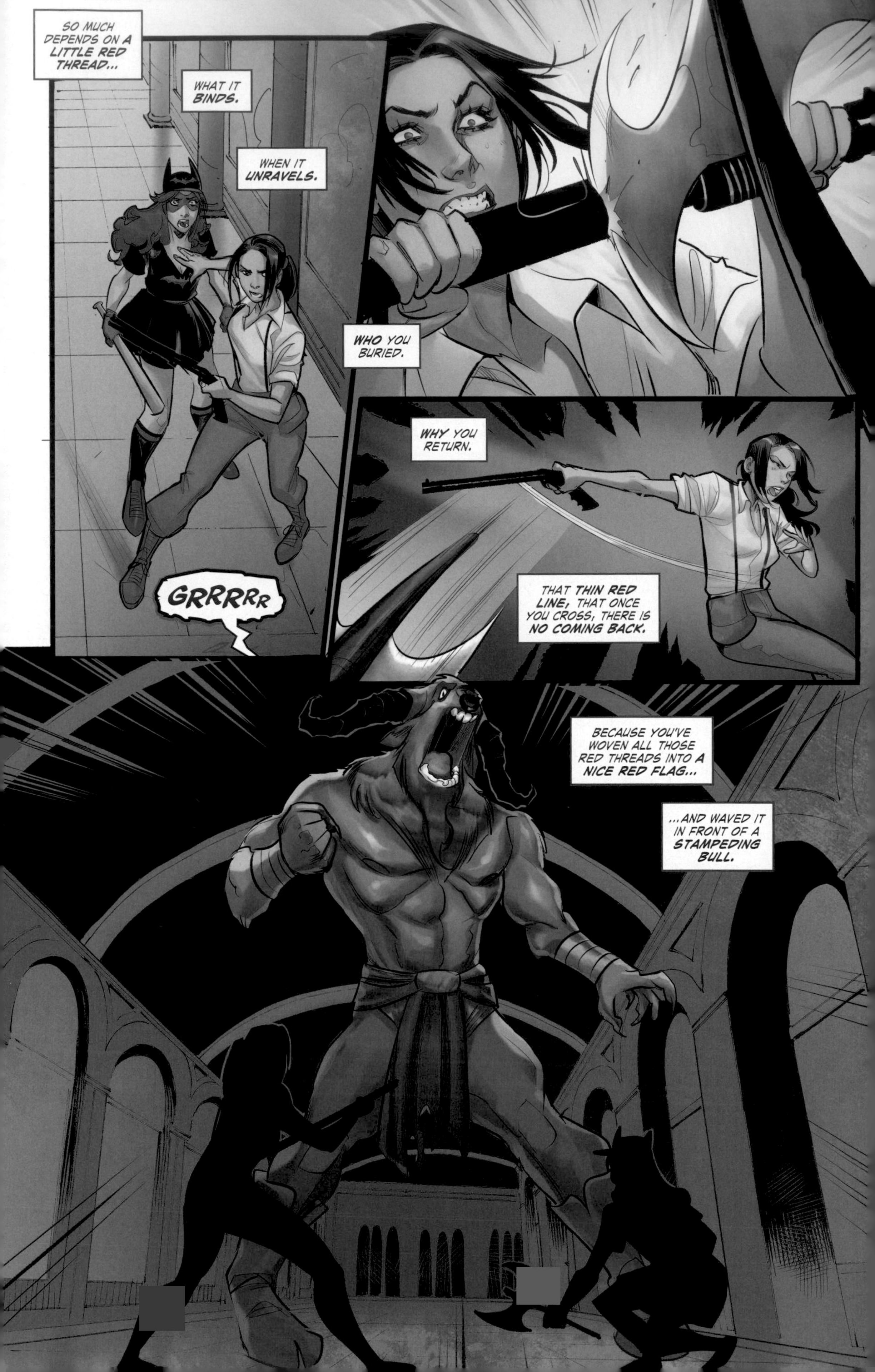
SO MUCH DEPENDS ON A LITTLE RED THREAD...
WHAT IT BINDS.
WHEN IT UNRAVELS.
GRRRRR
WHO YOU BURIED.
WHY YOU RETURN.
THAT THIN RED LINE, THAT ONCE YOU CROSS, THERE IS NO COMING BACK.
BECAUSE YOU'VE WOVEN ALL THOSE RED THREADS INTO A NICE RED FLAG...
...AND WAVED IT IN FRONT OF A STAMPEDING BULL.

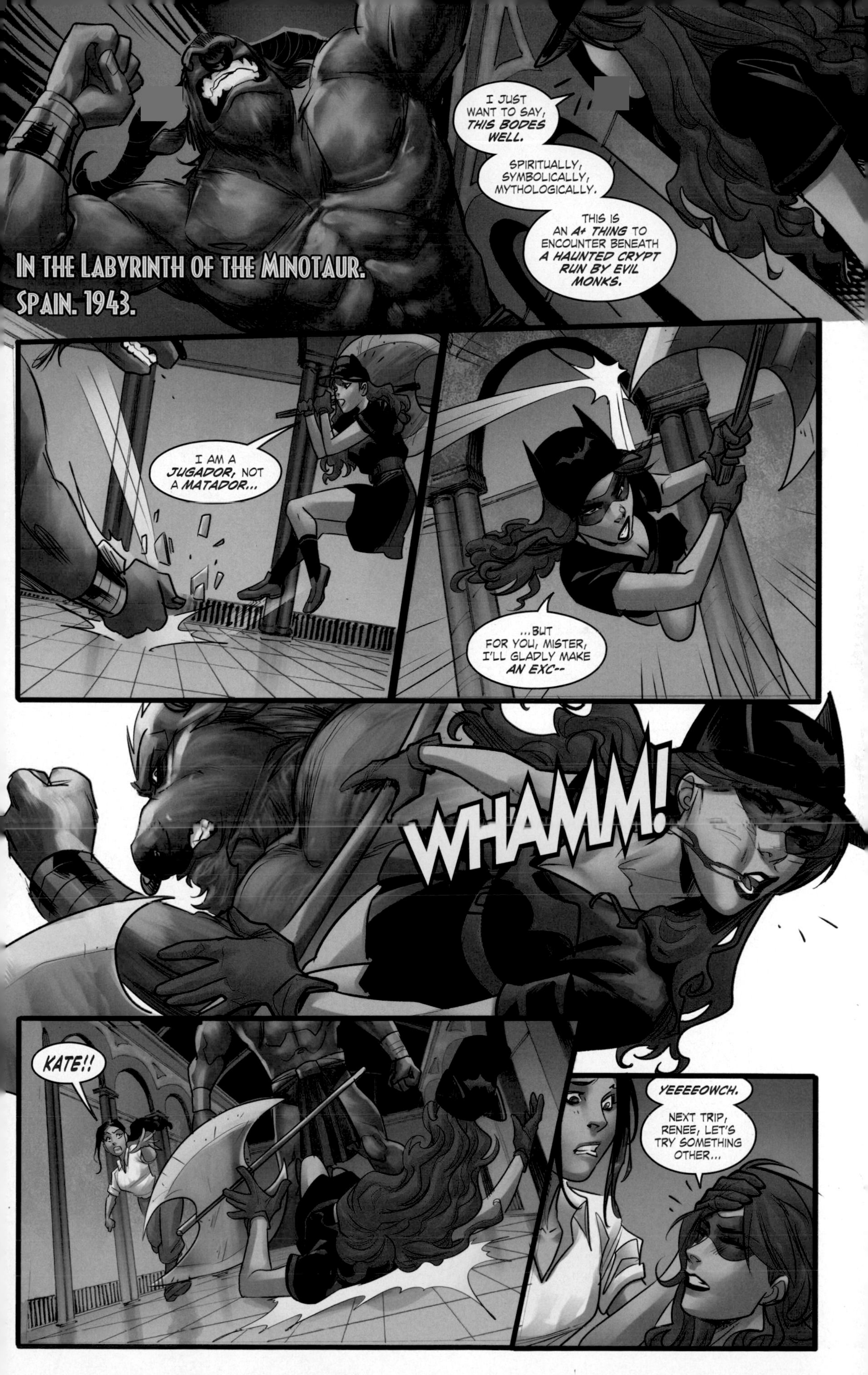

In the Labyrinth of the Minotaur.
Spain. 1943.
I JUST WANT TO SAY, THIS BODES WELL.
SPIRITUALLY, SYMBOLICALLY, MYTHOLOGICALLY.
THIS IS AN A+ THING TO ENCOUNTER BENEATH A HAUNTED CRYPT RUN BY EVIL MONKS.
I AM A JUGADOR, NOT A MATADOR...
...BUT FOR YOU, MISTER, I'LL GLADLY MAKE AN EXC--
WHAMM!
KATE!!
YEEEEOWCH.
NEXT TRIP, RENEE, LET'S TRY SOMETHING OTHER...

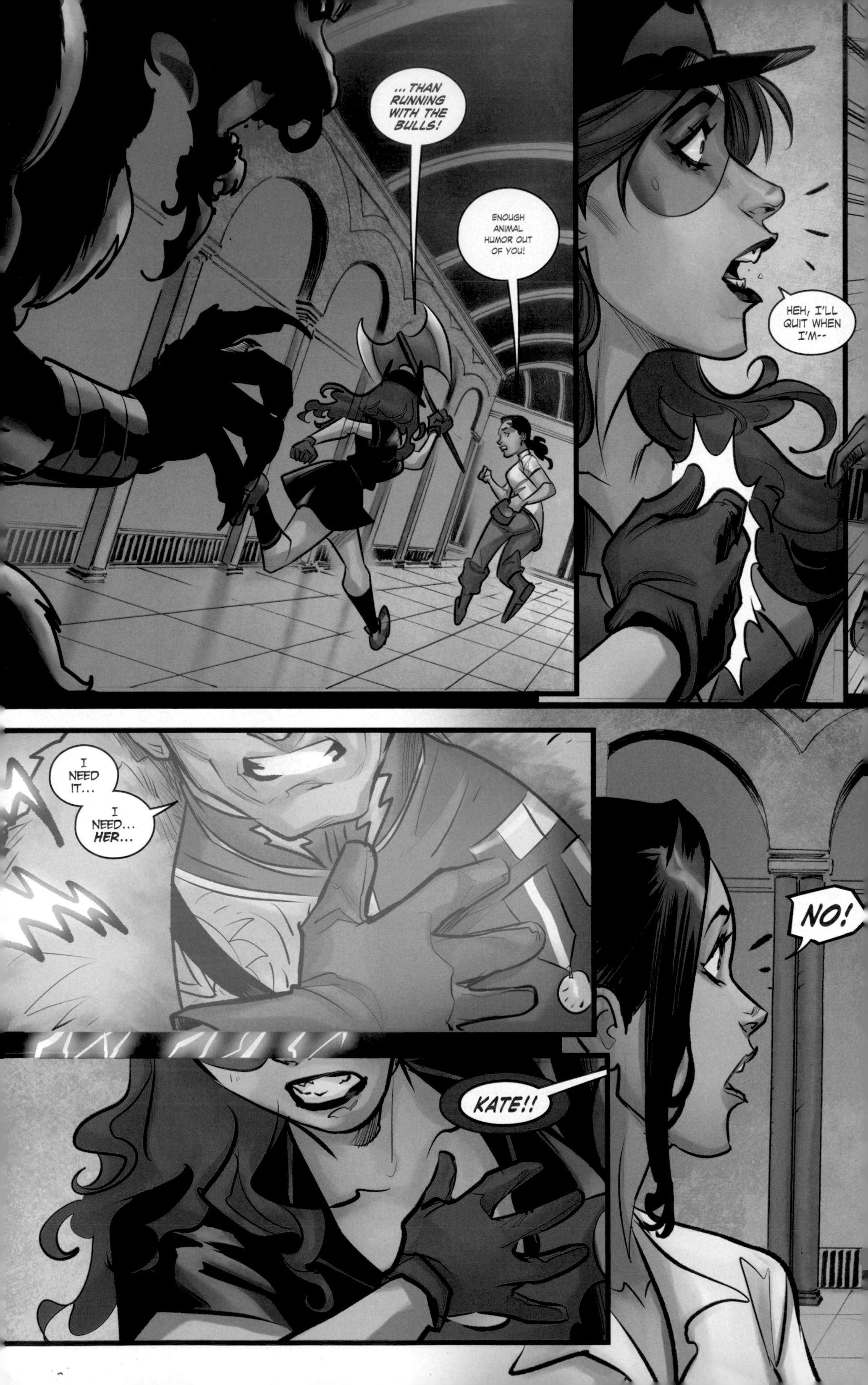
...THAN RUNNING WITH THE BULLS!
ENOUGH ANIMAL HUMOR OUT OF YOU!
HEH, I'LL QUIT WHEN I'M--
I NEED IT...
I NEED... HER...
NO!
KATE!!

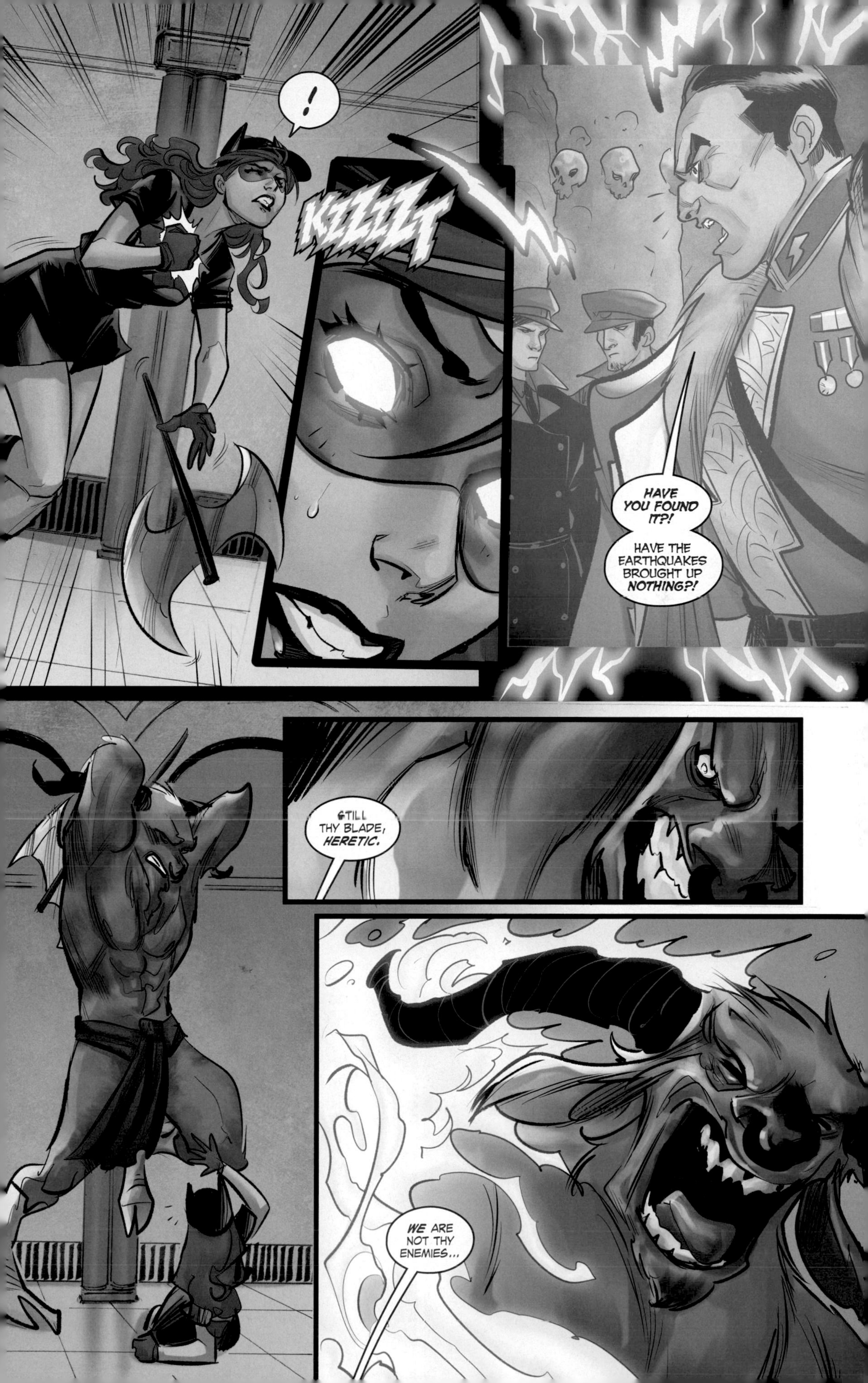
!
KZZZZT
HAVE YOU FOUND IT?!
HAVE THE EARTHQUAKES BROUGHT UP NOTHING?!
STILL THY BLADE, HERETIC.
WE ARE NOT THY ENEMIES...

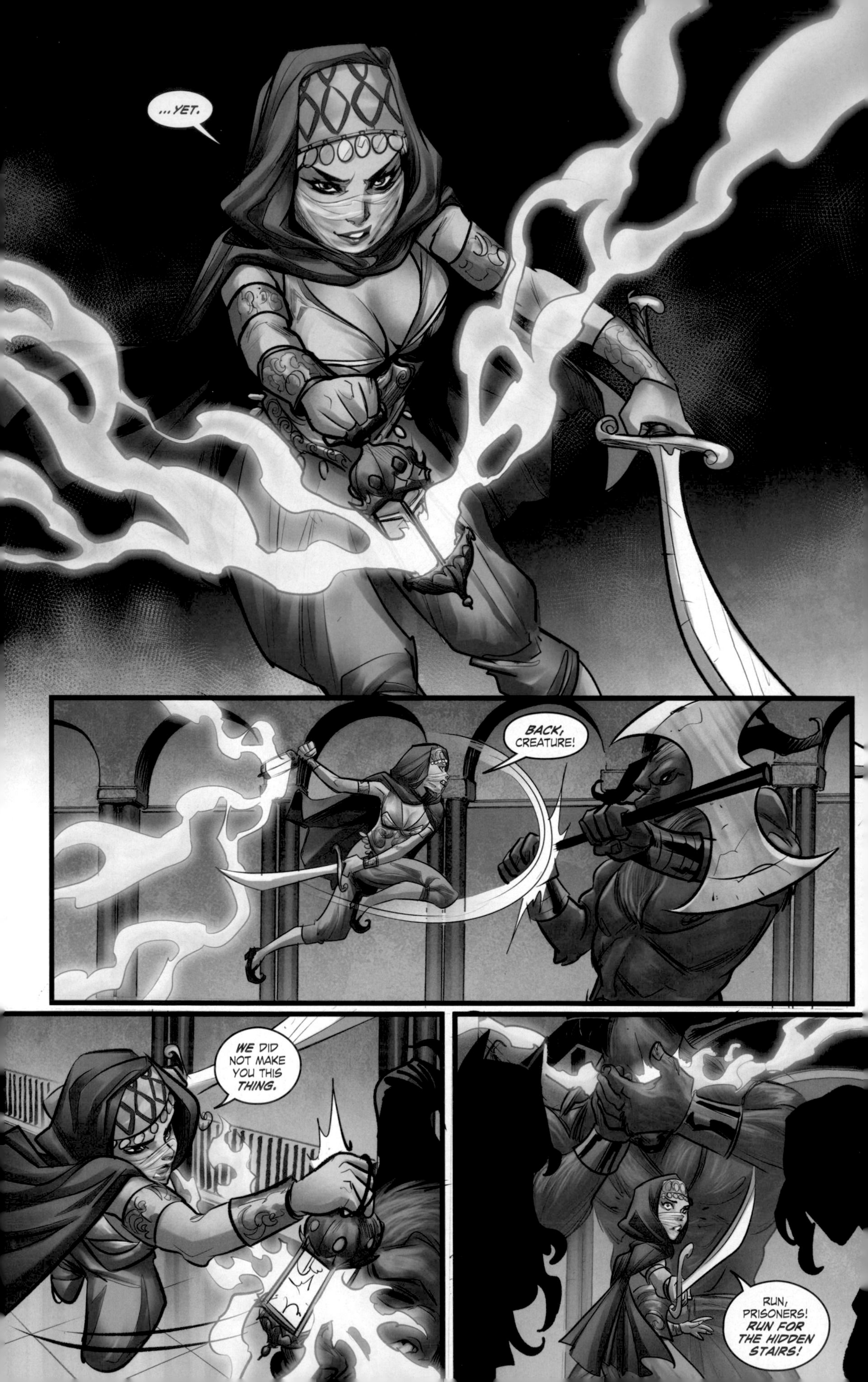
...YET.
BACK, CREATURE!
WE DID NOT MAKE YOU THIS THING.
RUN, PRISONERS! RUN FOR THE HIDDEN STAIRS!

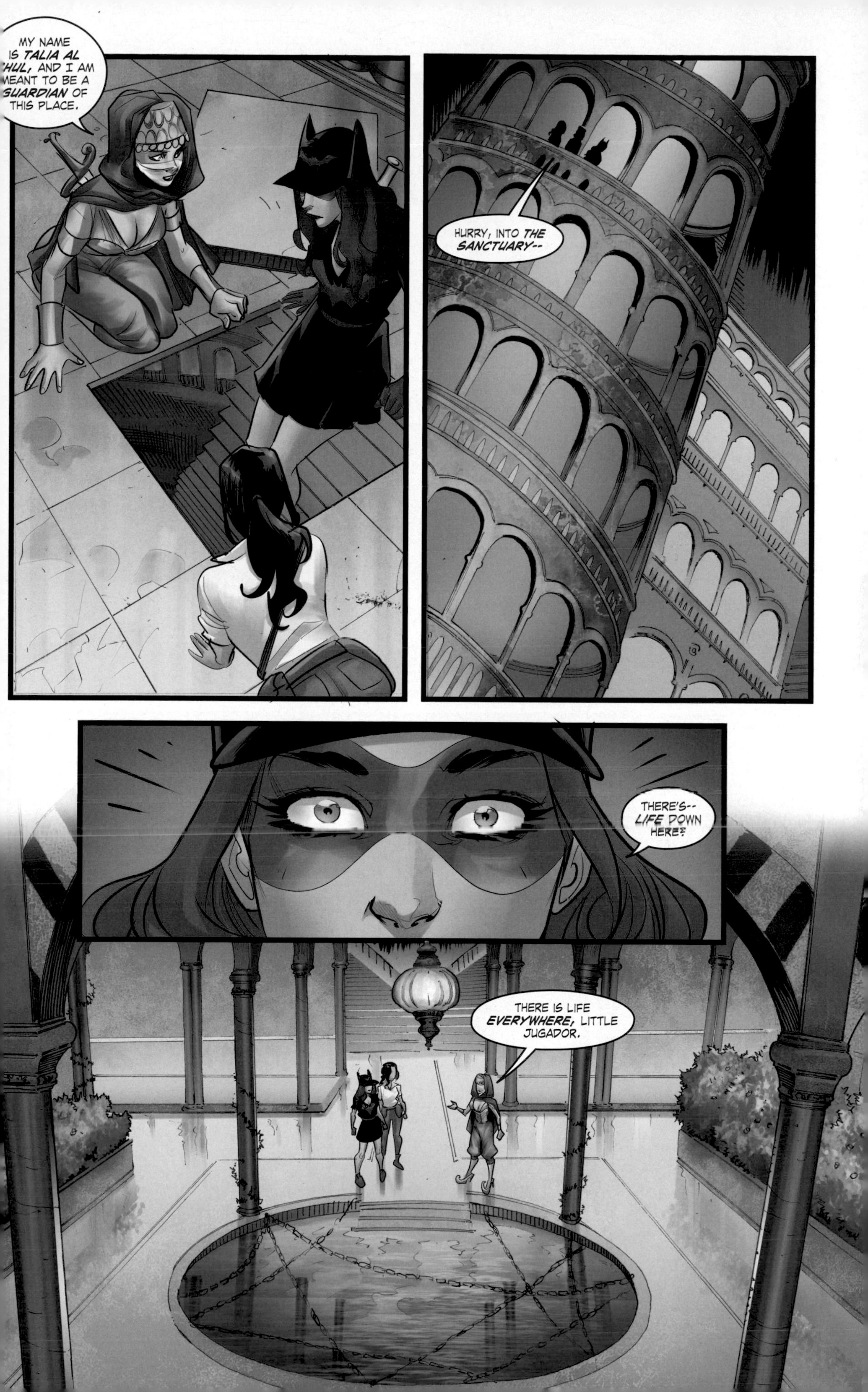
MY NAME IS TALIA AL GHUL, AND I AM MEANT TO BE A GUARDIAN OF THIS PLACE.
HURRY, INTO THE SANCTUARY--
THERE'S-- LIFE DOWN HERE?
THERE IS LIFE EVERYWHERE, LITTLE JUGADOR.

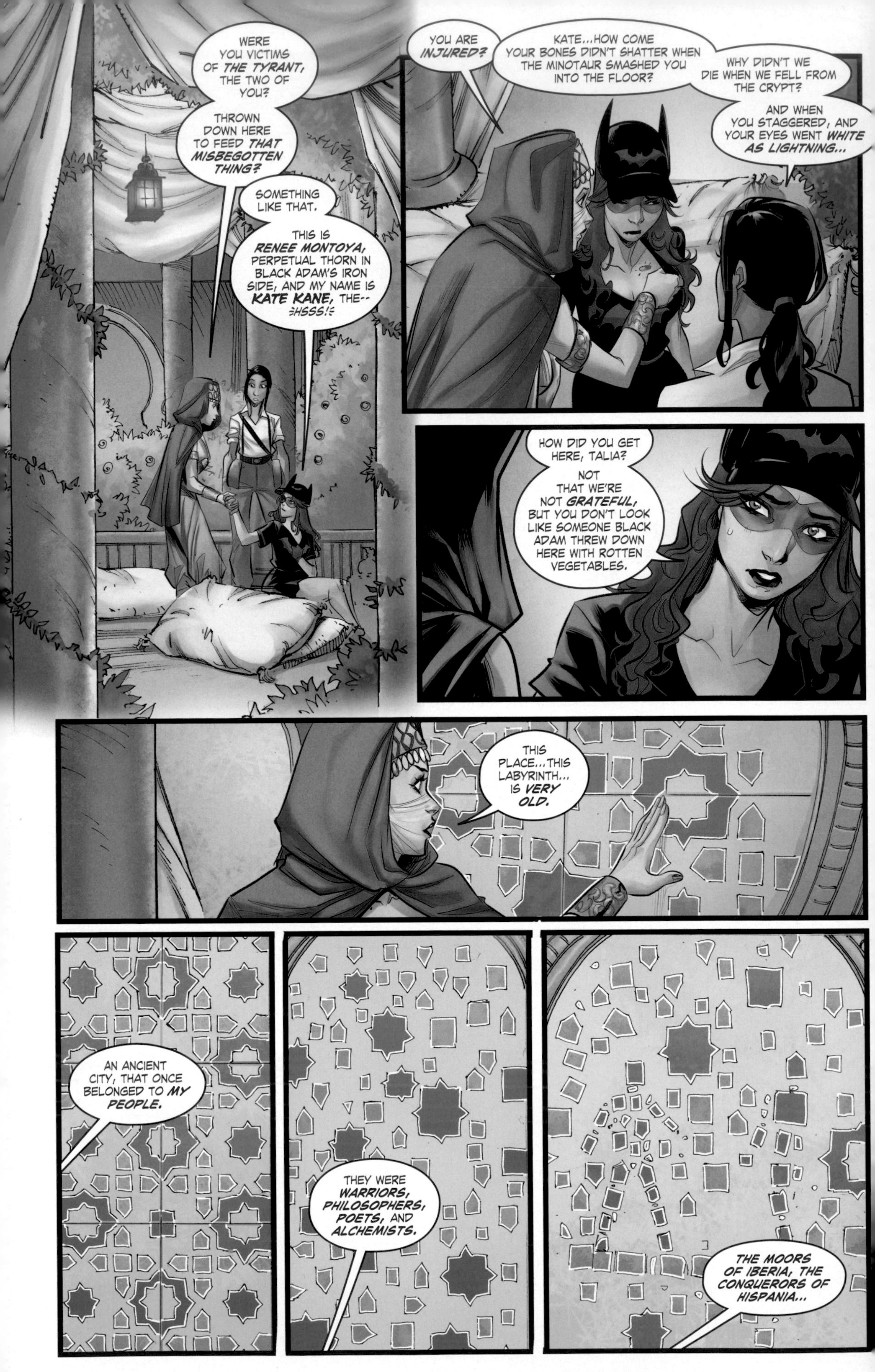

WERE YOU VICTIMS OF THE TYRANT, THE TWO OF YOU?
THROWN DOWN HERE TO FEED THAT MISBEGOTTEN THING?
SOMETHING LIKE THAT.
THIS IS RENEE MONTOYA, PERPETUAL THORN IN BLACK ADAM'S IRON SIDE, AND MY NAME IS KATE KANE, THE-- HSSS!
YOU ARE INJURED?
KATE...HOW COME YOUR BONES DIDN'T SHATTER WHEN THE MINOTAUR SMASHED YOU INTO THE FLOOR?
WHY DIDN'T WE DIE WHEN WE FELL FROM THE CRYPT?
AND WHEN YOU STAGGERED, AND YOUR EYES WENT WHITE AS LIGHTNING...
HOW DID YOU GET HERE, TALIA?
NOT THAT WE'RE NOT GRATEFUL, BUT YOU DON'T LOOK LIKE SOMEONE BLACK ADAM THREW DOWN HERE WITH ROTTEN VEGETABLES.
THIS PLACE...THIS LABYRINTH... IS VERY OLD.
AN ANCIENT CITY, THAT ONCE BELONGED TO MY PEOPLE.
THEY WERE WARRIORS, PHILOSOPHERS, POETS, AND ALCHEMISTS.
THE MOORS OF IBERIA, THE CONQUERORS OF HISPANIA...

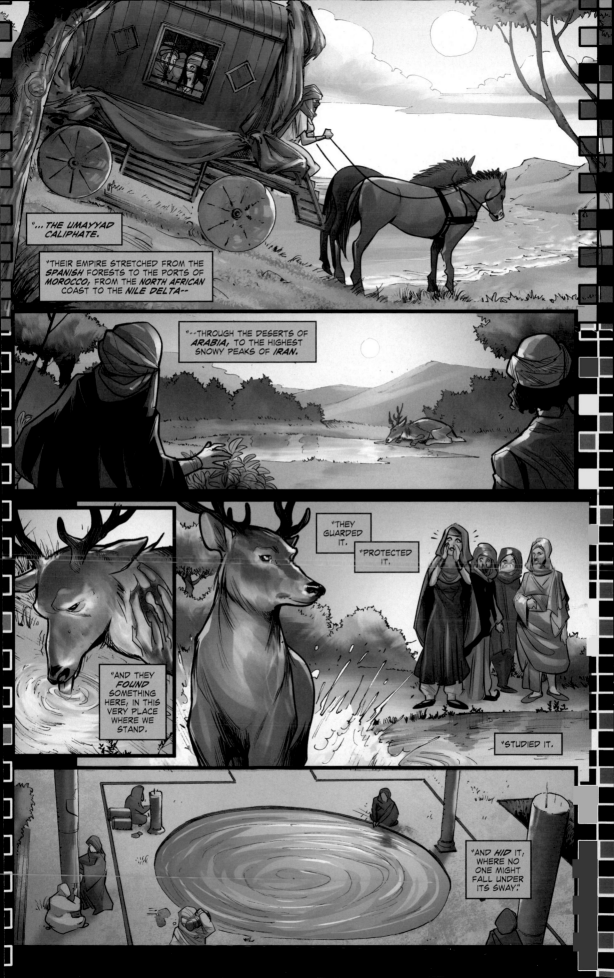

"...THE UMAYYAD CALIPHATE.

"THEIR EMPIRE STRETCHED FROM THE *SPANISH* FORESTS TO THE PORTS OF *MOROCCO,* FROM THE *NORTH AFRICAN* COAST TO THE *NILE DELTA--*

"--THROUGH THE DESERTS OF *ARABIA,* TO THE HIGHEST SNOWY PEAKS OF *IRAN.*

"THEY GUARDED IT.

"PROTECTED IT.

"AND THEY *FOUND* SOMETHING HERE, IN THIS VERY PLACE WHERE WE STAND.

"STUDIED IT.

"AND *HID* IT, WHERE NO ONE MIGHT FALL UNDER ITS SWAY."

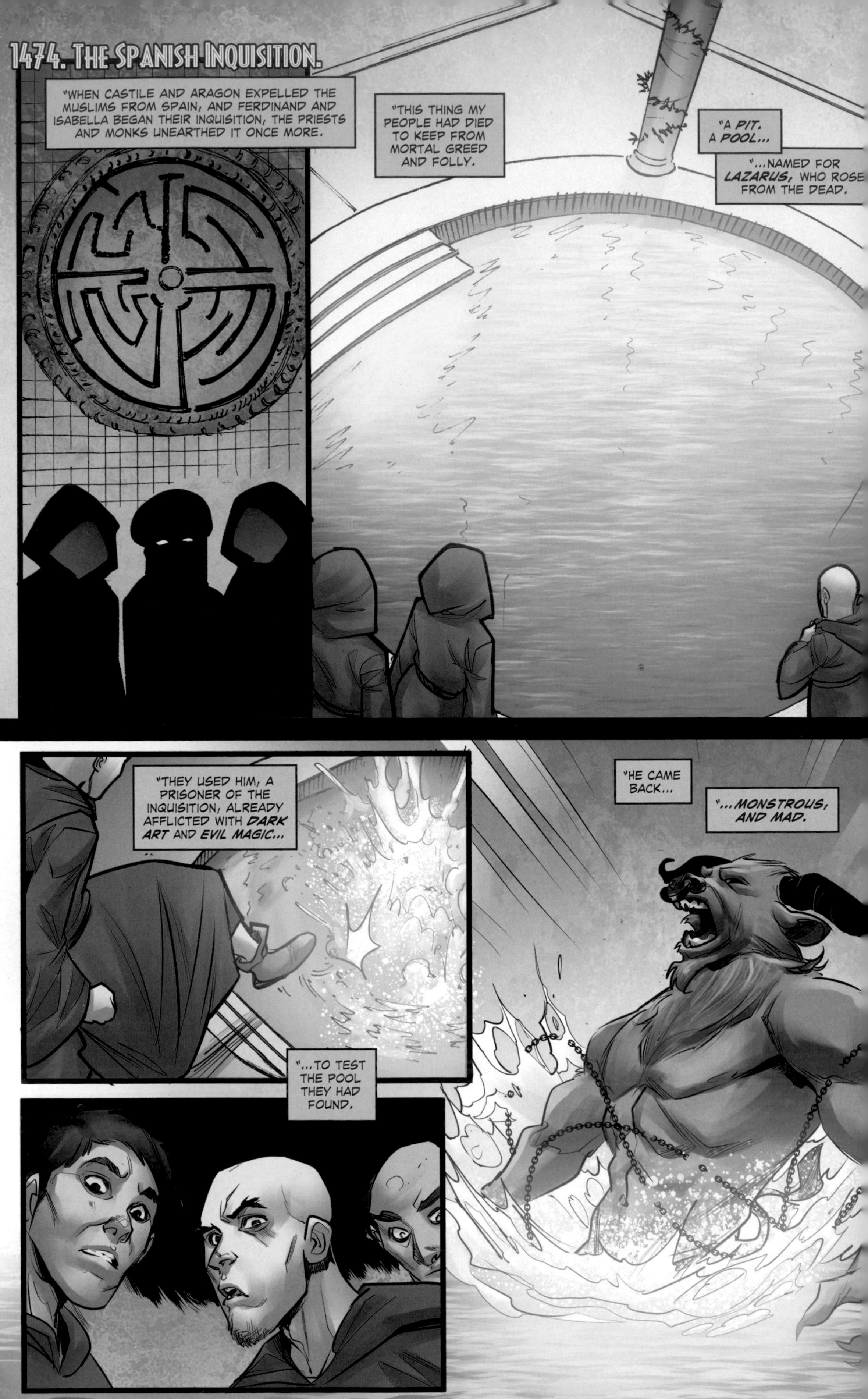
1474. The Spanish Inquisition.
"WHEN CASTILE AND ARAGON EXPELLED THE MUSLIMS FROM SPAIN, AND FERDINAND AND ISABELLA BEGAN THEIR INQUISITION, THE PRIESTS AND MONKS UNEARTHED IT ONCE MORE.
"THIS THING MY PEOPLE HAD DIED TO KEEP FROM MORTAL GREED AND FOLLY.
"A PIT. A POOL...
"...NAMED FOR LAZARUS, WHO ROSE FROM THE DEAD.
"THEY USED HIM, A PRISONER OF THE INQUISITION, ALREADY AFFLICTED WITH DARK ART AND EVIL MAGIC...
"...TO TEST THE POOL THEY HAD FOUND.
"HE CAME BACK...
"...MONSTROUS, AND MAD.

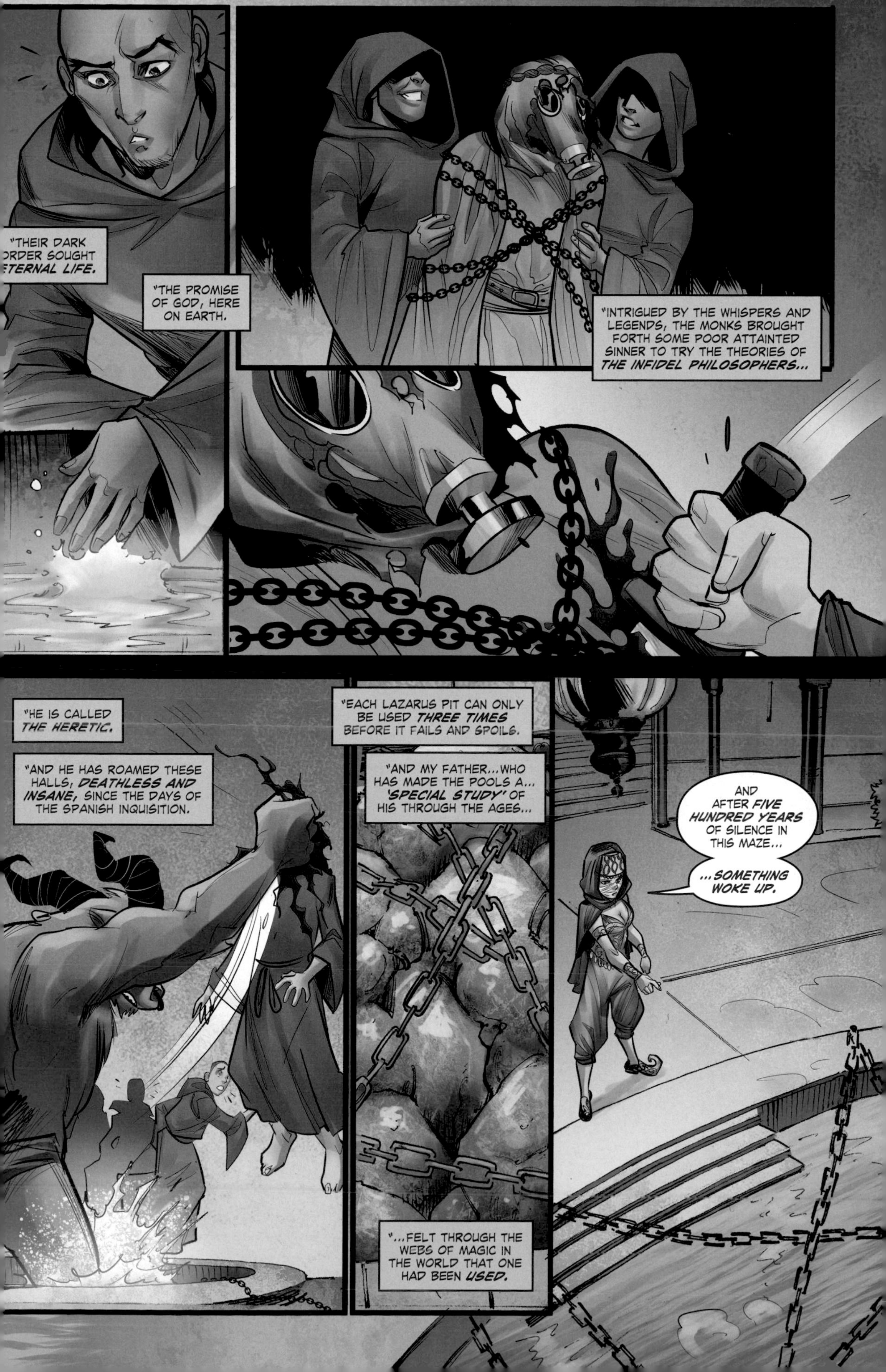
"THEIR DARK ORDER SOUGHT ETERNAL LIFE.
"THE PROMISE OF GOD, HERE ON EARTH.
"INTRIGUED BY THE WHISPERS AND LEGENDS, THE MONKS BROUGHT FORTH SOME POOR ATTAINTED SINNER TO TRY THE THEORIES OF THE INFIDEL PHILOSOPHERS...
"HE IS CALLED THE HERETIC.
"AND HE HAS ROAMED THESE HALLS, DEATHLESS AND INSANE, SINCE THE DAYS OF THE SPANISH INQUISITION.
"EACH LAZARUS PIT CAN ONLY BE USED THREE TIMES BEFORE IT FAILS AND SPOILS.
"AND MY FATHER...WHO HAS MADE THE POOLS A... 'SPECIAL STUDY' OF HIS THROUGH THE AGES...
"...FELT THROUGH THE WEBS OF MAGIC IN THE WORLD THAT ONE HAD BEEN USED.
AND AFTER FIVE HUNDRED YEARS OF SILENCE IN THIS MAZE...
...SOMETHING WOKE UP.

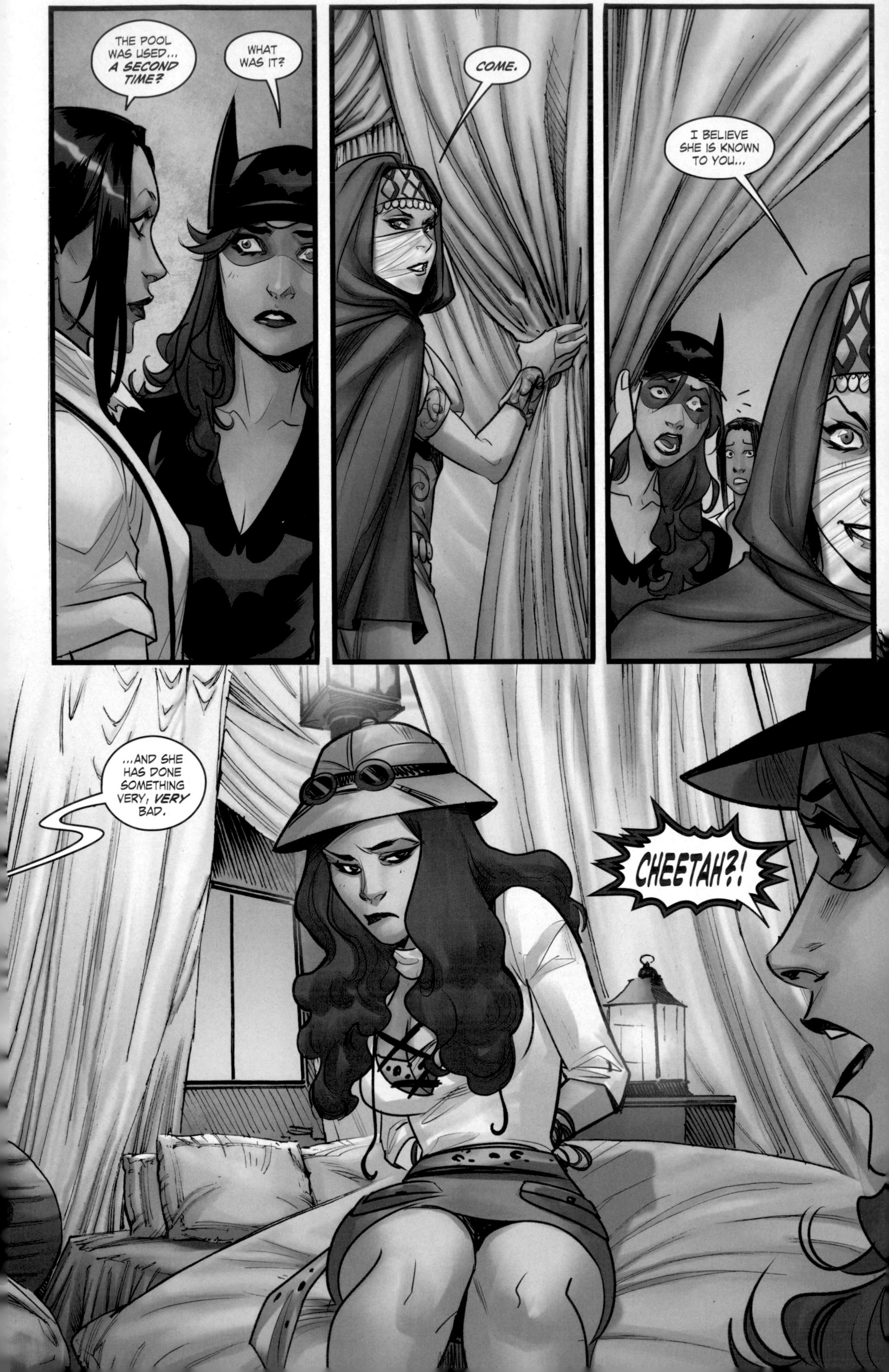
THE POOL WAS USED... *A SECOND TIME?*
WHAT WAS IT?
COME.
I BELIEVE SHE IS KNOWN TO YOU...
...AND SHE HAS DONE SOMETHING VERY, *VERY* BAD.
CHEETAH?!

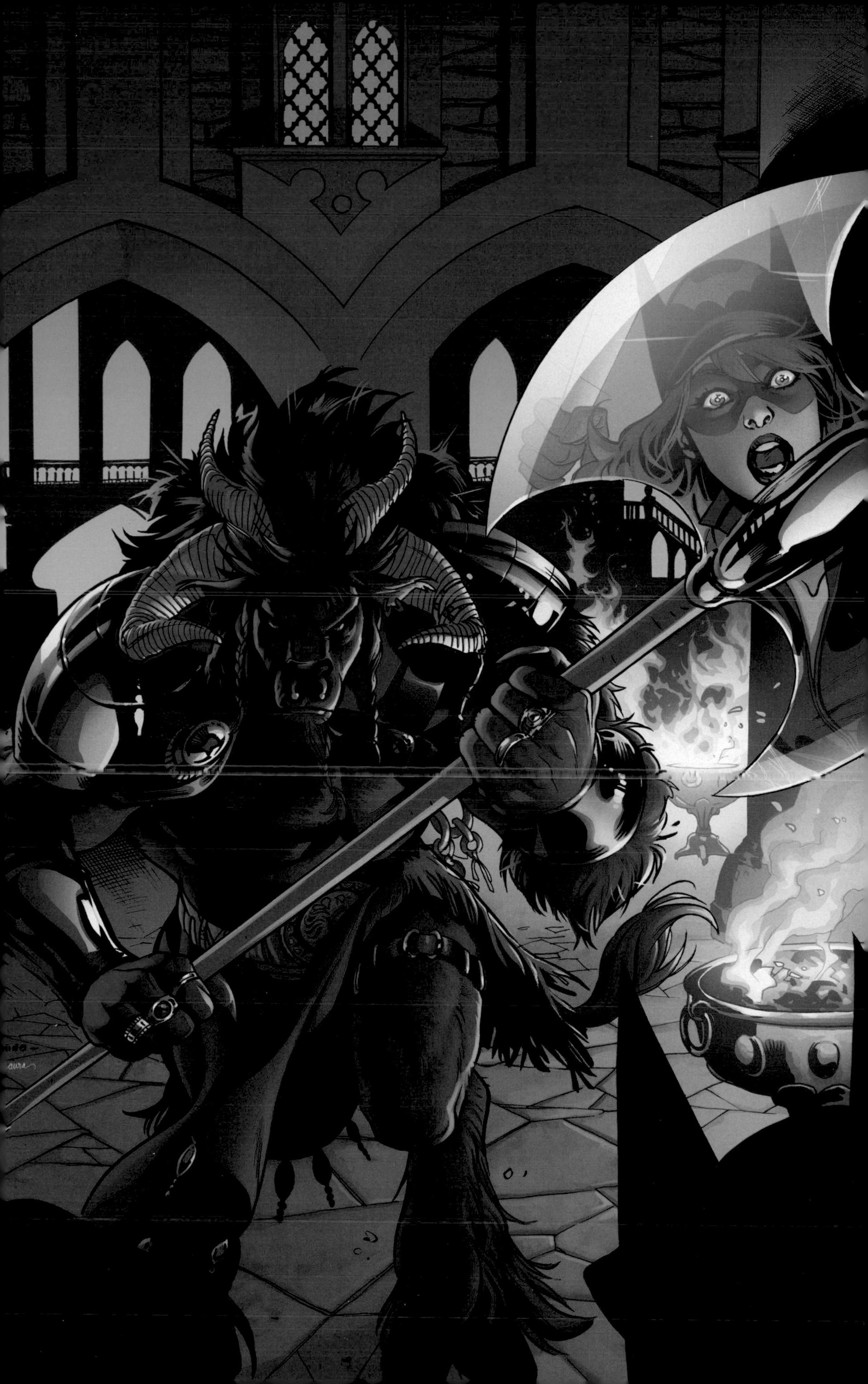

WAR BONDS

PARTS FIVE and SIX

Written by
MARGUERITE BENNETT

Art by
SIYA OUM

Colors by
J. NANJAN

Cover by
EMANUELA LUPACCHINO
and **LAURA MARTIN**

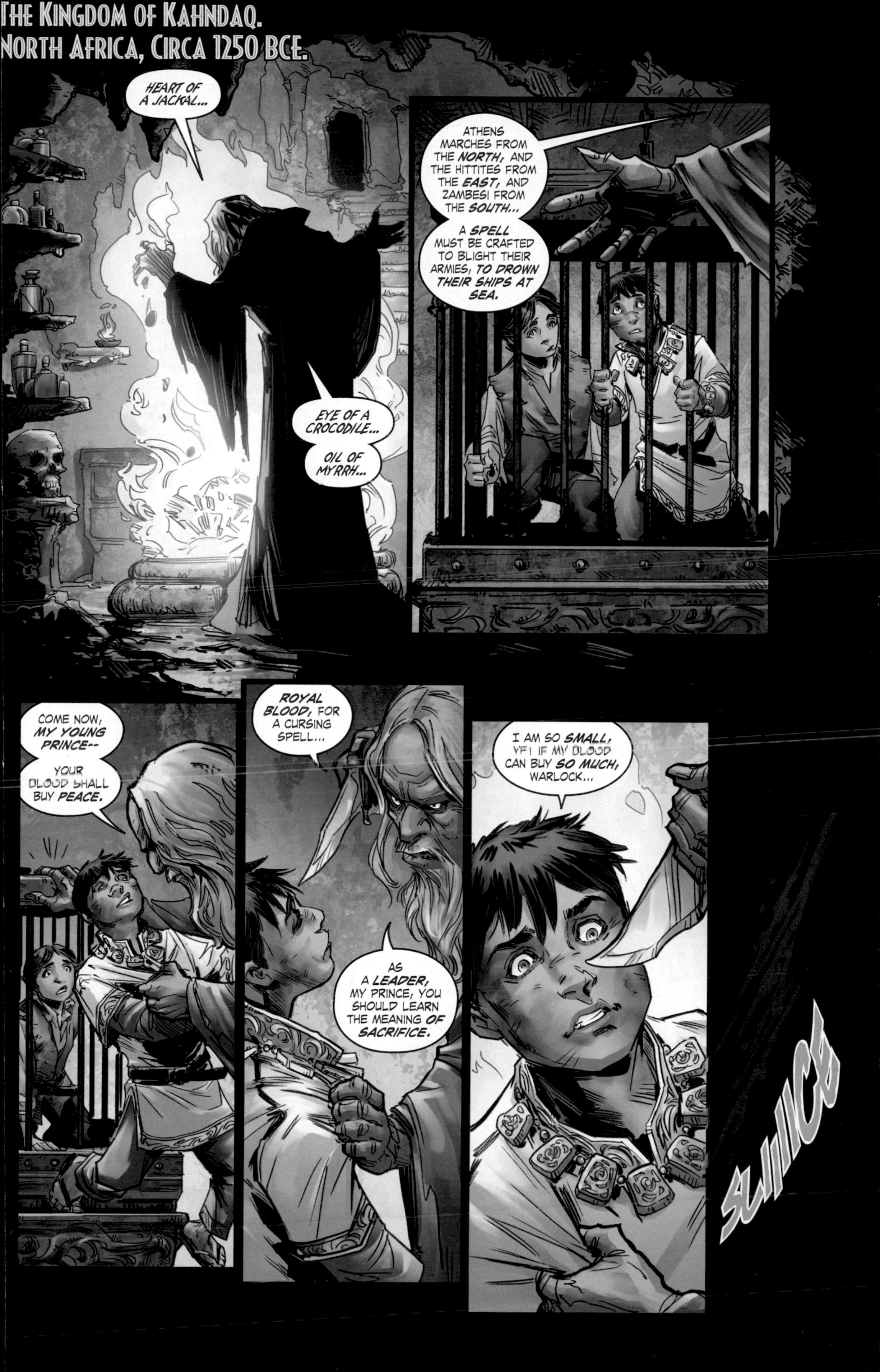

THE KINGDOM OF KAHNDAQ.
NORTH AFRICA, CIRCA 1250 BCE.
HEART OF A JACKAL...
EYE OF A CROCODILE...
OIL OF MYRRH...
ATHENS MARCHES FROM THE NORTH, AND THE HITTITES FROM THE EAST, AND ZAMBESI FROM THE SOUTH...
A SPELL MUST BE CRAFTED TO BLIGHT THEIR ARMIES, TO DROWN THEIR SHIPS AT SEA.
COME NOW, MY YOUNG PRINCE--
YOUR BLOOD SHALL BUY PEACE.
ROYAL BLOOD, FOR A CURSING SPELL...
AS A LEADER, MY PRINCE, YOU SHOULD LEARN THE MEANING OF SACRIFICE.
I AM SO SMALL, YET IF MY BLOOD CAN BUY SO MUCH, WARLOCK...
SLIIICE

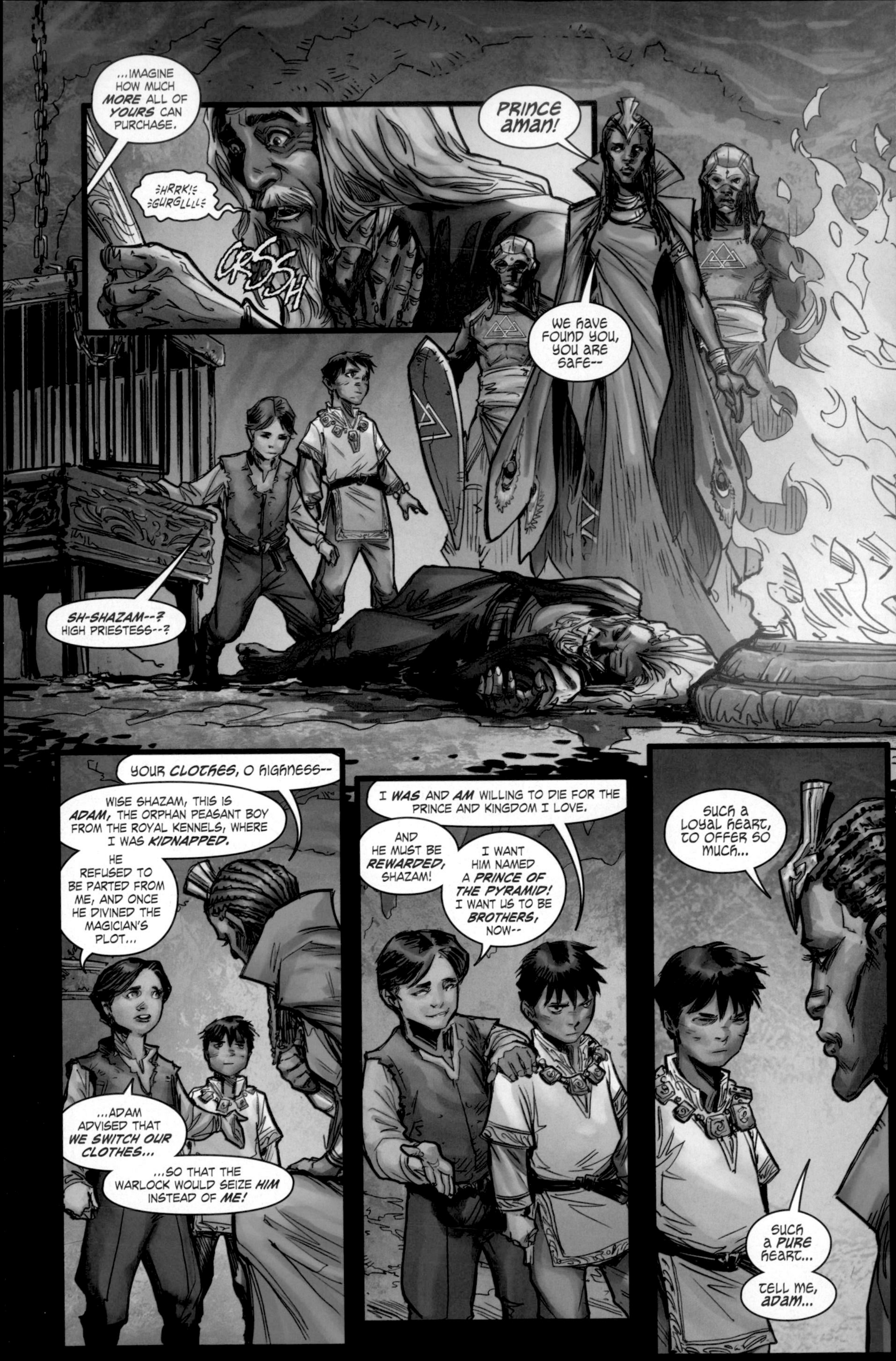

...IMAGINE HOW MUCH MORE ALL OF YOURS CAN PURCHASE.
HRRK! GURGLLLL
CRSSH
PRINCE AMAN!
WE HAVE FOUND YOU, YOU ARE SAFE--
SH-SHAZAM--? HIGH PRIESTESS--?
YOUR CLOTHES, O HIGHNESS--
WISE SHAZAM, THIS IS ADAM, THE ORPHAN PEASANT BOY FROM THE ROYAL KENNELS, WHERE I WAS KIDNAPPED.
HE REFUSED TO BE PARTED FROM ME, AND ONCE HE DIVINED THE MAGICIAN'S PLOT...
...ADAM ADVISED THAT WE SWITCH OUR CLOTHES...
...SO THAT THE WARLOCK WOULD SEIZE HIM INSTEAD OF ME!
I WAS AND AM WILLING TO DIE FOR THE PRINCE AND KINGDOM I LOVE.
AND HE MUST BE REWARDED, SHAZAM!
I WANT HIM NAMED A PRINCE OF THE PYRAMID! I WANT US TO BE BROTHERS, NOW--
SUCH A LOYAL HEART, TO OFFER SO MUCH...
SUCH A PURE HEART...
TELL ME, ADAM...

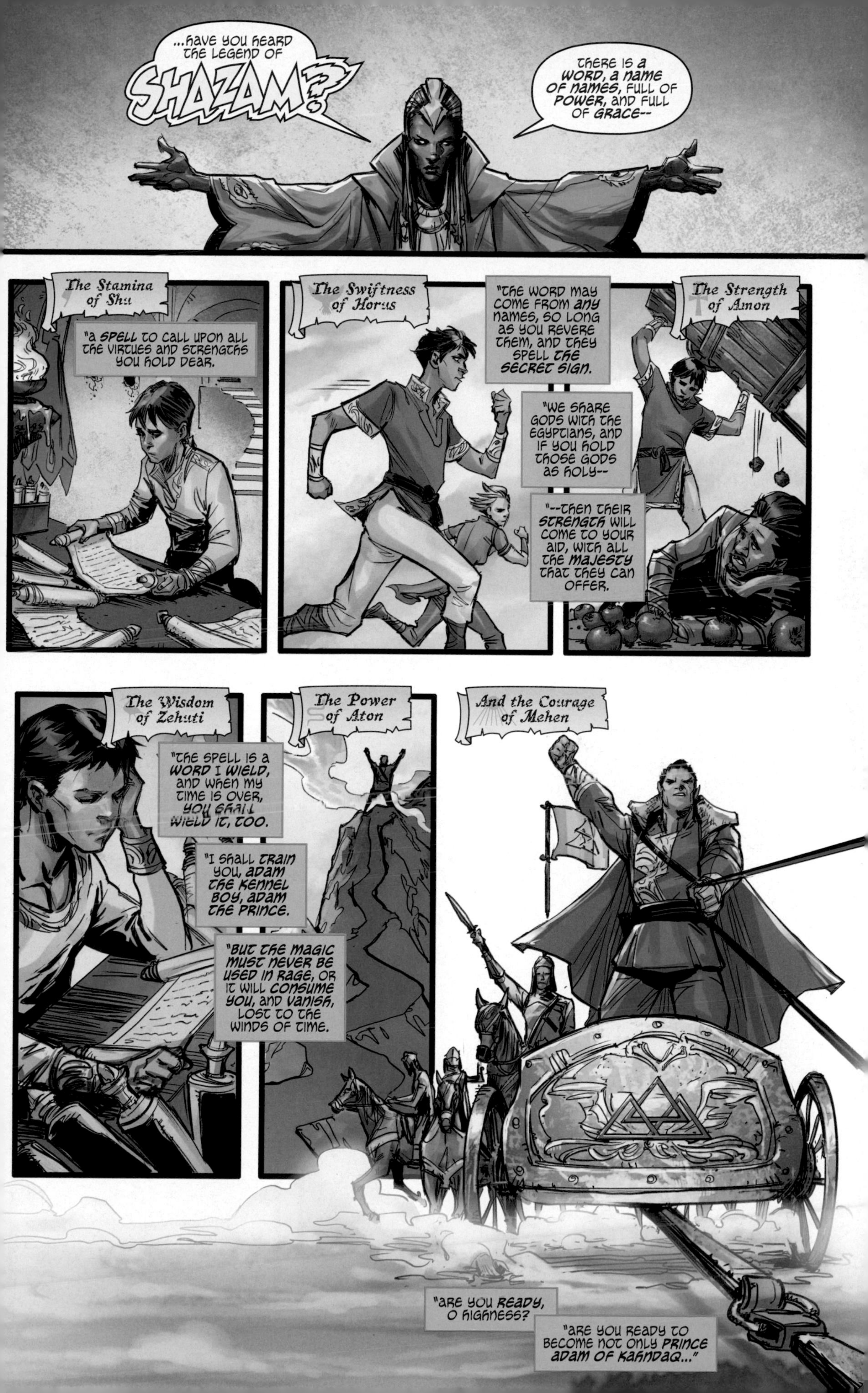

...HAVE YOU HEARD THE LEGEND OF SHAZAM?
THERE IS A WORD, A NAME OF NAMES, FULL OF POWER, AND FULL OF GRACE--
The Stamina of Shu
"A SPELL TO CALL UPON ALL THE VIRTUES AND STRENGTHS YOU HOLD DEAR.
The Swiftness of Horus
"THE WORD MAY COME FROM ANY NAMES, SO LONG AS YOU REVERE THEM, AND THEY SPELL THE SECRET SIGN.
"WE SHARE GODS WITH THE EGYPTIANS, AND IF YOU HOLD THOSE GODS AS HOLY--
"--THEN THEIR STRENGTH WILL COME TO YOUR AID, WITH ALL THE MAJESTY THAT THEY CAN OFFER.
The Strength of Amon
The Wisdom of Zehuti
"THE SPELL IS A WORD I WIELD, AND WHEN MY TIME IS OVER, YOU SHALL WIELD IT, TOO.
"I SHALL TRAIN YOU, ADAM THE KENNEL BOY, ADAM THE PRINCE.
"BUT THE MAGIC MUST NEVER BE USED IN RAGE, OR IT WILL CONSUME YOU, AND VANISH, LOST TO THE WINDS OF TIME.
The Power of Aton
And the Courage of Mehen
"ARE YOU READY, O HIGHNESS?
"ARE YOU READY TO BECOME NOT ONLY PRINCE ADAM OF KAHNDAQ..."

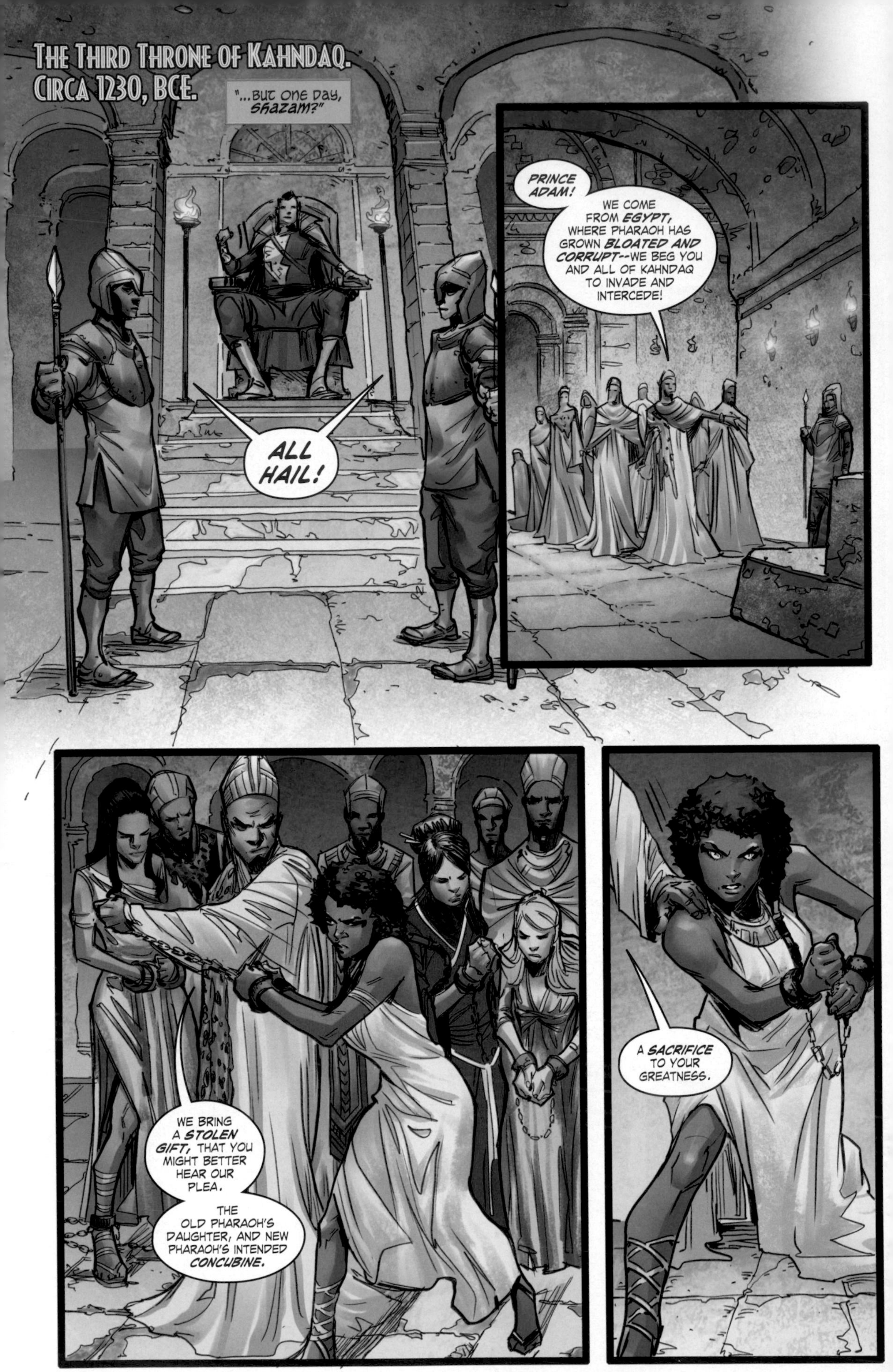
THE THIRD THRONE OF KAHNDAQ.
CIRCA 1230, BCE.
"...BUT ONE DAY, SHAZAM?"
ALL HAIL!
PRINCE ADAM!
WE COME FROM EGYPT, WHERE PHARAOH HAS GROWN BLOATED AND CORRUPT--WE BEG YOU AND ALL OF KAHNDAQ TO INVADE AND INTERCEDE!
WE BRING A STOLEN GIFT, THAT YOU MIGHT BETTER HEAR OUR PLEA.
THE OLD PHARAOH'S DAUGHTER, AND NEW PHARAOH'S INTENDED CONCUBINE.
A SACRIFICE TO YOUR GREATNESS.

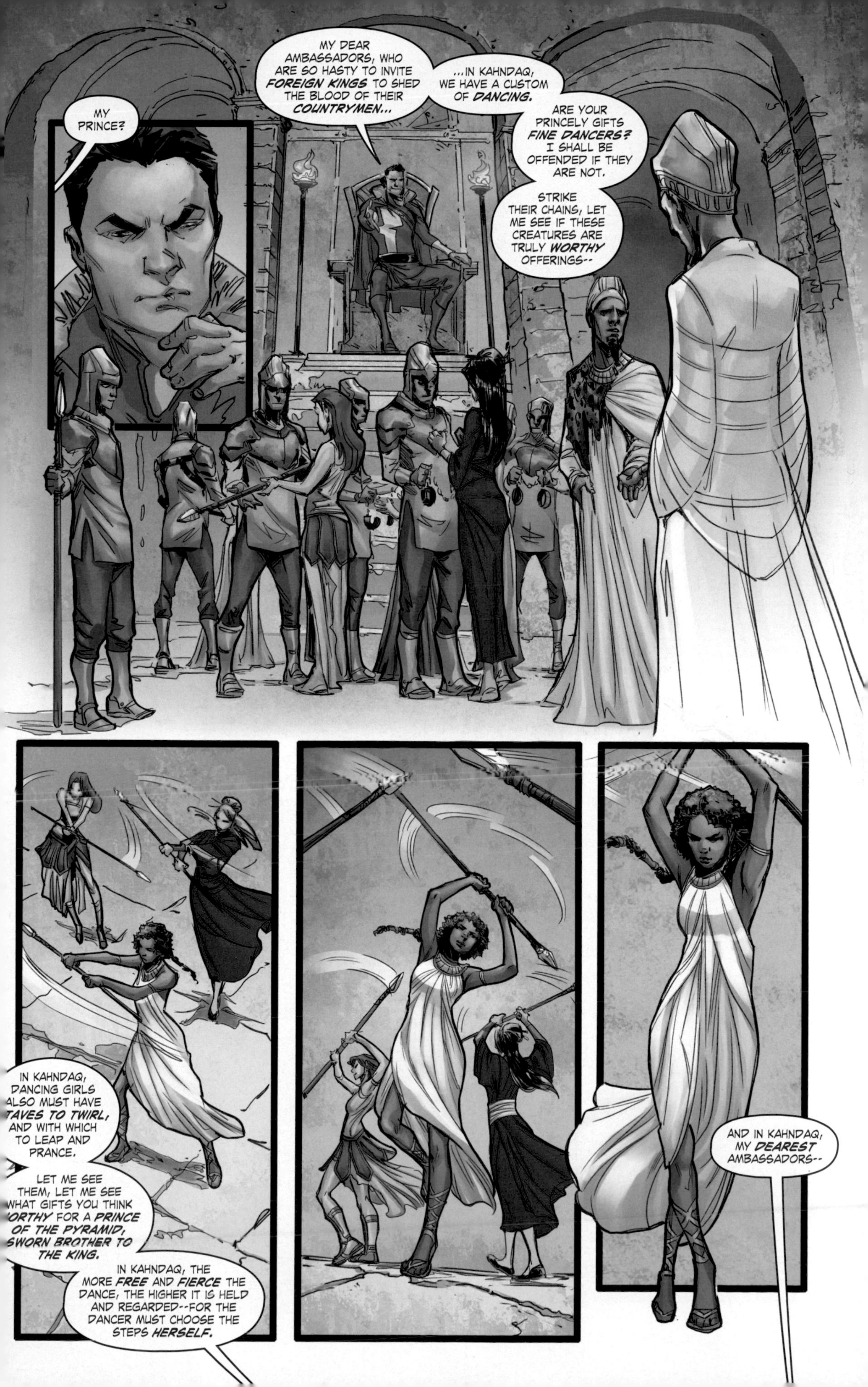
MY PRINCE?
MY DEAR AMBASSADORS, WHO ARE SO HASTY TO INVITE FOREIGN KINGS TO SHED THE BLOOD OF THEIR COUNTRYMEN...
...IN KAHNDAQ, WE HAVE A CUSTOM OF DANCING.
ARE YOUR PRINCELY GIFTS FINE DANCERS? I SHALL BE OFFENDED IF THEY ARE NOT.
STRIKE THEIR CHAINS, LET ME SEE IF THESE CREATURES ARE TRULY WORTHY OFFERINGS--
IN KAHNDAQ, DANCING GIRLS ALSO MUST HAVE STAVES TO TWIRL, AND WITH WHICH TO LEAP AND PRANCE.
LET ME SEE THEM, LET ME SEE WHAT GIFTS YOU THINK WORTHY FOR A PRINCE OF THE PYRAMID, SWORN BROTHER TO THE KING.
IN KAHNDAQ, THE MORE FREE AND FIERCE THE DANCE, THE HIGHER IT IS HELD AND REGARDED--FOR THE DANCER MUST CHOOSE THE STEPS HERSELF.
AND IN KAHNDAQ, MY DEAREST AMBASSADORS--

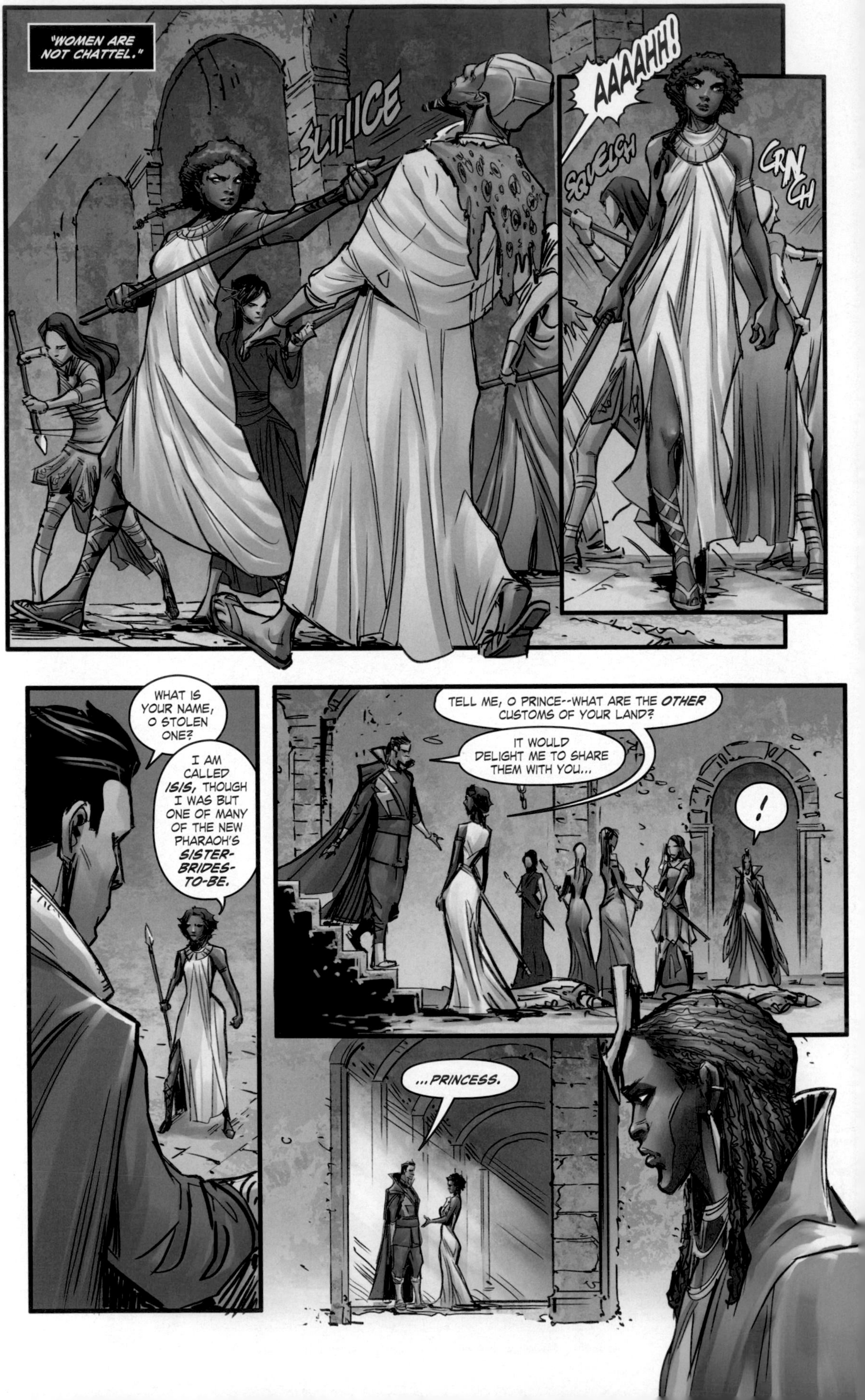
"WOMEN ARE NOT CHATTEL."
SLIIIICE
AAAAHH!
SQUELCH
CRNCH
WHAT IS YOUR NAME, O STOLEN ONE?
I AM CALLED ISIS, THOUGH I WAS BUT ONE OF MANY OF THE NEW PHARAOH'S SISTER-BRIDES-TO-BE.
TELL ME, O PRINCE--WHAT ARE THE OTHER CUSTOMS OF YOUR LAND?
IT WOULD DELIGHT ME TO SHARE THEM WITH YOU...
!
...PRINCESS.

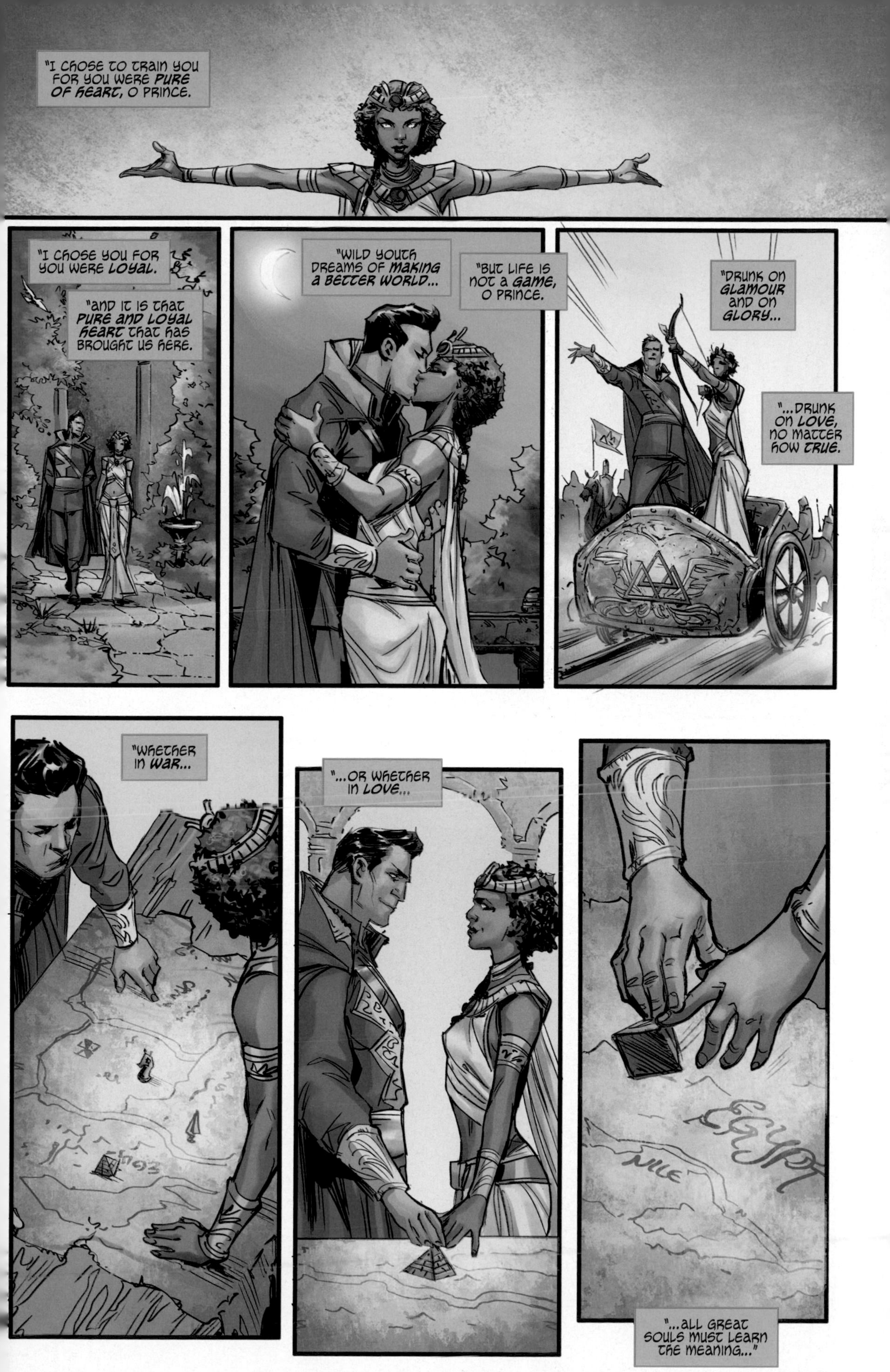
"I CHOSE TO TRAIN YOU FOR YOU WERE PURE OF HEART, O PRINCE.
"I CHOSE YOU FOR YOU WERE LOYAL.
"AND IT IS THAT PURE AND LOYAL HEART THAT HAS BROUGHT US HERE.
"WILD YOUTH DREAMS OF MAKING A BETTER WORLD...
"BUT LIFE IS NOT A GAME, O PRINCE.
"DRUNK ON GLAMOUR AND ON GLORY...
"...DRUNK ON LOVE, NO MATTER HOW TRUE.
"WHETHER IN WAR...
"...OR WHETHER IN LOVE...
EGYPT
NILE
"...ALL GREAT SOULS MUST LEARN THE MEANING..."

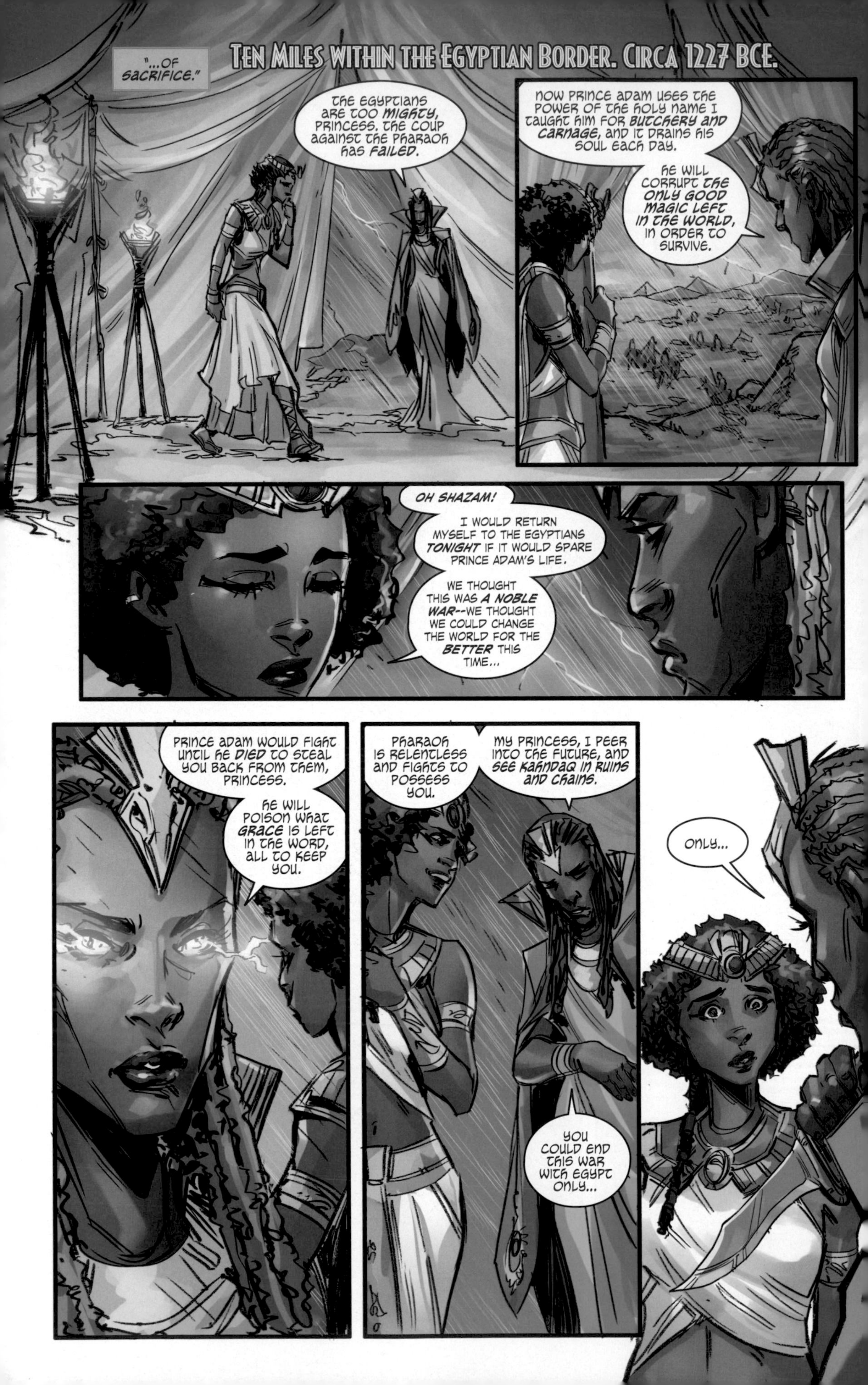

"...OF SACRIFICE."
TEN MILES WITHIN THE EGYPTIAN BORDER. CIRCA 1227 BCE.
THE EGYPTIANS ARE TOO MIGHTY, PRINCESS. THE COUP AGAINST THE PHARAOH HAS FAILED.
NOW PRINCE ADAM USES THE POWER OF THE HOLY NAME I TAUGHT HIM FOR BUTCHERY AND CARNAGE, AND IT DRAINS HIS SOUL EACH DAY.
HE WILL CORRUPT THE ONLY GOOD MAGIC LEFT IN THE WORLD, IN ORDER TO SURVIVE.
OH SHAZAM!
I WOULD RETURN MYSELF TO THE EGYPTIANS TONIGHT IF IT WOULD SPARE PRINCE ADAM'S LIFE.
WE THOUGHT THIS WAS A NOBLE WAR--WE THOUGHT WE COULD CHANGE THE WORLD FOR THE BETTER THIS TIME...
PRINCE ADAM WOULD FIGHT UNTIL HE DIED TO STEAL YOU BACK FROM THEM, PRINCESS.
HE WILL POISON WHAT GRACE IS LEFT IN THE WORD, ALL TO KEEP YOU.
PHARAOH IS RELENTLESS AND FIGHTS TO POSSESS YOU.
MY PRINCESS, I PEER INTO THE FUTURE, AND SEE KAHNDAQ IN RUINS AND CHAINS.
YOU COULD END THIS WAR WITH EGYPT ONLY...
ONLY...

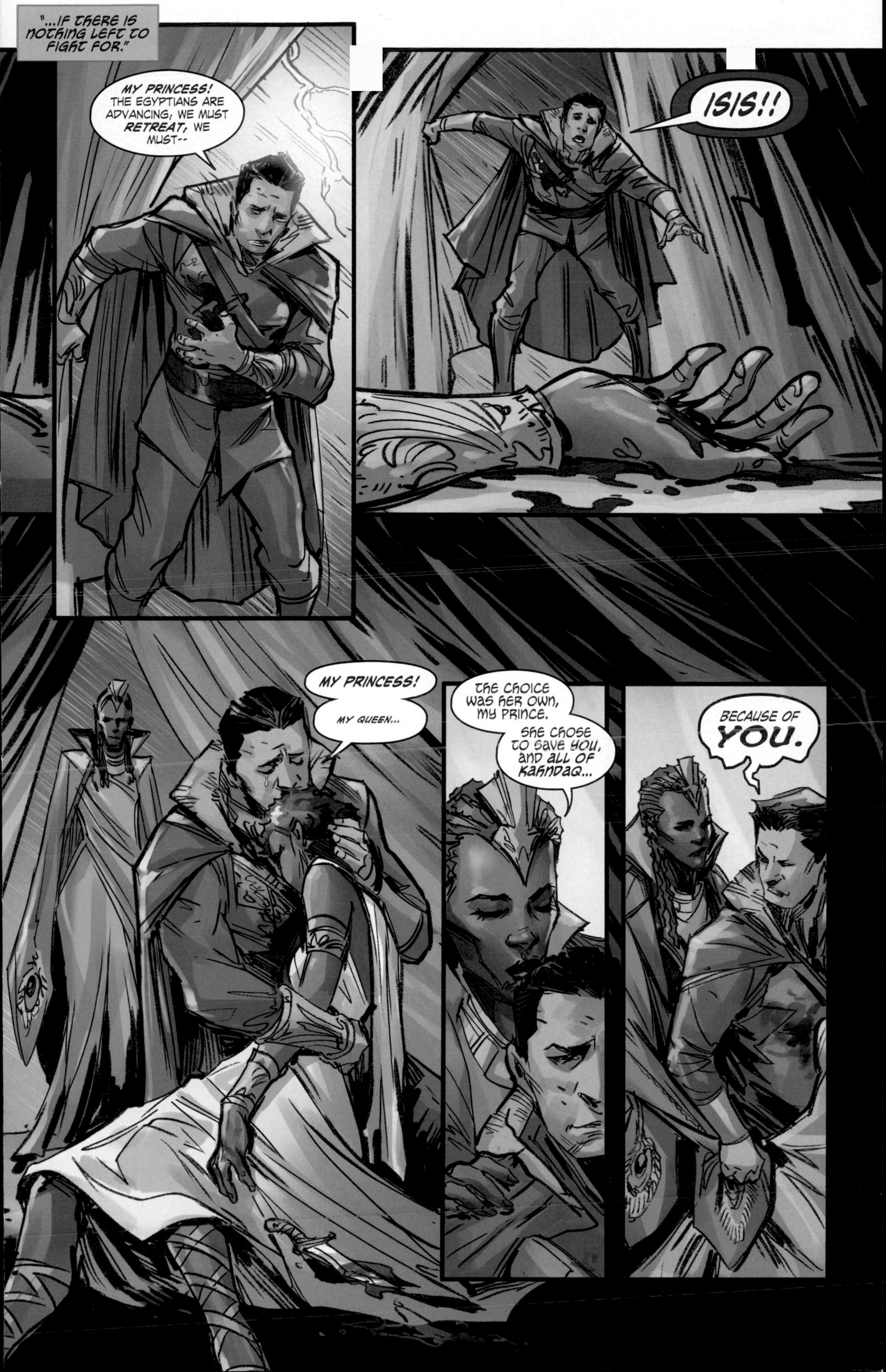
"...IF THERE IS NOTHING LEFT TO FIGHT FOR."
MY PRINCESS! THE EGYPTIANS ARE ADVANCING, WE MUST RETREAT, WE MUST--
ISIS!!
MY PRINCESS!
MY QUEEN...
THE CHOICE WAS HER OWN, MY PRINCE.
SHE CHOSE TO SAVE YOU, AND ALL OF KAHNDAQ...
BECAUSE OF YOU.

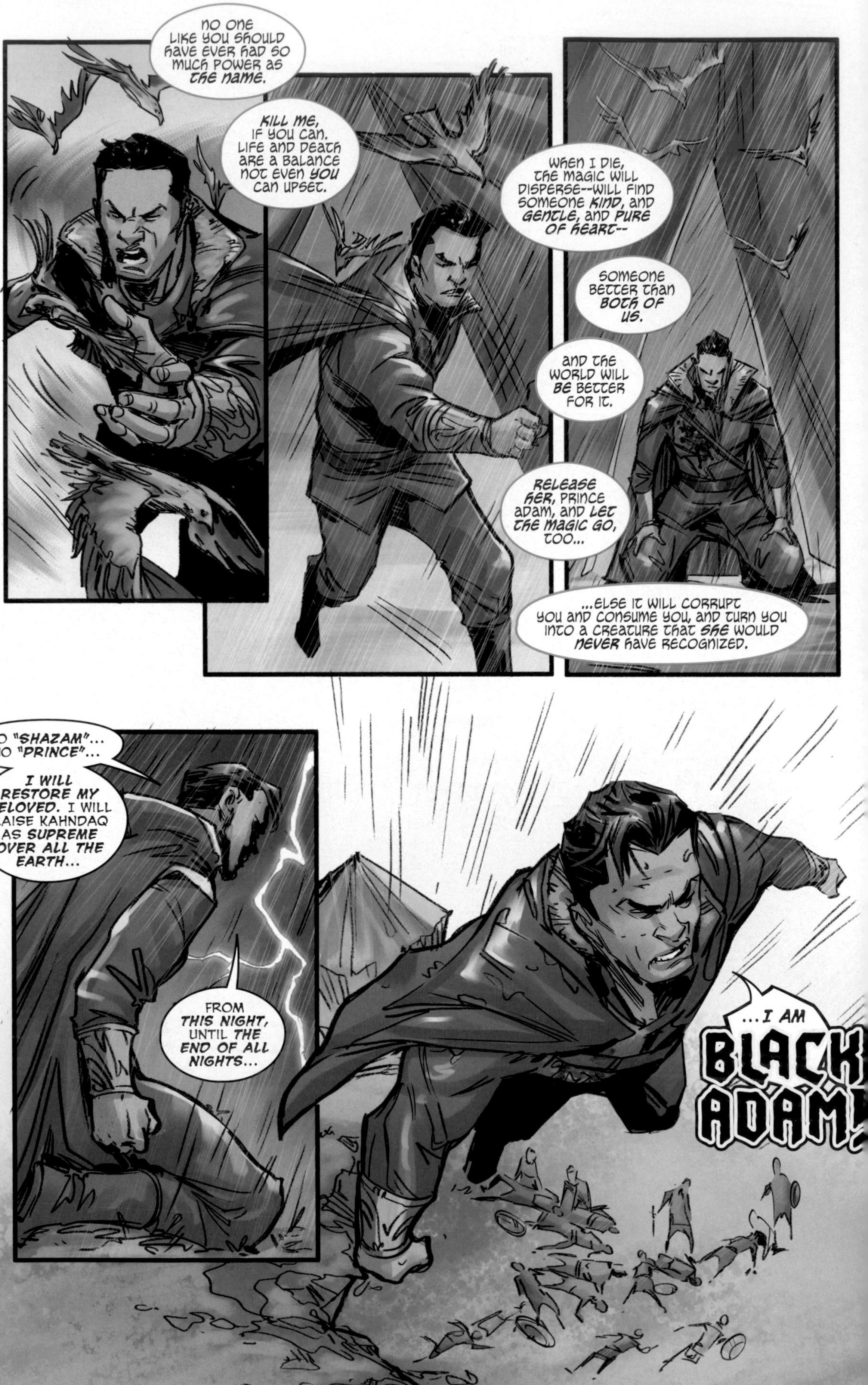
NO ONE LIKE YOU SHOULD HAVE EVER HAD SO MUCH POWER AS THE NAME.
KILL ME, IF YOU CAN. LIFE AND DEATH ARE A BALANCE NOT EVEN YOU CAN UPSET.
WHEN I DIE, THE MAGIC WILL DISPERSE--WILL FIND SOMEONE KIND, AND GENTLE, AND PURE OF HEART--
SOMEONE BETTER THAN BOTH OF US.
AND THE WORLD WILL BE BETTER FOR IT.
RELEASE HER, PRINCE ADAM, AND LET THE MAGIC GO, TOO...
...ELSE IT WILL CORRUPT YOU AND CONSUME YOU, AND TURN YOU INTO A CREATURE THAT SHE WOULD NEVER HAVE RECOGNIZED.
NO "SHAZAM"... NO "PRINCE"...
I WILL RESTORE MY BELOVED. I WILL RAISE KAHNDAQ AS SUPREME OVER ALL THE EARTH...
FROM THIS NIGHT, UNTIL THE END OF ALL NIGHTS...
...I AM
BLACK ADAM!

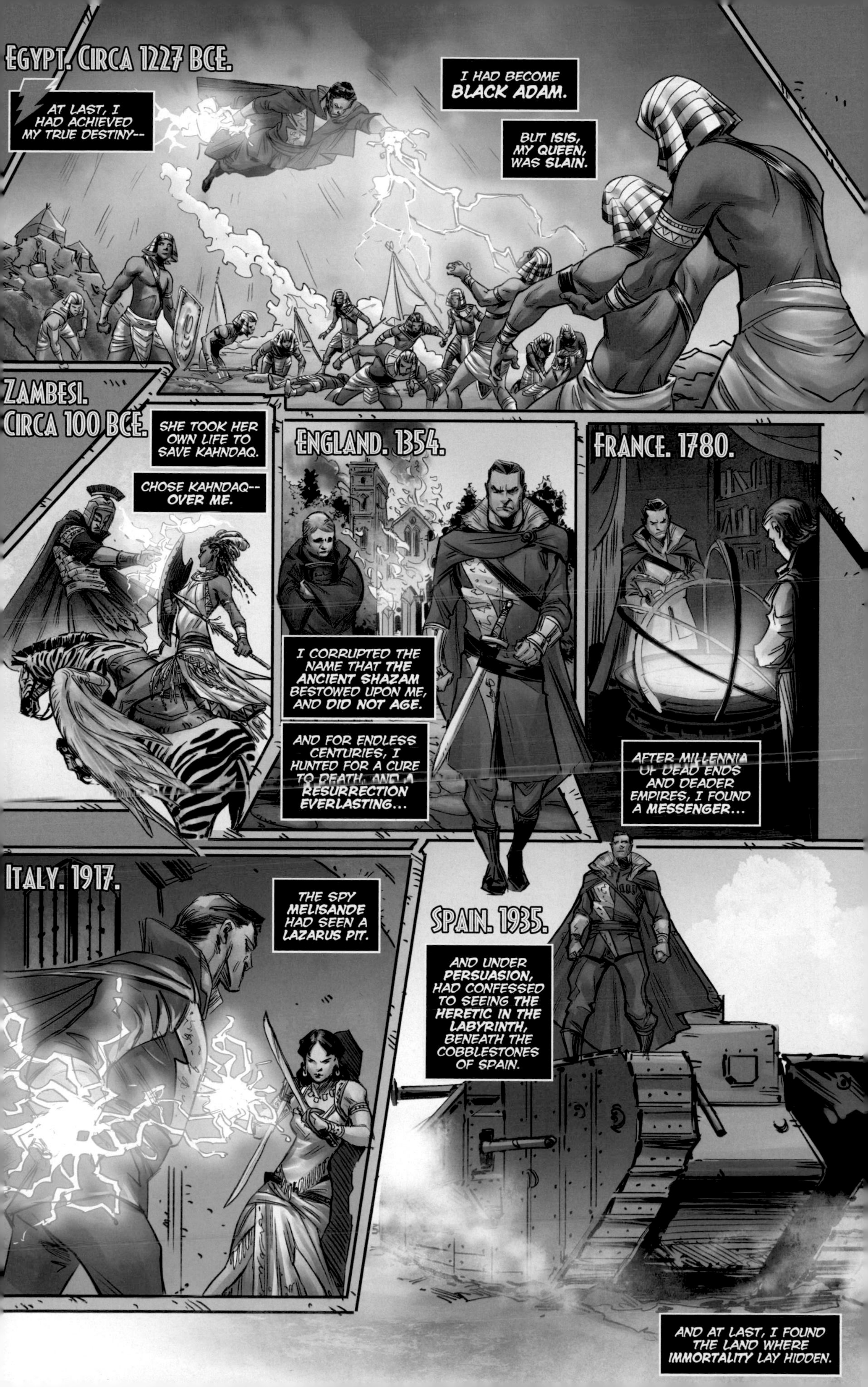

EGYPT. CIRCA 1227 BCE.
AT LAST, I HAD ACHIEVED MY TRUE DESTINY--
I HAD BECOME BLACK ADAM.
BUT ISIS, MY QUEEN, WAS SLAIN.
ZAMBESI. CIRCA 100 BCE.
SHE TOOK HER OWN LIFE TO SAVE KAHNDAQ.
CHOSE KAHNDAQ-- OVER ME.
ENGLAND. 1354.
I CORRUPTED THE NAME THAT THE ANCIENT SHAZAM BESTOWED UPON ME, AND DID NOT AGE.
AND FOR ENDLESS CENTURIES, I HUNTED FOR A CURE TO DEATH, AND A RESURRECTION EVERLASTING...
FRANCE. 1780.
AFTER MILLENNIA OF DEAD ENDS AND DEADER EMPIRES, I FOUND A MESSENGER...
ITALY. 1917.
THE SPY MELISANDE HAD SEEN A LAZARUS PIT.
SPAIN. 1935.
AND UNDER PERSUASION, HAD CONFESSED TO SEEING THE HERETIC IN THE LABYRINTH, BENEATH THE COBBLESTONES OF SPAIN.
AND AT LAST, I FOUND THE LAND WHERE IMMORTALITY LAY HIDDEN.

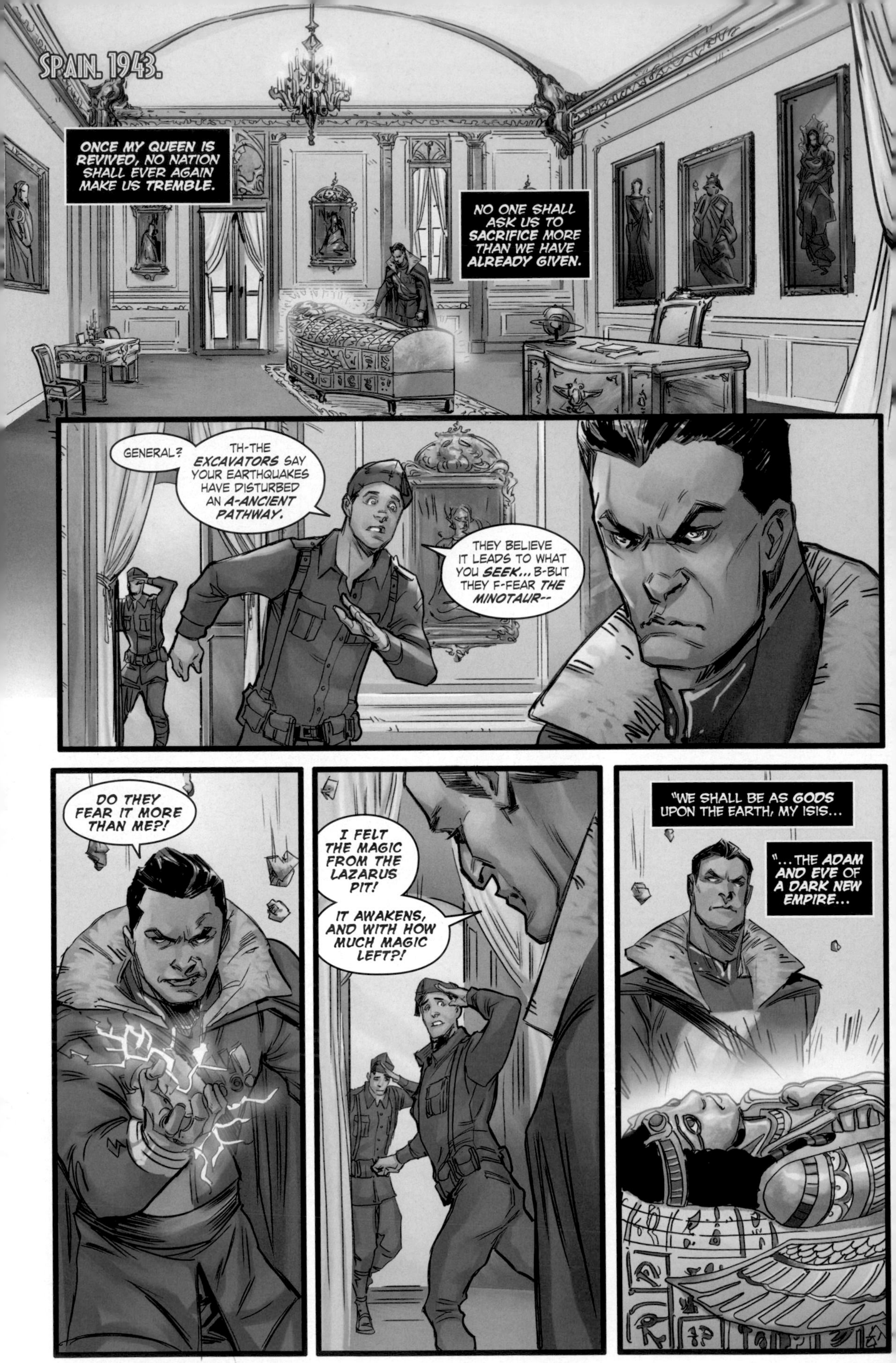
SPAIN. 1943.
ONCE MY QUEEN IS REVIVED, NO NATION SHALL EVER AGAIN MAKE US TREMBLE.
NO ONE SHALL ASK US TO SACRIFICE MORE THAN WE HAVE ALREADY GIVEN.
GENERAL?
TH-THE EXCAVATORS SAY YOUR EARTHQUAKES HAVE DISTURBED AN A-ANCIENT PATHWAY.
THEY BELIEVE IT LEADS TO WHAT YOU SEEK... B-BUT THEY F-FEAR THE MINOTAUR--
DO THEY FEAR IT MORE THAN ME?!
I FELT THE MAGIC FROM THE LAZARUS PIT!
IT AWAKENS, AND WITH HOW MUCH MAGIC LEFT?!
"WE SHALL BE AS GODS UPON THE EARTH, MY ISIS...
"...THE ADAM AND EVE OF A DARK NEW EMPIRE...

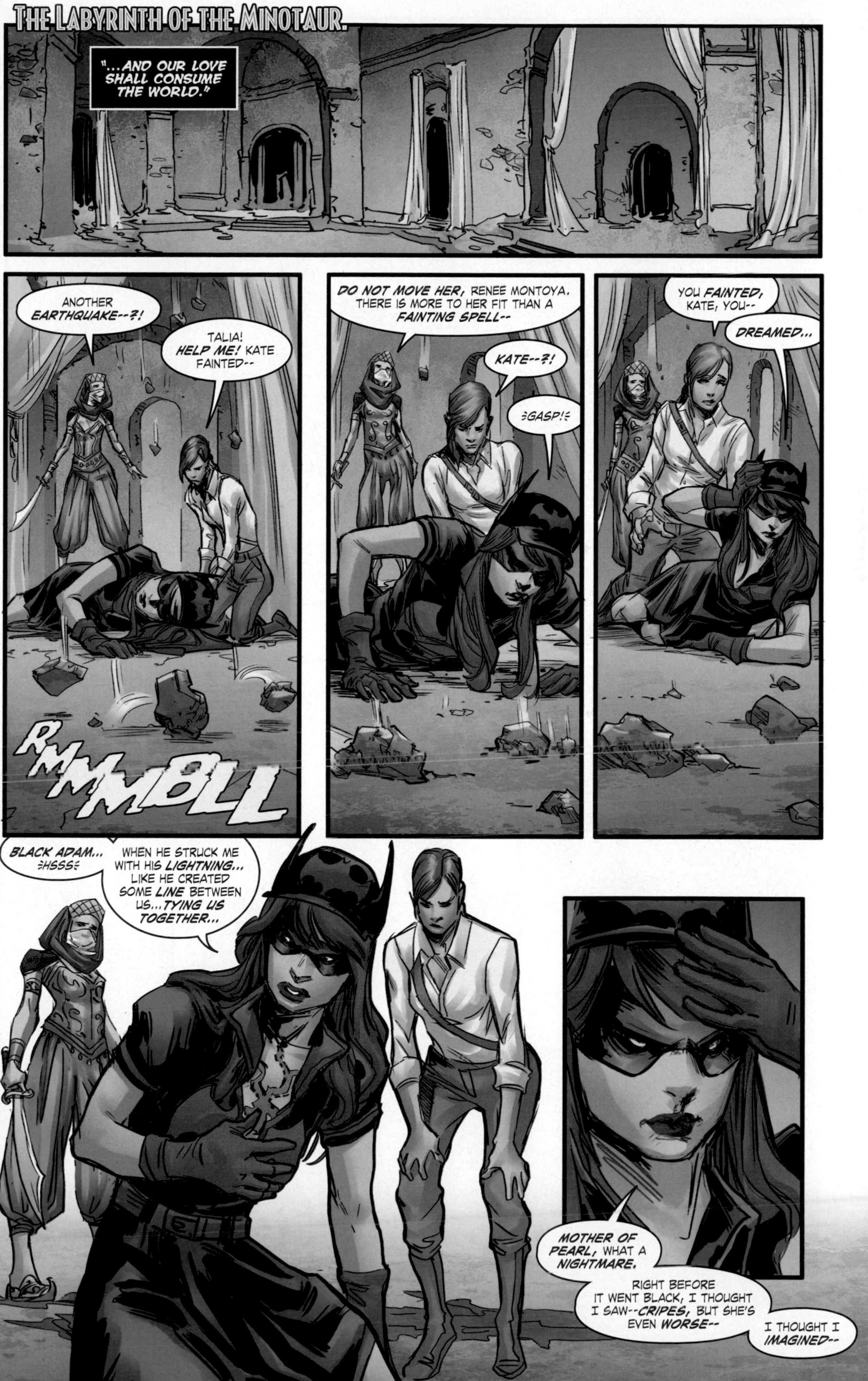
THE LABYRINTH OF THE MINOTAUR.
"...AND OUR LOVE SHALL CONSUME THE WORLD."
ANOTHER EARTHQUAKE--?!
TALIA! HELP ME! KATE FAINTED--
RMMMBLL
DO NOT MOVE HER, RENEE MONTOYA. THERE IS MORE TO HER FIT THAN A FAINTING SPELL--
KATE--?!
GASP!
YOU FAINTED, KATE, YOU--
DREAMED...
BLACK ADAM... HSSS
WHEN HE STRUCK ME WITH HIS LIGHTNING... LIKE HE CREATED SOME LINE BETWEEN US...TYING US TOGETHER...
MOTHER OF PEARL, WHAT A NIGHTMARE.
RIGHT BEFORE IT WENT BLACK, I THOUGHT I SAW--CRIPES, BUT SHE'S EVEN WORSE--
I THOUGHT I IMAGINED--

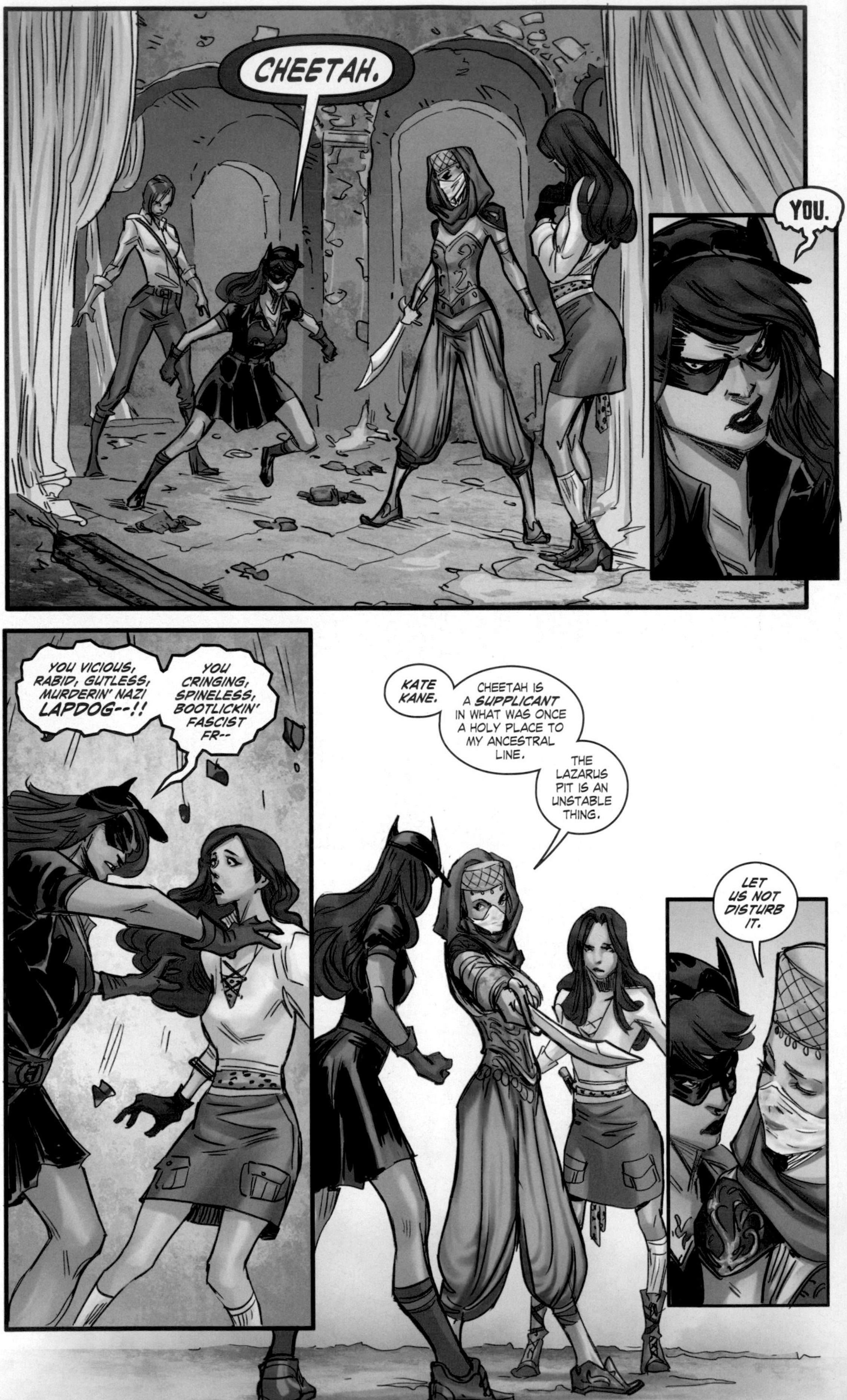
CHEETAH.
YOU.
YOU VICIOUS, RABID, GUTLESS, MURDERIN' NAZI LAPDOG--!!
YOU CRINGING, SPINELESS, BOOTLICKIN' FASCIST FR--
KATE KANE.
CHEETAH IS A SUPPLICANT IN WHAT WAS ONCE A HOLY PLACE TO MY ANCESTRAL LINE.
THE LAZARUS PIT IS AN UNSTABLE THING.
LET US NOT DISTURB IT.

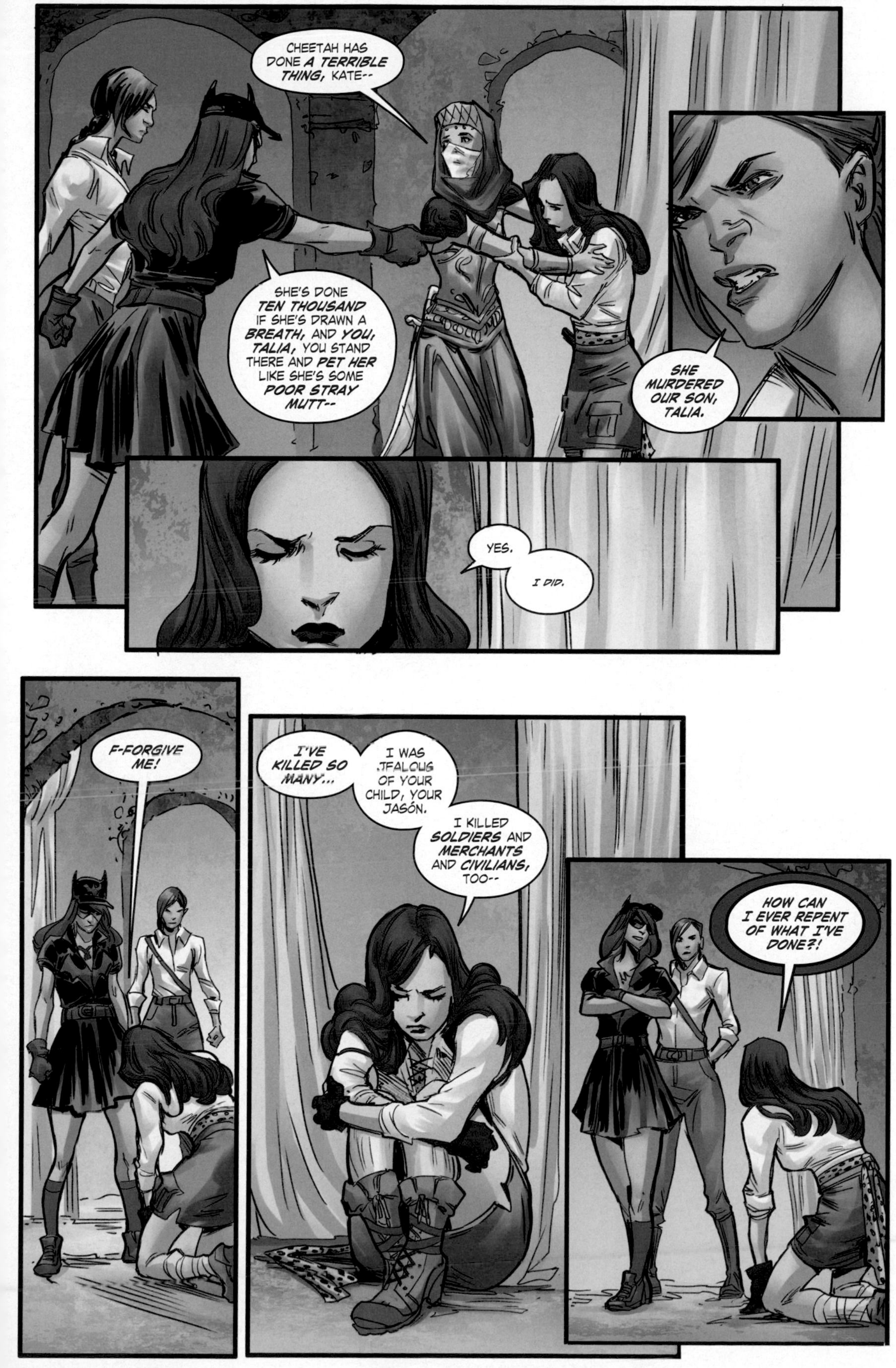
CHEETAH HAS DONE A TERRIBLE THING, KATE--
SHE'S DONE TEN THOUSAND IF SHE'S DRAWN A BREATH, AND YOU, TALIA, YOU STAND THERE AND PET HER LIKE SHE'S SOME POOR STRAY MUTT--
SHE MURDERED OUR SON, TALIA.
YES.
I DID.
F-FORGIVE ME!
I'VE KILLED SO MANY...
I WAS JEALOUS OF YOUR CHILD, YOUR JASÓN.
I KILLED SOLDIERS AND MERCHANTS AND CIVILIANS, TOO--
HOW CAN I EVER REPENT OF WHAT I'VE DONE?!

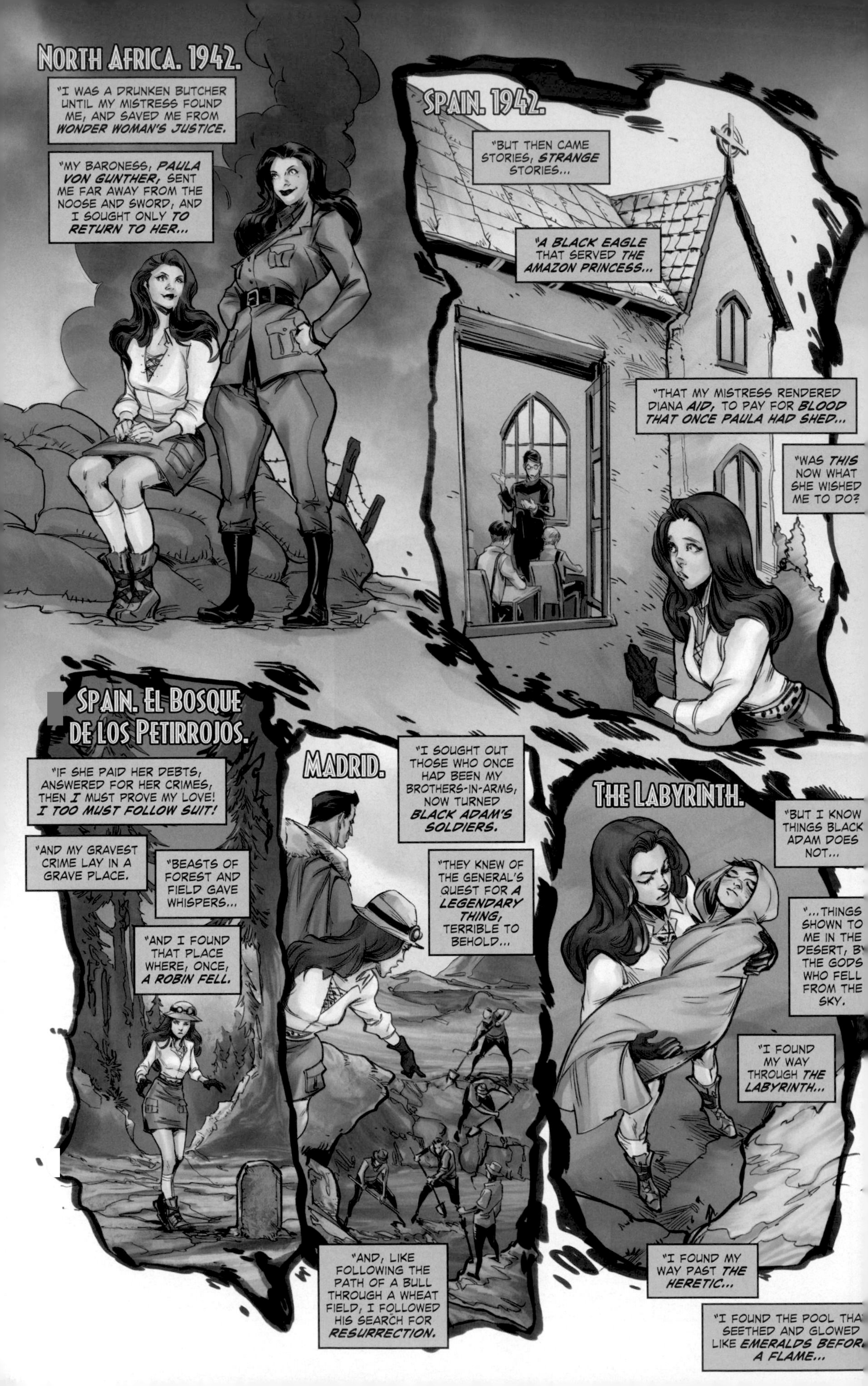
North Africa. 1942.
"I WAS A DRUNKEN BUTCHER UNTIL MY MISTRESS FOUND ME, AND SAVED ME FROM WONDER WOMAN'S JUSTICE.
"MY BARONESS, PAULA VON GUNTHER, SENT ME FAR AWAY FROM THE NOOSE AND SWORD, AND I SOUGHT ONLY TO RETURN TO HER...
Spain. 1942.
"BUT THEN CAME STORIES, STRANGE STORIES...
"A BLACK EAGLE THAT SERVED THE AMAZON PRINCESS...
"THAT MY MISTRESS RENDERED DIANA AID, TO PAY FOR BLOOD THAT ONCE PAULA HAD SHED...
"WAS THIS NOW WHAT SHE WISHED ME TO DO?
Spain. El Bosque de los Petirrojos.
"IF SHE PAID HER DEBTS, ANSWERED FOR HER CRIMES, THEN I MUST PROVE MY LOVE! I TOO MUST FOLLOW SUIT!
"AND MY GRAVEST CRIME LAY IN A GRAVE PLACE.
"BEASTS OF FOREST AND FIELD GAVE WHISPERS...
"AND I FOUND THAT PLACE WHERE, ONCE, A ROBIN FELL.
Madrid.
"I SOUGHT OUT THOSE WHO ONCE HAD BEEN MY BROTHERS-IN-ARMS, NOW TURNED BLACK ADAM'S SOLDIERS.
"THEY KNEW OF THE GENERAL'S QUEST FOR A LEGENDARY THING, TERRIBLE TO BEHOLD...
"AND, LIKE FOLLOWING THE PATH OF A BULL THROUGH A WHEAT FIELD, I FOLLOWED HIS SEARCH FOR RESURRECTION.
The Labyrinth.
"BUT I KNOW THINGS BLACK ADAM DOES NOT...
"...THINGS SHOWN TO ME IN THE DESERT, BY THE GODS WHO FELL FROM THE SKY.
"I FOUND MY WAY THROUGH THE LABYRINTH...
"I FOUND MY WAY PAST THE HERETIC...
"I FOUND THE POOL THAT SEETHED AND GLOWED LIKE EMERALDS BEFORE A FLAME...

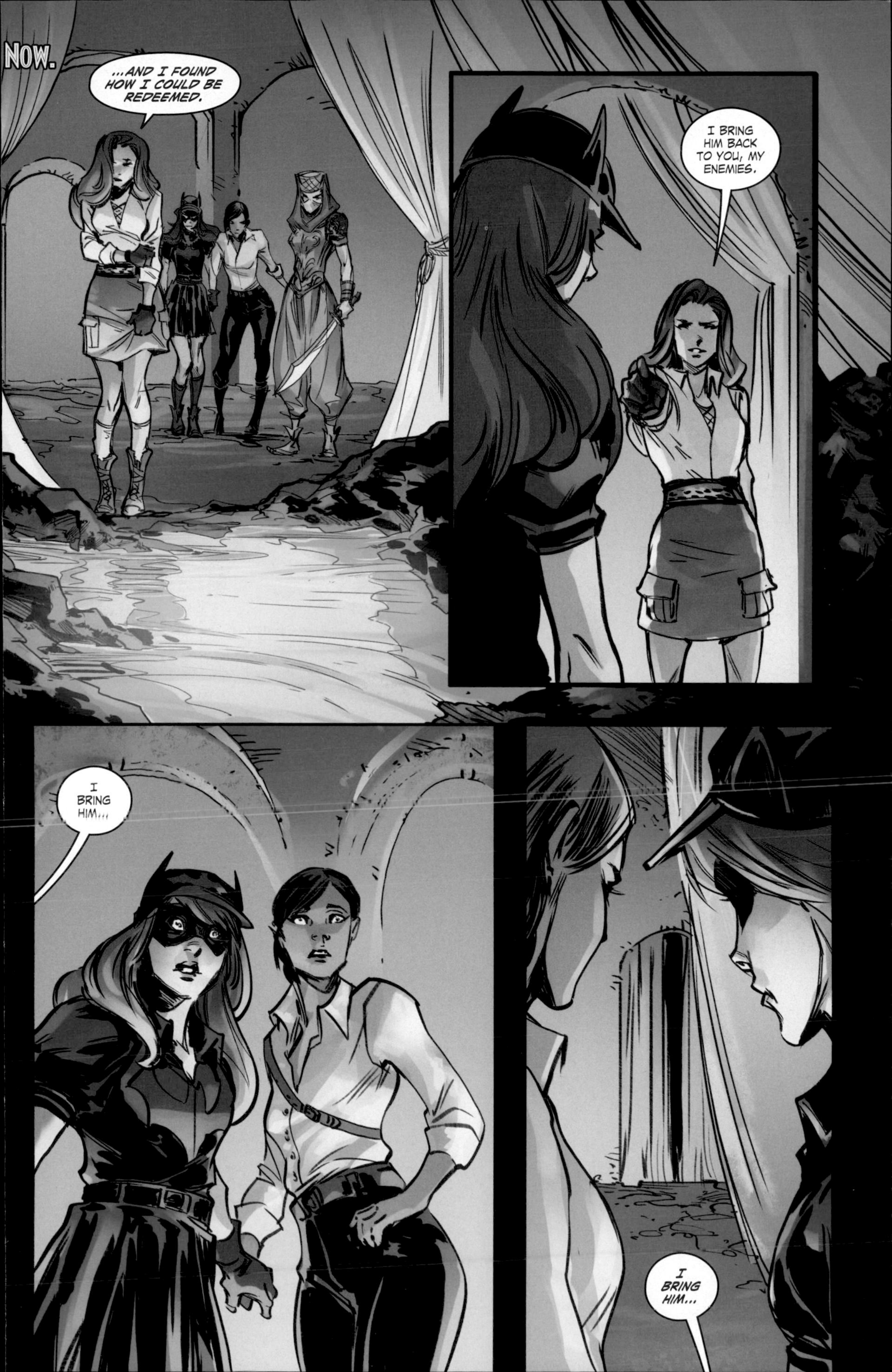
NOW.
...AND I FOUND HOW I COULD BE REDEEMED.
I BRING HIM BACK TO YOU, MY ENEMIES.
I BRING HIM...
I BRING HIM...

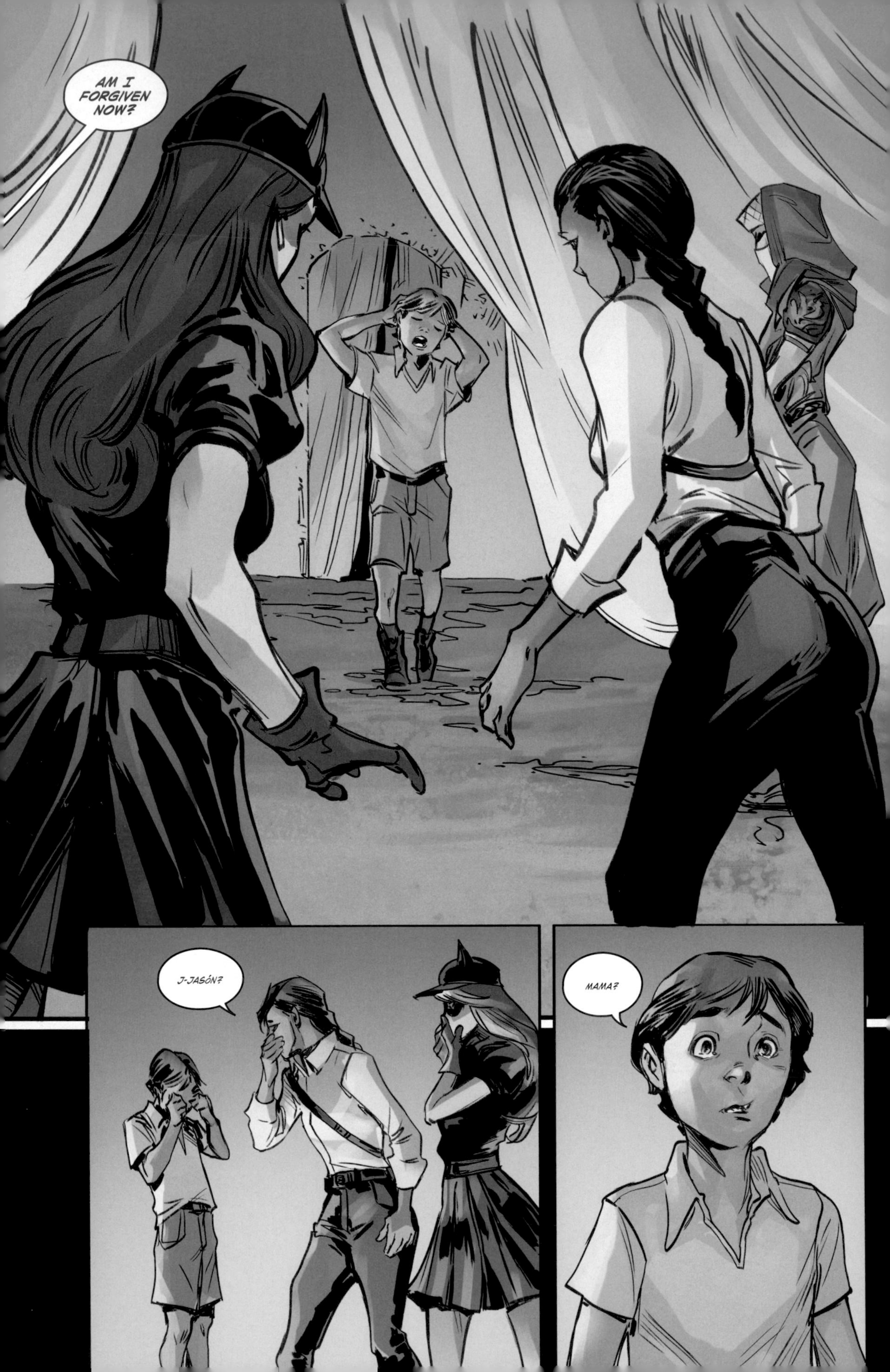
AM I FORGIVEN NOW?
J-JASÓN?
MAMA?

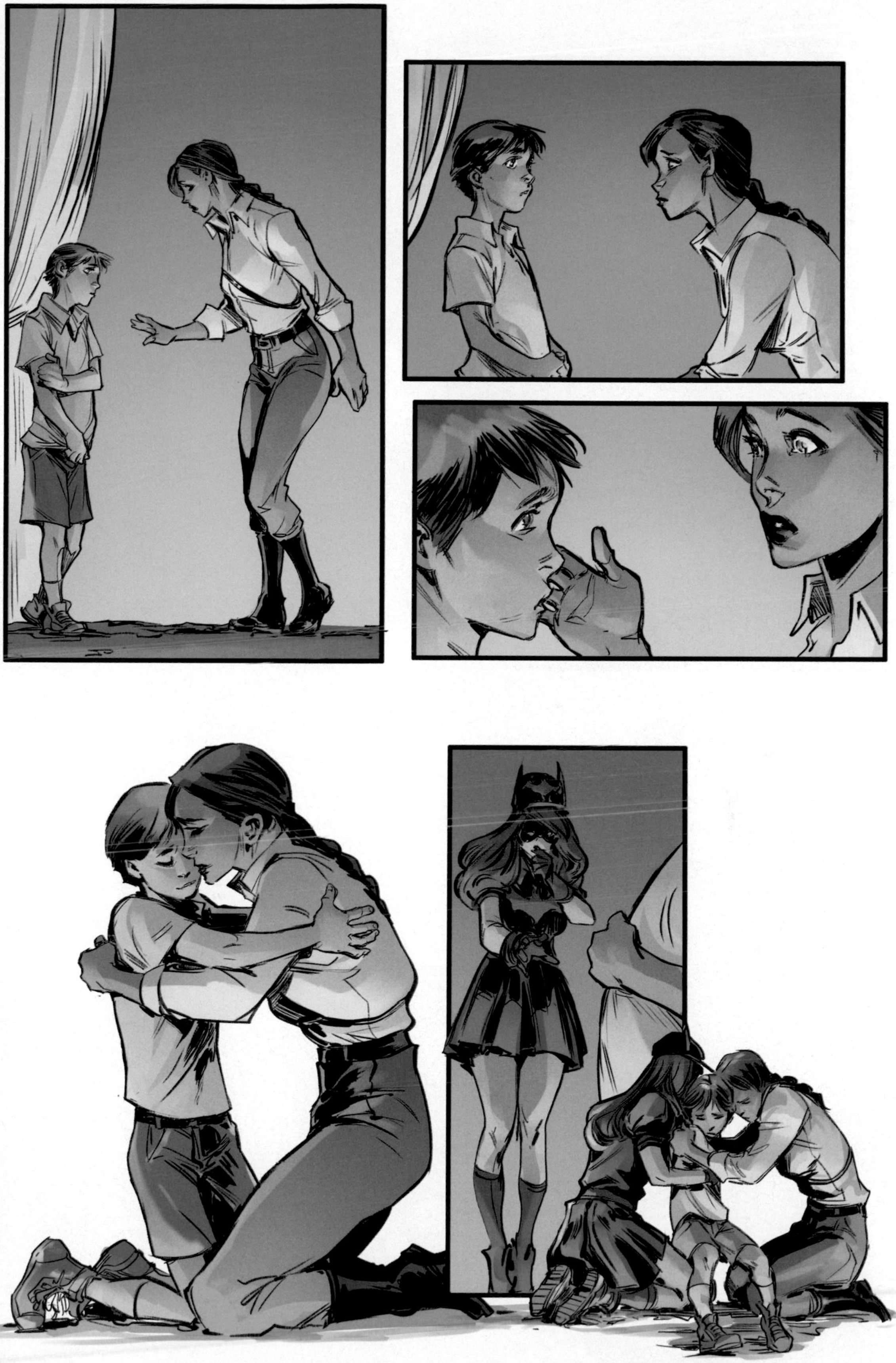

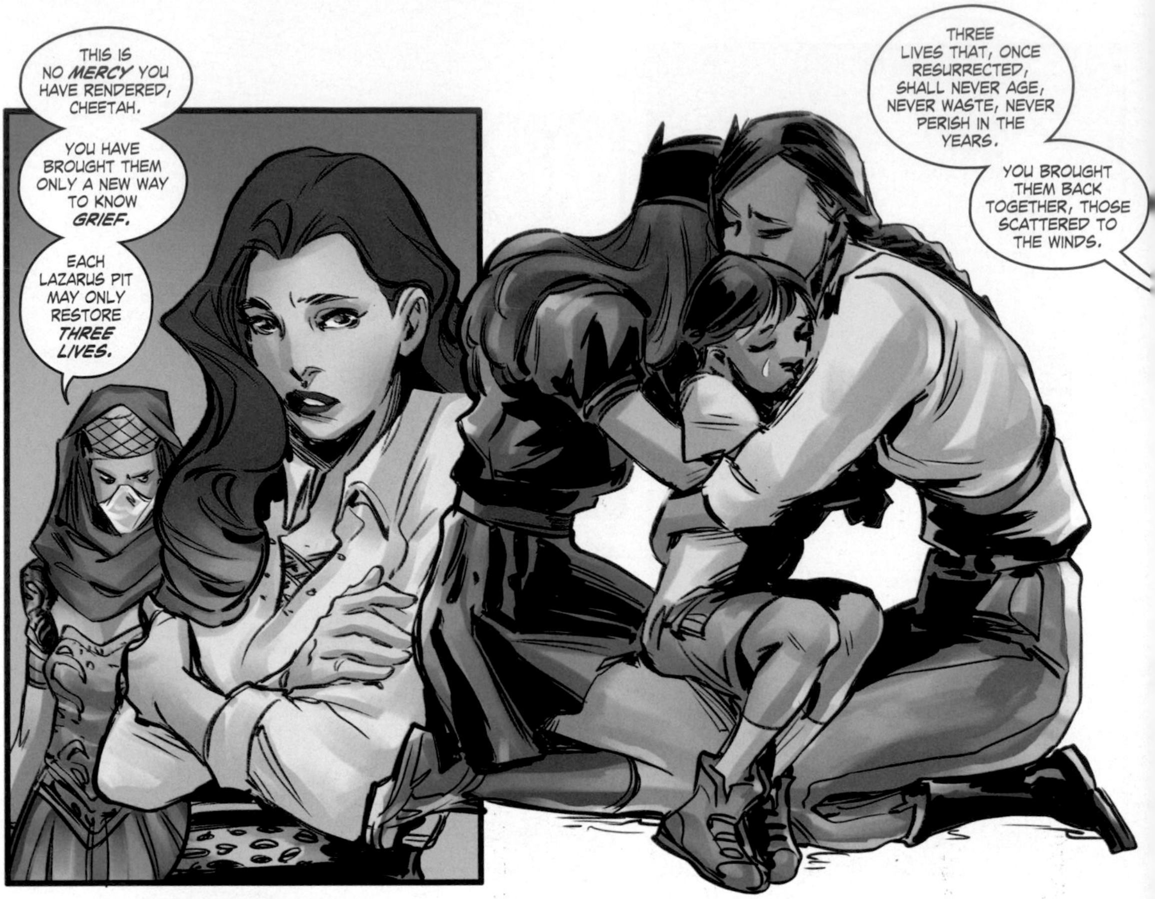
THIS IS NO MERCY YOU HAVE RENDERED, CHEETAH.
YOU HAVE BROUGHT THEM ONLY A NEW WAY TO KNOW GRIEF.
EACH LAZARUS PIT MAY ONLY RESTORE THREE LIVES.
THREE LIVES THAT, ONCE RESURRECTED, SHALL NEVER AGE, NEVER WASTE, NEVER PERISH IN THE YEARS.
YOU BROUGHT THEM BACK TOGETHER, THOSE SCATTERED TO THE WINDS.

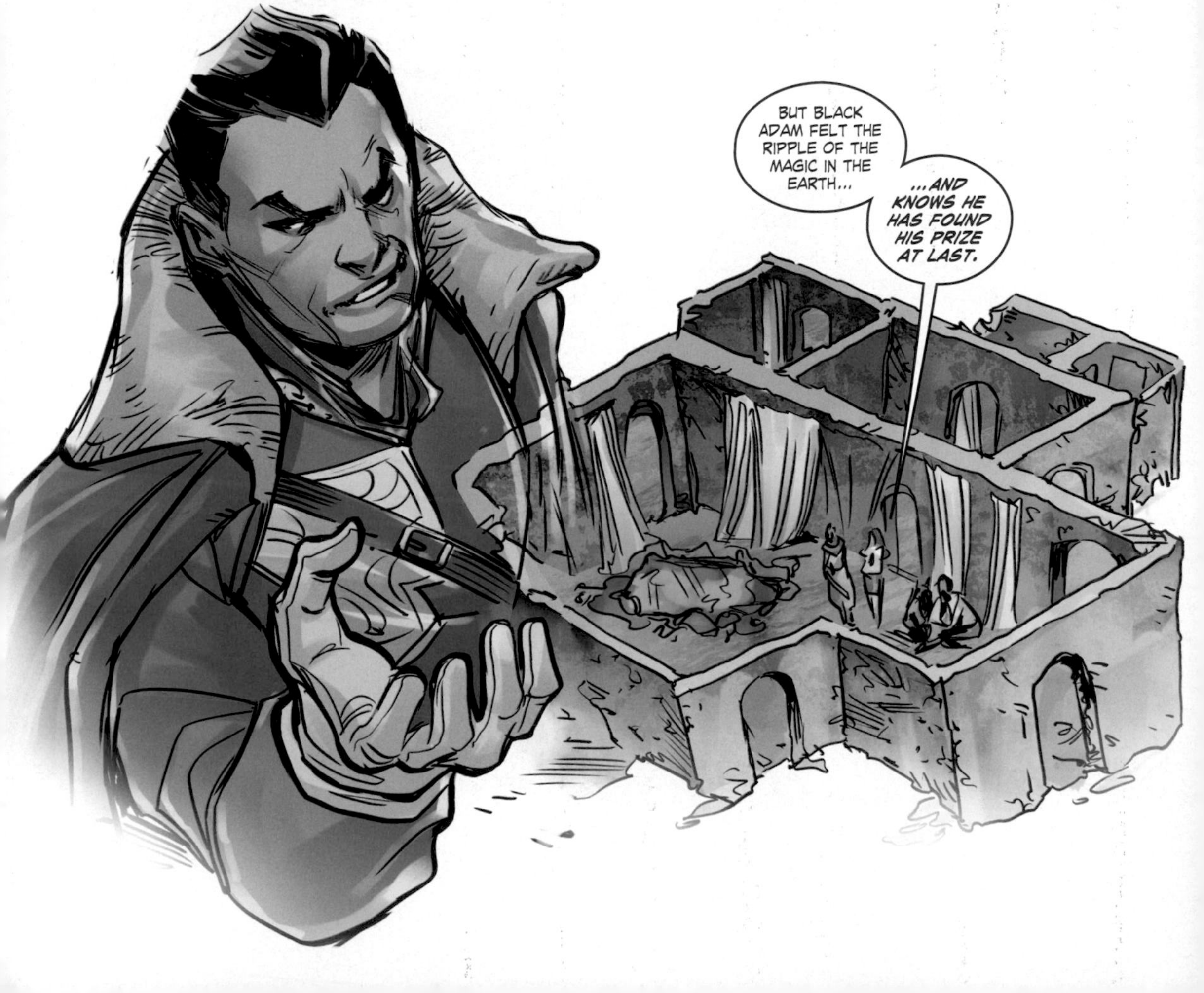
BUT BLACK ADAM FELT THE RIPPLE OF THE MAGIC IN THE EARTH...
...AND KNOWS HE HAS FOUND HIS PRIZE AT LAST.

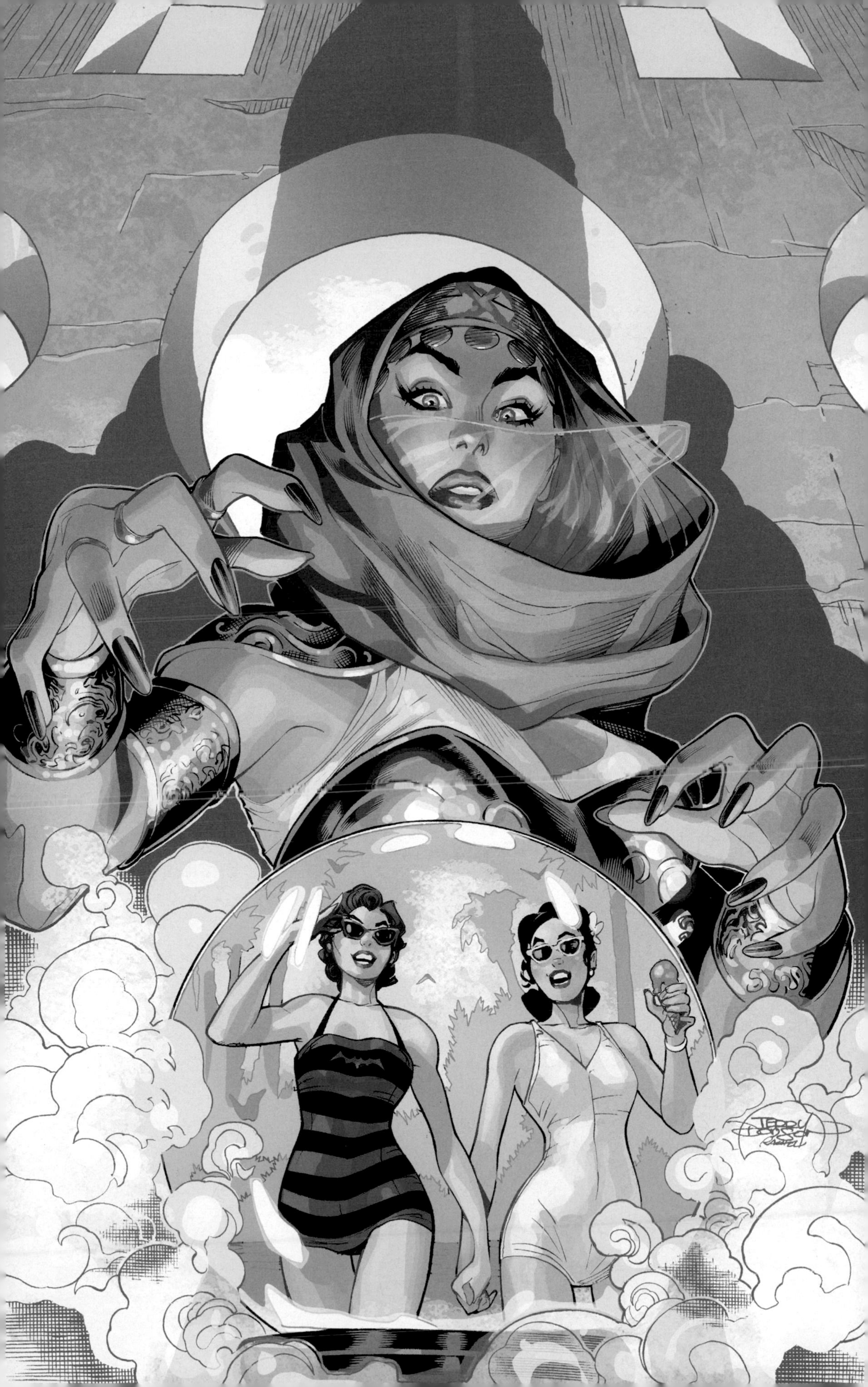

WAR BONDS

PARTS SEVEN *and* EIGHT

Written by
MARGUERITE BENNETT

Art by
MIRKA ANDOLFO
and **DAVID HAHN**

Colors by
J. NANJAN

Cover by
TERRY *and* **RACHEL DODSON**

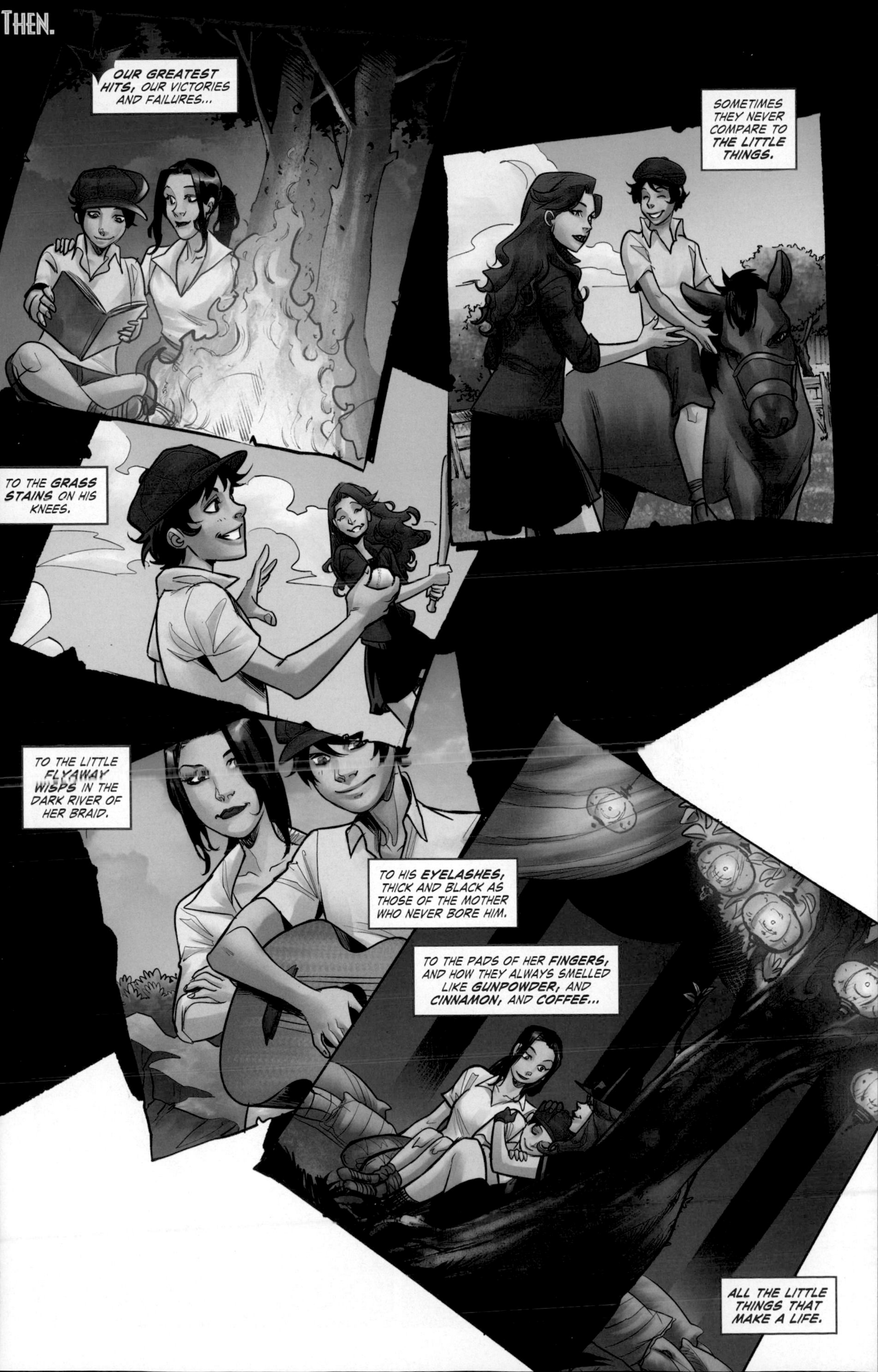
THEN.
OUR GREATEST HITS, OUR VICTORIES AND FAILURES...
SOMETIMES THEY NEVER COMPARE TO THE LITTLE THINGS.
TO THE GRASS STAINS ON HIS KNEES.
TO THE LITTLE FLYAWAY WISPS IN THE DARK RIVER OF HER BRAID.
TO HIS EYELASHES, THICK AND BLACK AS THOSE OF THE MOTHER WHO NEVER BORE HIM.
TO THE PADS OF HER FINGERS, AND HOW THEY ALWAYS SMELLED LIKE GUNPOWDER, AND CINNAMON, AND COFFEE...
ALL THE LITTLE THINGS THAT MAKE A LIFE.

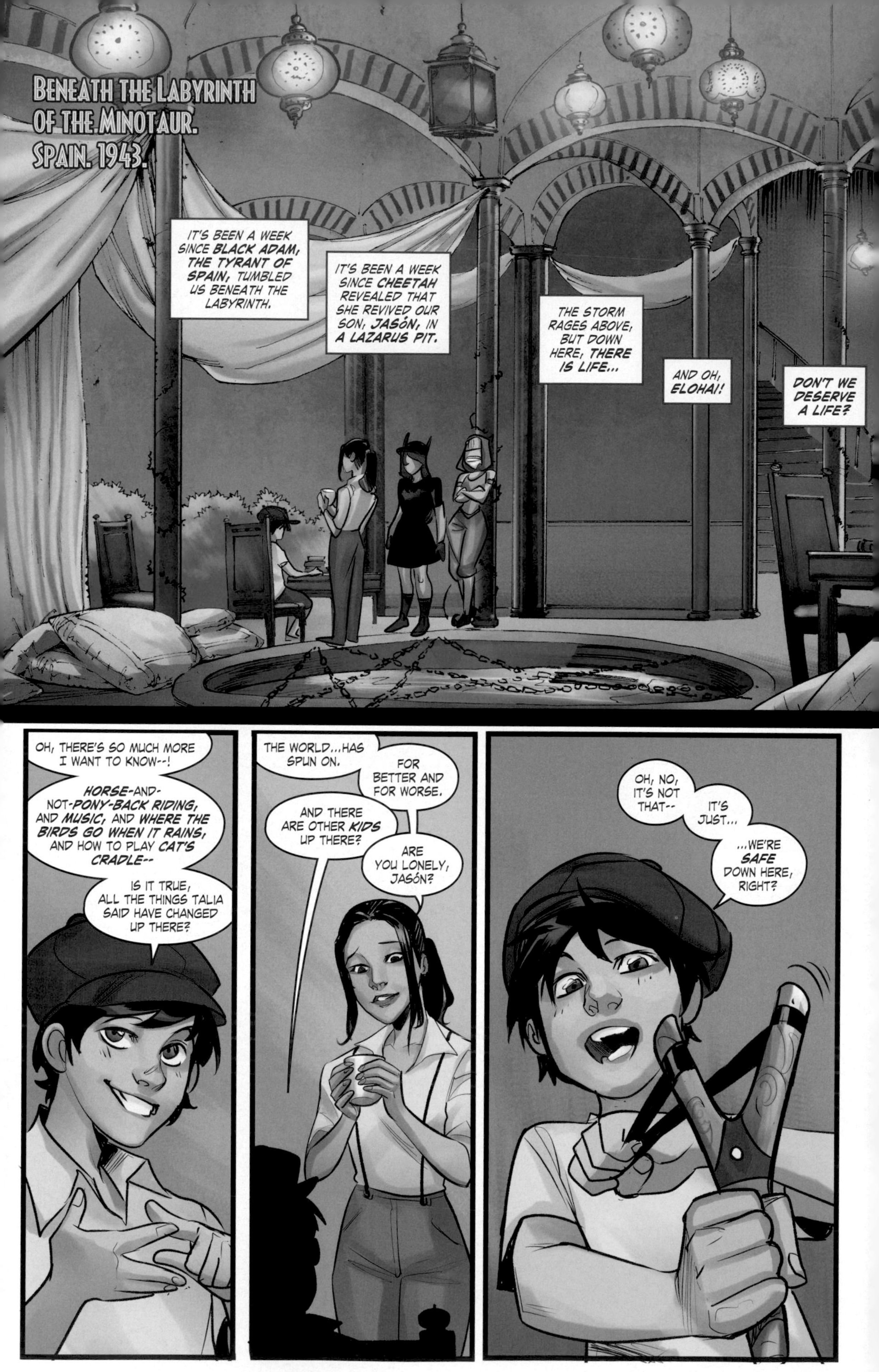
BENEATH THE LABYRINTH OF THE MINOTAUR. SPAIN. 1943.
IT'S BEEN A WEEK SINCE BLACK ADAM, THE TYRANT OF SPAIN, TUMBLED US BENEATH THE LABYRINTH.
IT'S BEEN A WEEK SINCE CHEETAH REVEALED THAT SHE REVIVED OUR SON, JASÓN, IN A LAZARUS PIT.
THE STORM RAGES ABOVE, BUT DOWN HERE, THERE IS LIFE...
AND OH, ELOHAI!
DON'T WE DESERVE A LIFE?
OH, THERE'S SO MUCH MORE I WANT TO KNOW--!
HORSE-AND-NOT-PONY-BACK RIDING, AND MUSIC, AND WHERE THE BIRDS GO WHEN IT RAINS, AND HOW TO PLAY CAT'S CRADLE--
IS IT TRUE, ALL THE THINGS TALIA SAID HAVE CHANGED UP THERE?
THE WORLD...HAS SPUN ON.
FOR BETTER AND FOR WORSE.
AND THERE ARE OTHER KIDS UP THERE?
ARE YOU LONELY, JASÓN?
OH, NO, IT'S NOT THAT--
IT'S JUST...
...WE'RE SAFE DOWN HERE, RIGHT?

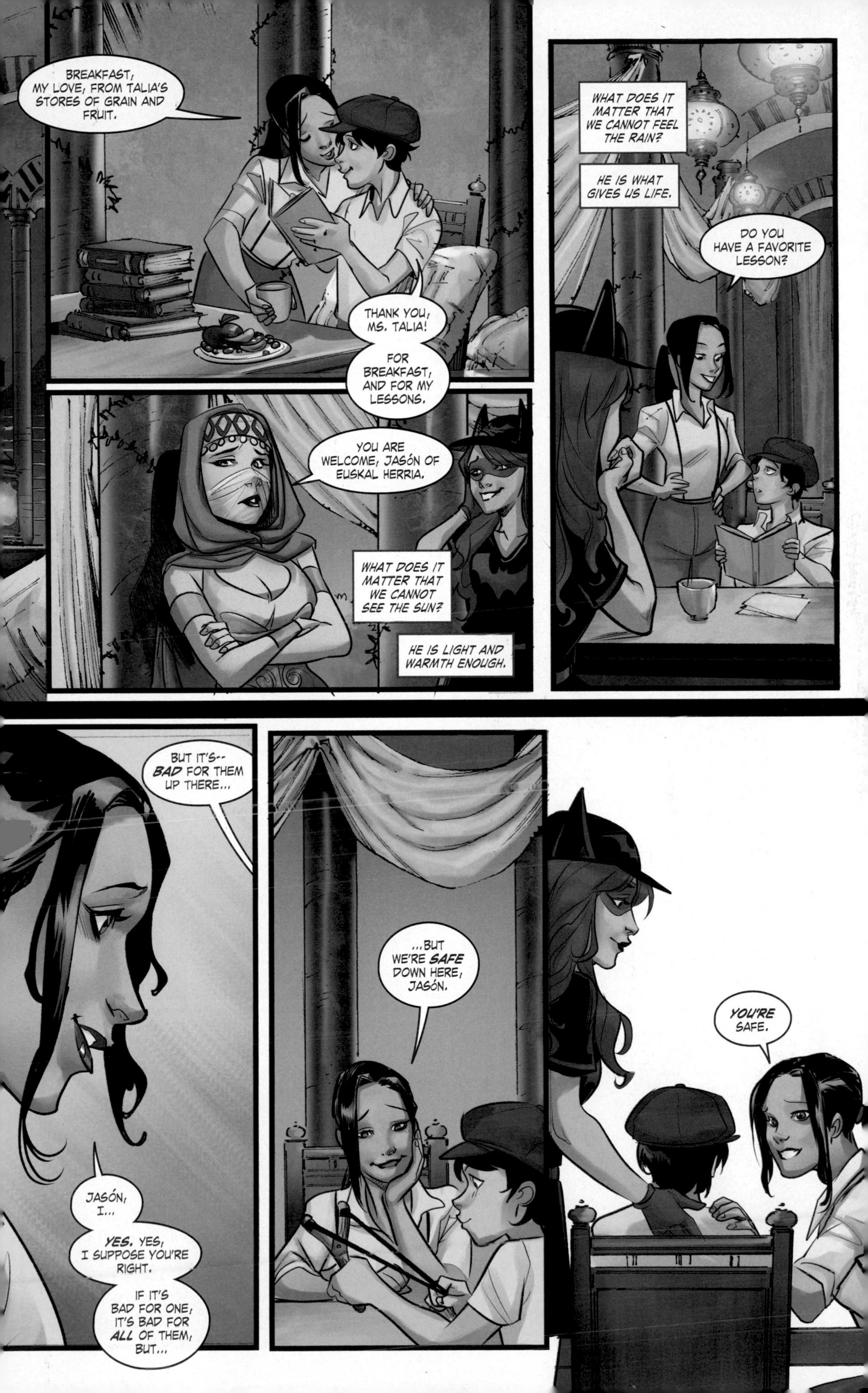
BREAKFAST, MY LOVE, FROM TALIA'S STORES OF GRAIN AND FRUIT.
THANK YOU, MS. TALIA!
FOR BREAKFAST, AND FOR MY LESSONS.
YOU ARE WELCOME, JASÓN OF EUSKAL HERRIA.
WHAT DOES IT MATTER THAT WE CANNOT SEE THE SUN?
HE IS LIGHT AND WARMTH ENOUGH.
WHAT DOES IT MATTER THAT WE CANNOT FEEL THE RAIN?
HE IS WHAT GIVES US LIFE.
DO YOU HAVE A FAVORITE LESSON?
BUT IT'S-- BAD FOR THEM UP THERE...
JASÓN, I...
YES. YES, I SUPPOSE YOU'RE RIGHT.
IF IT'S BAD FOR ONE, IT'S BAD FOR ALL OF THEM, BUT...
...BUT WE'RE SAFE DOWN HERE, JASÓN.
YOU'RE SAFE.

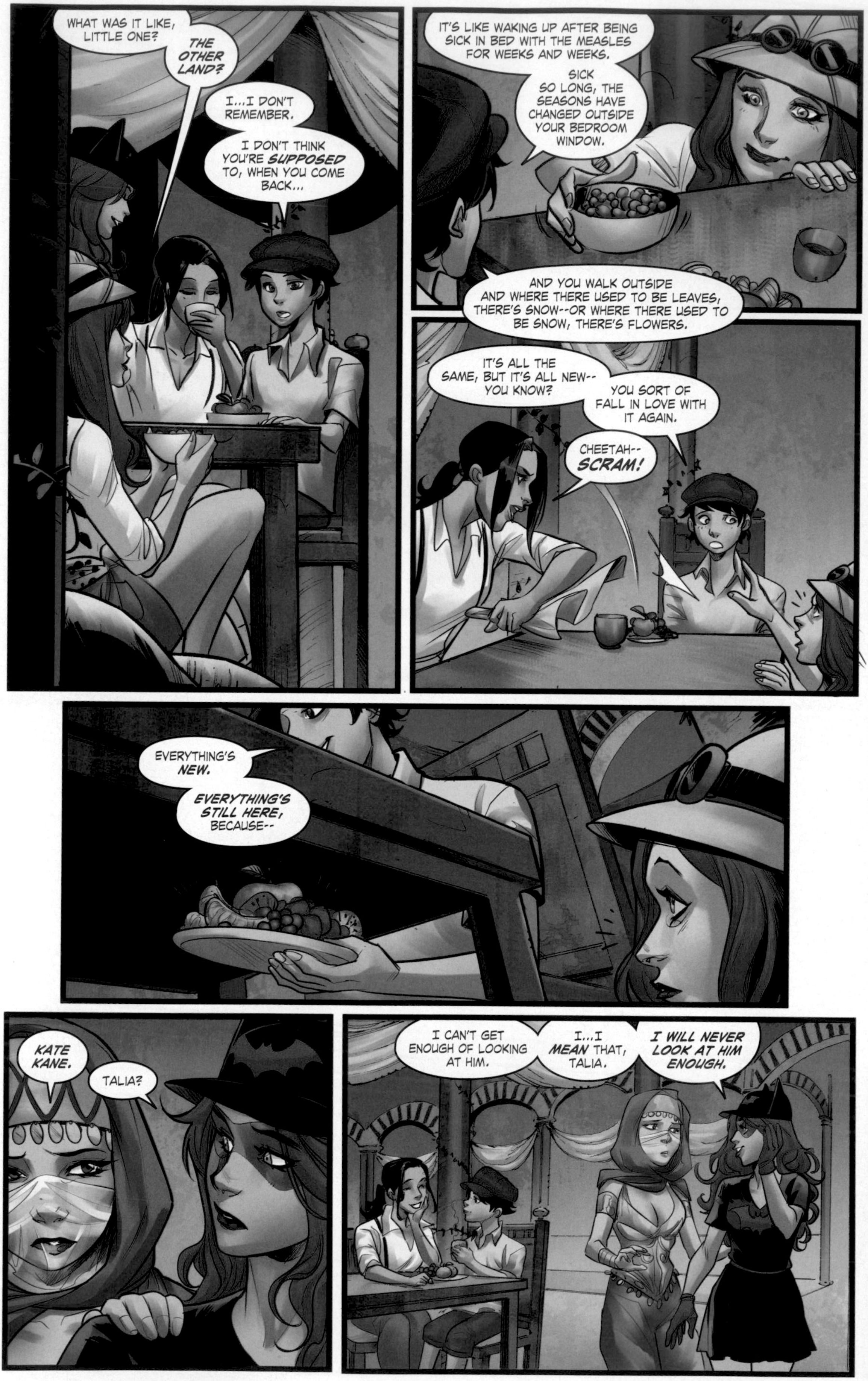
WHAT WAS IT LIKE, LITTLE ONE?
THE OTHER LAND?
I...I DON'T REMEMBER.
I DON'T THINK YOU'RE SUPPOSED TO, WHEN YOU COME BACK...
IT'S LIKE WAKING UP AFTER BEING SICK IN BED WITH THE MEASLES FOR WEEKS AND WEEKS.
SICK SO LONG, THE SEASONS HAVE CHANGED OUTSIDE YOUR BEDROOM WINDOW.
AND YOU WALK OUTSIDE AND WHERE THERE USED TO BE LEAVES, THERE'S SNOW--OR WHERE THERE USED TO BE SNOW, THERE'S FLOWERS.
IT'S ALL THE SAME, BUT IT'S ALL NEW-- YOU KNOW?
YOU SORT OF FALL IN LOVE WITH IT AGAIN.
CHEETAH-- SCRAM!
EVERYTHING'S NEW.
EVERYTHING'S STILL HERE, BECAUSE--
KATE KANE.
TALIA?
I CAN'T GET ENOUGH OF LOOKING AT HIM.
I...I MEAN THAT, TALIA.
I WILL NEVER LOOK AT HIM ENOUGH.

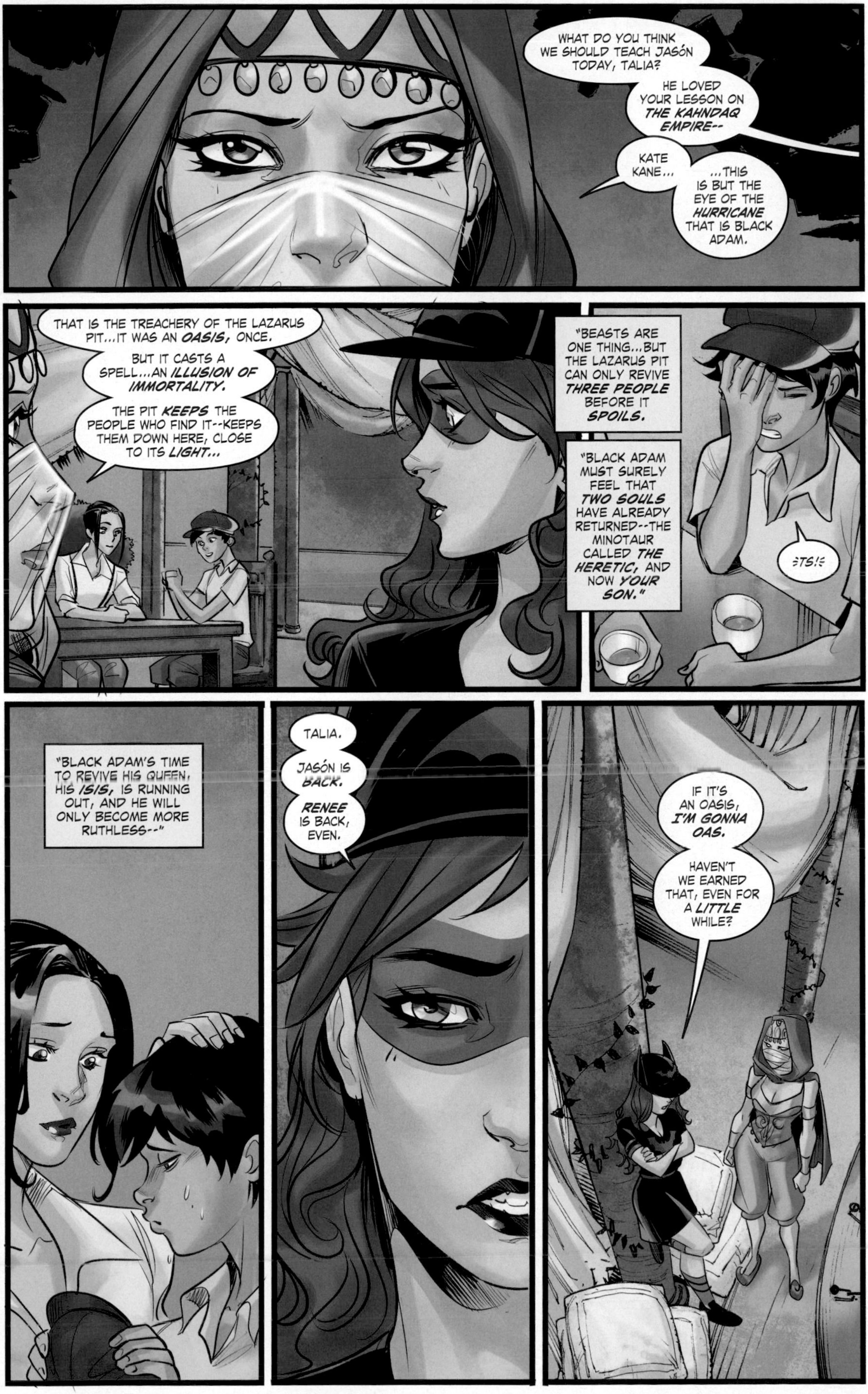

WHAT DO YOU THINK WE SHOULD TEACH JASÓN TODAY, TALIA?
HE LOVED YOUR LESSON ON THE KAHNDAQ EMPIRE--
KATE KANE...
...THIS IS BUT THE EYE OF THE HURRICANE THAT IS BLACK ADAM.
THAT IS THE TREACHERY OF THE LAZARUS PIT...IT WAS AN OASIS, ONCE.
BUT IT CASTS A SPELL...AN ILLUSION OF IMMORTALITY.
THE PIT KEEPS THE PEOPLE WHO FIND IT--KEEPS THEM DOWN HERE, CLOSE TO ITS LIGHT...
"BEASTS ARE ONE THING...BUT THE LAZARUS PIT CAN ONLY REVIVE THREE PEOPLE BEFORE IT SPOILS.
"BLACK ADAM MUST SURELY FEEL THAT TWO SOULS HAVE ALREADY RETURNED--THE MINOTAUR CALLED THE HERETIC, AND NOW YOUR SON."
TS!
"BLACK ADAM'S TIME TO REVIVE HIS QUEEN, HIS ISIS, IS RUNNING OUT, AND HE WILL ONLY BECOME MORE RUTHLESS--"
TALIA.
JASÓN IS BACK.
RENEE IS BACK, EVEN.
IF IT'S AN OASIS, I'M GONNA OAS.
HAVEN'T WE EARNED THAT, EVEN FOR A LITTLE WHILE?

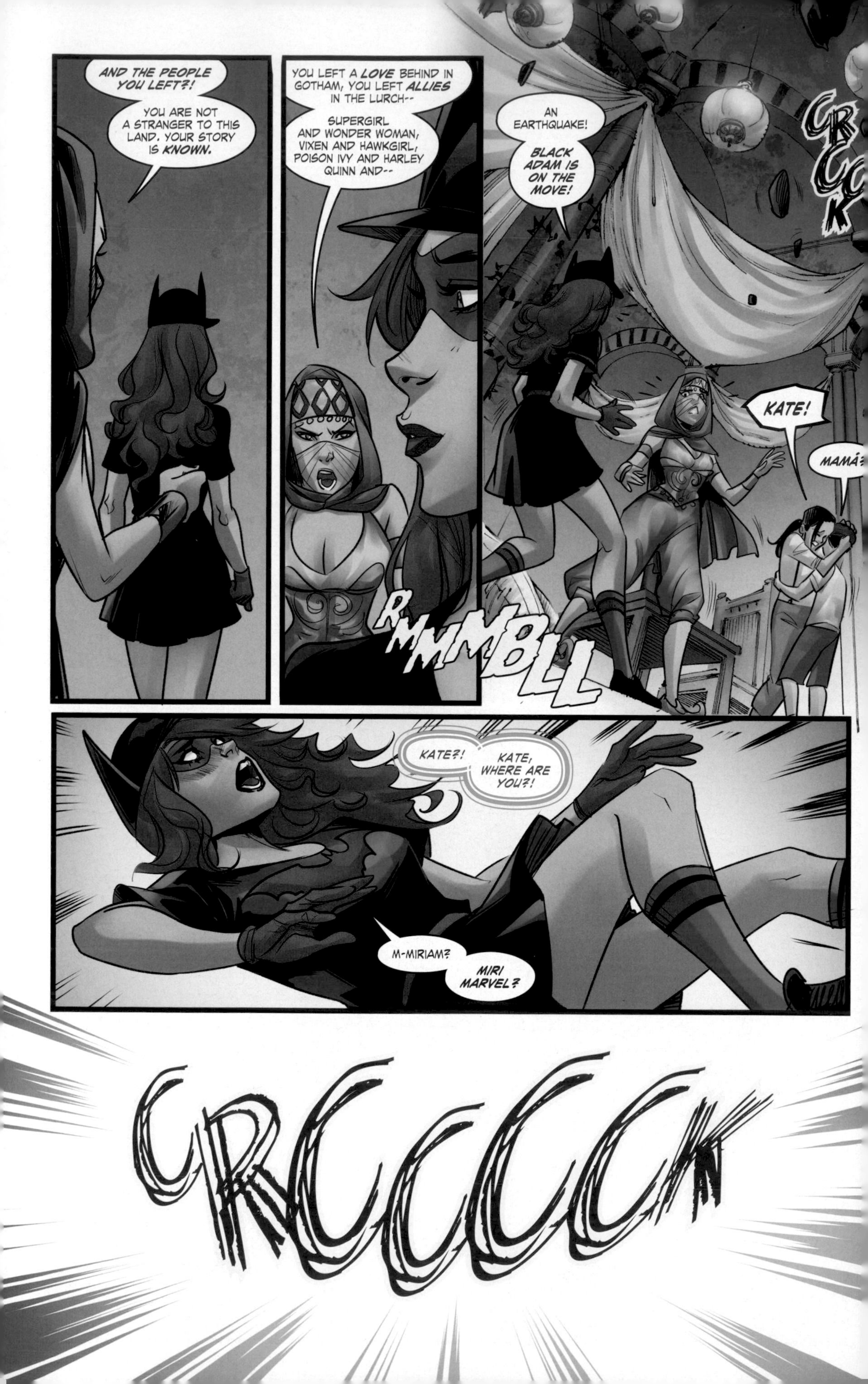
AND THE PEOPLE YOU LEFT?!
YOU ARE NOT A STRANGER TO THIS LAND. YOUR STORY IS KNOWN.
YOU LEFT A LOVE BEHIND IN GOTHAM, YOU LEFT ALLIES IN THE LURCH--
SUPERGIRL AND WONDER WOMAN, VIXEN AND HAWKGIRL, POISON IVY AND HARLEY QUINN AND--
RMMMBLL
AN EARTHQUAKE!
BLACK ADAM IS ON THE MOVE!
CRCCK
KATE!
MAMÁ
KATE?!
KATE, WHERE ARE YOU?!
M-MIRIAM?
MIRI MARVEL?
CRCCCCK

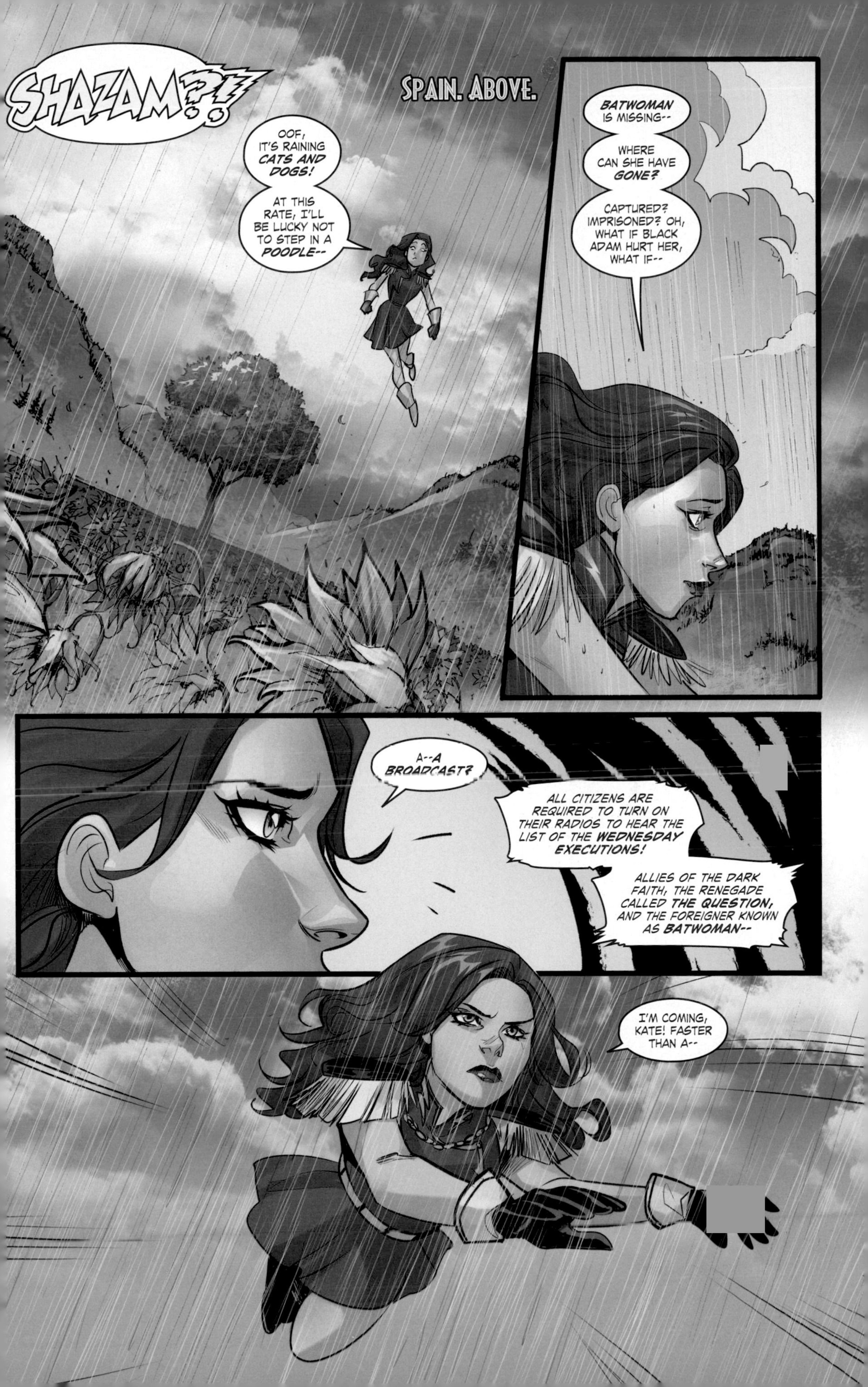
SHAZAM?!
SPAIN. ABOVE.
OOF, IT'S RAINING CATS AND DOGS!
AT THIS RATE, I'LL BE LUCKY NOT TO STEP IN A POODLE--
BATWOMAN IS MISSING--
WHERE CAN SHE HAVE GONE?
CAPTURED? IMPRISONED? OH, WHAT IF BLACK ADAM HURT HER, WHAT IF--
A--A BROADCAST?
ALL CITIZENS ARE REQUIRED TO TURN ON THEIR RADIOS TO HEAR THE LIST OF THE WEDNESDAY EXECUTIONS!
ALLIES OF THE DARK FAITH, THE RENEGADE CALLED THE QUESTION, AND THE FOREIGNER KNOWN AS BATWOMAN--
I'M COMING, KATE! FASTER THAN A--

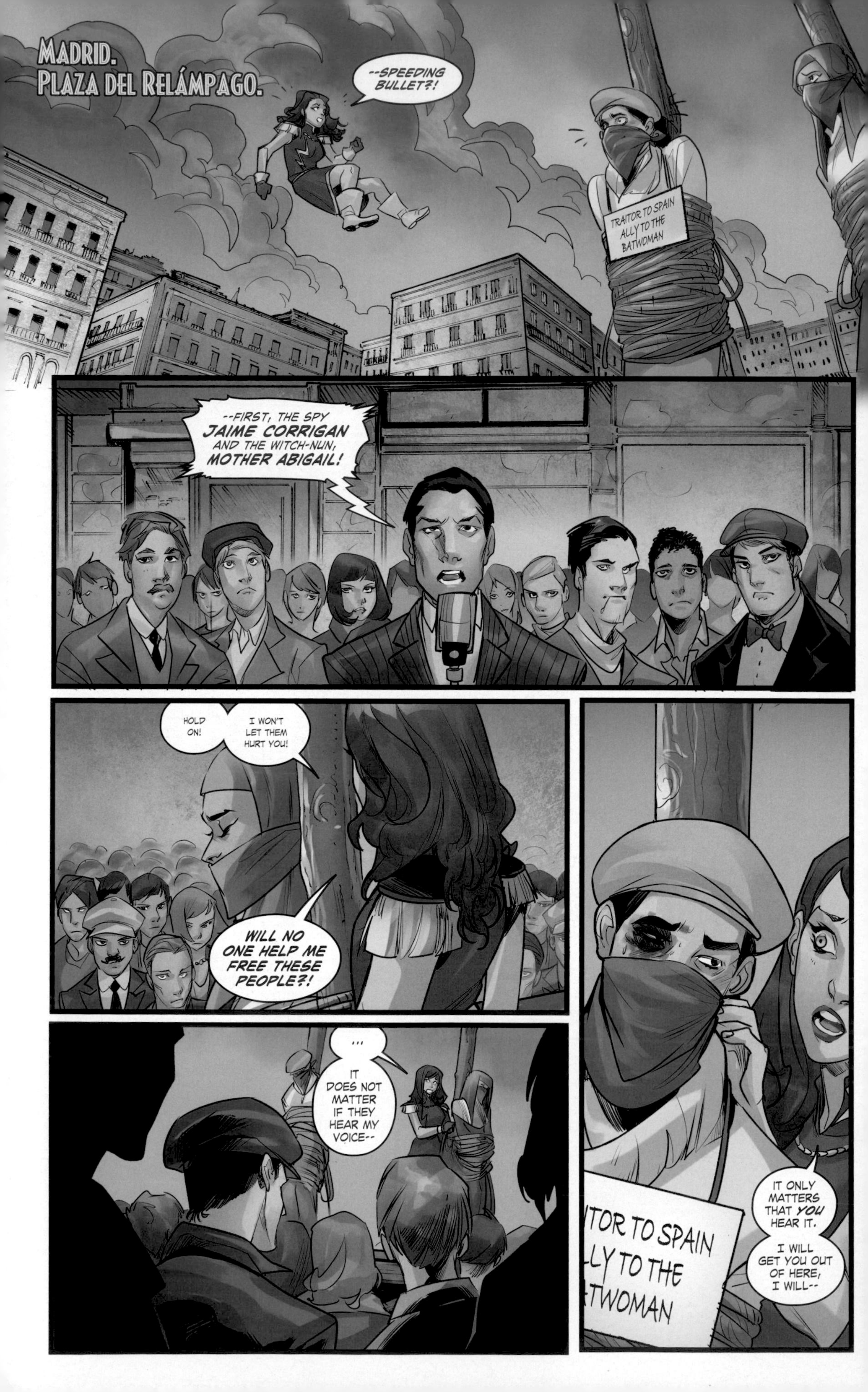

MADRID. PLAZA DEL RELÁMPAGO.
--SPEEDING BULLET?!
TRAITOR TO SPAIN ALLY TO THE BATWOMAN
--FIRST, THE SPY JAIME CORRIGAN AND THE WITCH-NUN, MOTHER ABIGAIL!
HOLD ON!
I WON'T LET THEM HURT YOU!
WILL NO ONE HELP ME FREE THESE PEOPLE?!
...
IT DOES NOT MATTER IF THEY HEAR MY VOICE--
TOR TO SPAIN
LLY TO THE
TWOMAN
IT ONLY MATTERS THAT YOU HEAR IT.
I WILL GET YOU OUT OF HERE, I WILL--

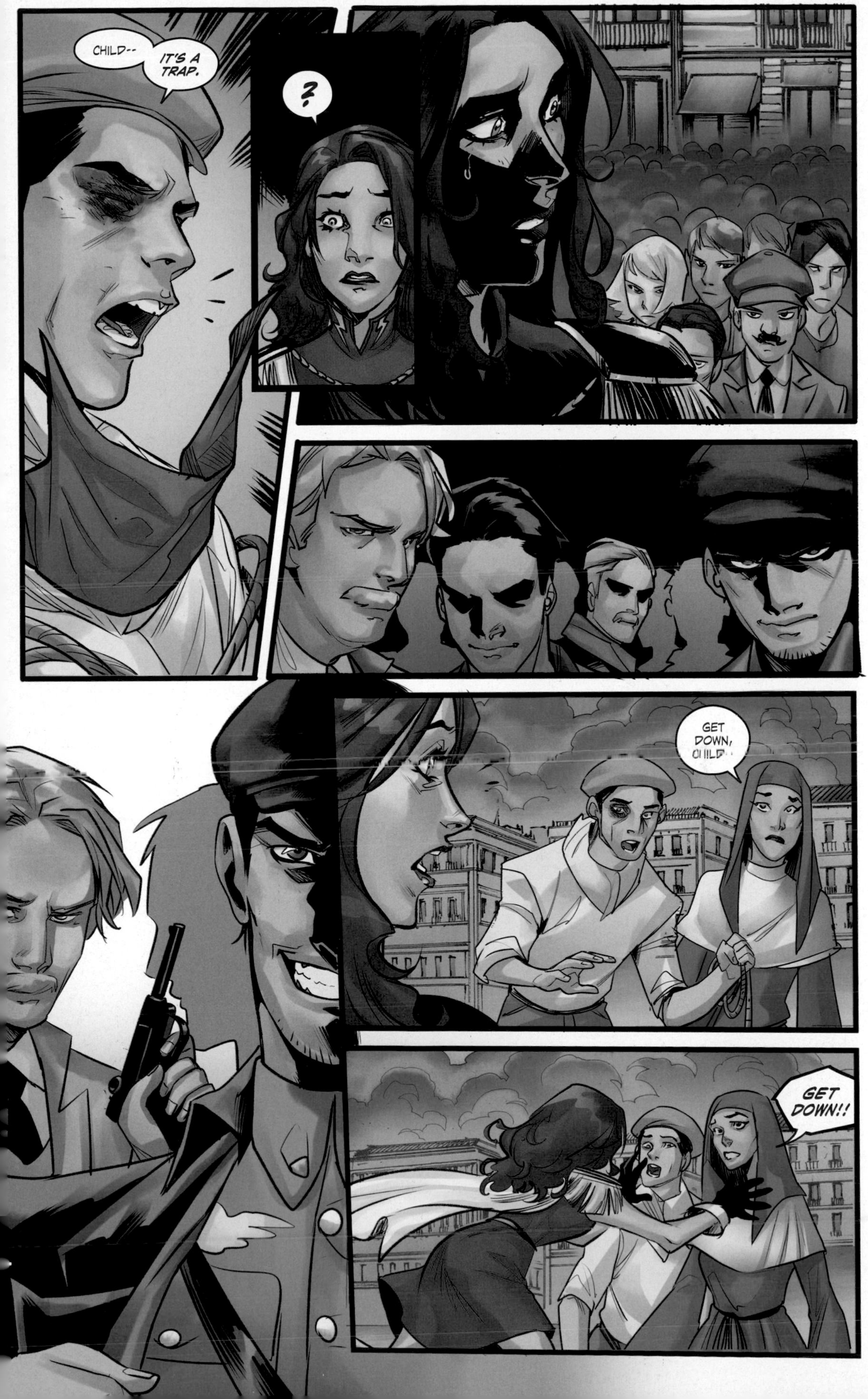
CHILD--
IT'S A TRAP.
?
GET DOWN, CHILD.
GET DOWN!!

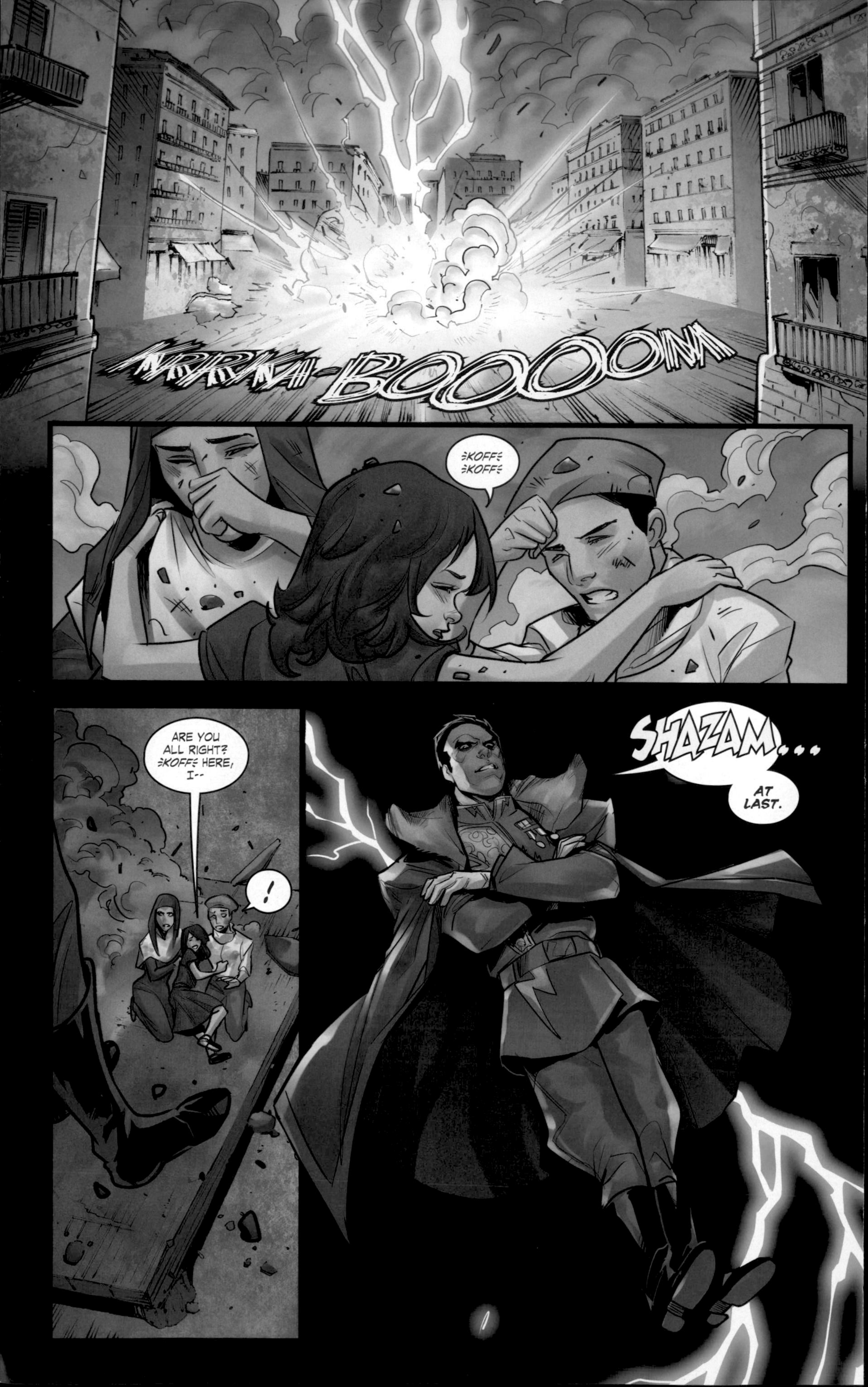

KRRRKA-BOOOOOM
÷KOFF÷ ÷KOFF÷
ARE YOU ALL RIGHT? ÷KOFF÷ HERE, I--
!
SHAZAM...
AT LAST.

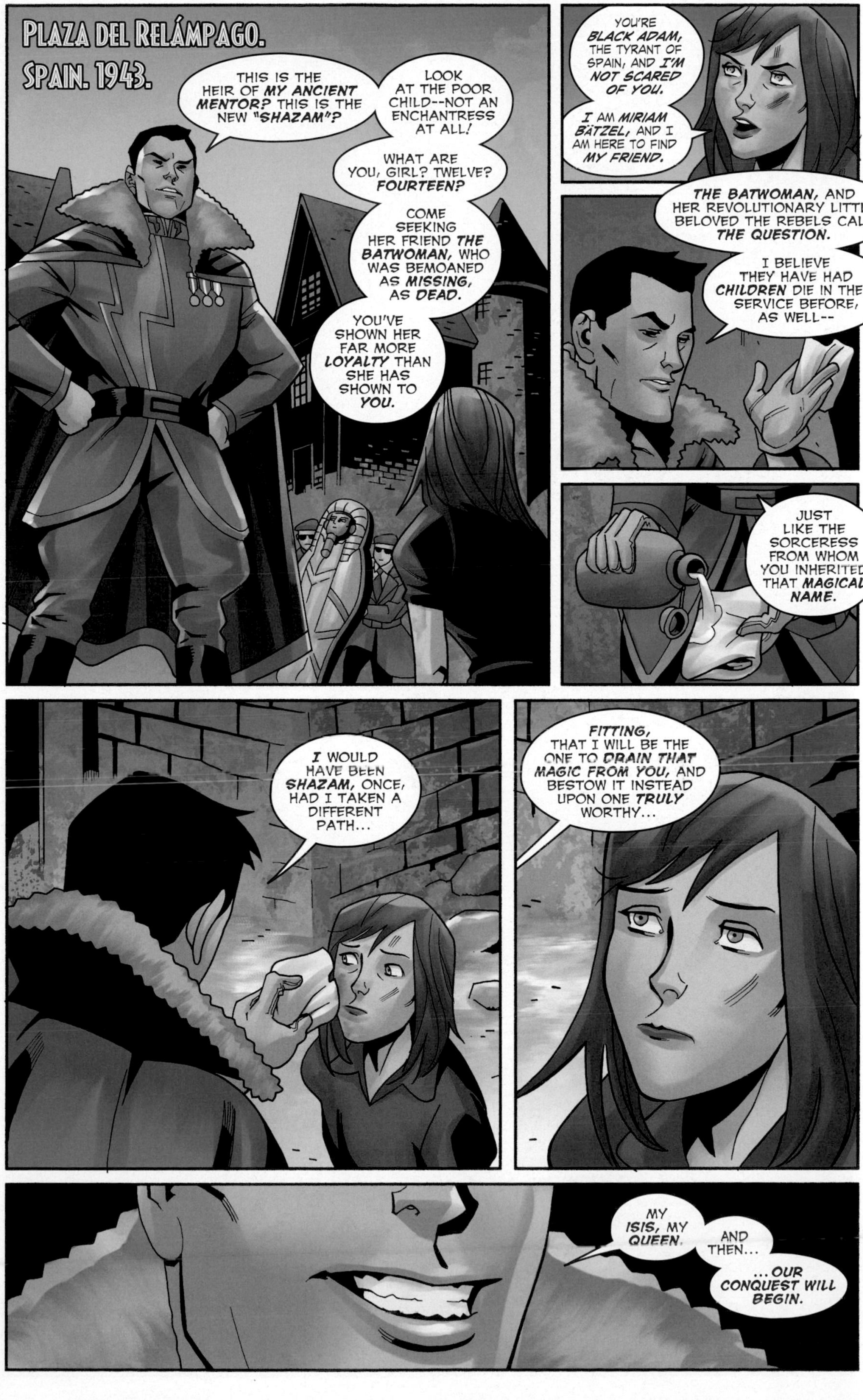
PLAZA DEL RELÁMPAGO. SPAIN. 1943.
THIS IS THE HEIR OF MY ANCIENT MENTOR? THIS IS THE NEW "SHAZAM"?
LOOK AT THE POOR CHILD--NOT AN ENCHANTRESS AT ALL!
WHAT ARE YOU, GIRL? TWELVE? FOURTEEN?
COME SEEKING HER FRIEND THE BATWOMAN, WHO WAS BEMOANED AS MISSING, AS DEAD.
YOU'VE SHOWN HER FAR MORE LOYALTY THAN SHE HAS SHOWN TO YOU.
YOU'RE BLACK ADAM, THE TYRANT OF SPAIN, AND I'M NOT SCARED OF YOU.
I AM MIRIAM BÄTZEL, AND I AM HERE TO FIND MY FRIEND.
THE BATWOMAN, AND HER REVOLUTIONARY LITTLE BELOVED THE REBELS CALL THE QUESTION.
I BELIEVE THEY HAVE HAD CHILDREN DIE IN THEIR SERVICE BEFORE, AS WELL--
JUST LIKE THE SORCERESS FROM WHOM YOU INHERITED THAT MAGICAL NAME.
I WOULD HAVE BEEN SHAZAM, ONCE, HAD I TAKEN A DIFFERENT PATH...
FITTING, THAT I WILL BE THE ONE TO DRAIN THAT MAGIC FROM YOU, AND BESTOW IT INSTEAD UPON ONE TRULY WORTHY...
MY ISIS, MY QUEEN.
AND THEN...
...OUR CONQUEST WILL BEGIN.

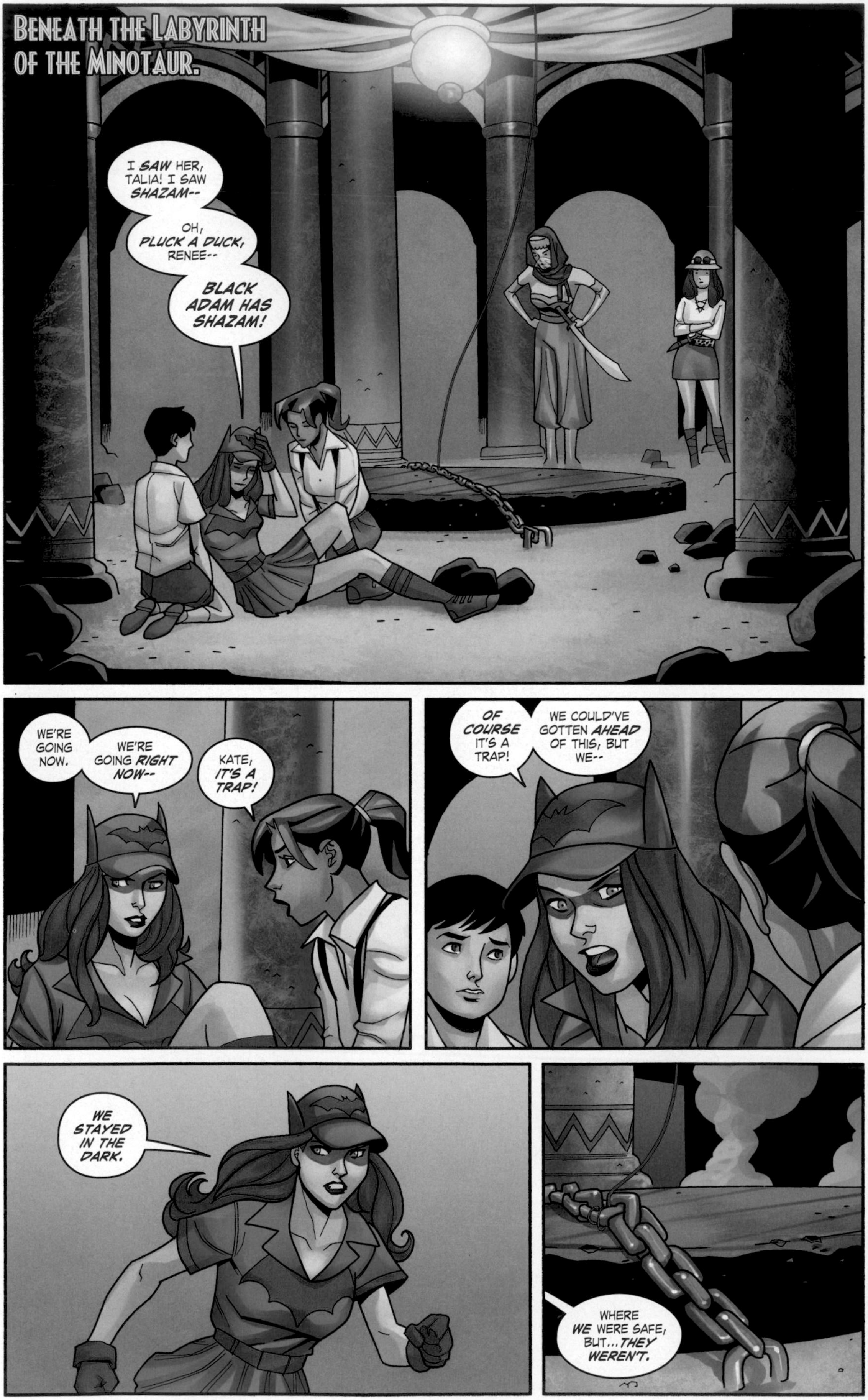
BENEATH THE LABYRINTH OF THE MINOTAUR.
I SAW HER, TALIA! I SAW SHAZAM--
OH, PLUCK A DUCK, RENEE--
BLACK ADAM HAS SHAZAM!
WE'RE GOING NOW.
WE'RE GOING RIGHT NOW--
KATE, IT'S A TRAP!
OF COURSE IT'S A TRAP!
WE COULD'VE GOTTEN AHEAD OF THIS, BUT WE--
WE STAYED IN THE DARK.
WHERE WE WERE SAFE, BUT...THEY WEREN'T.

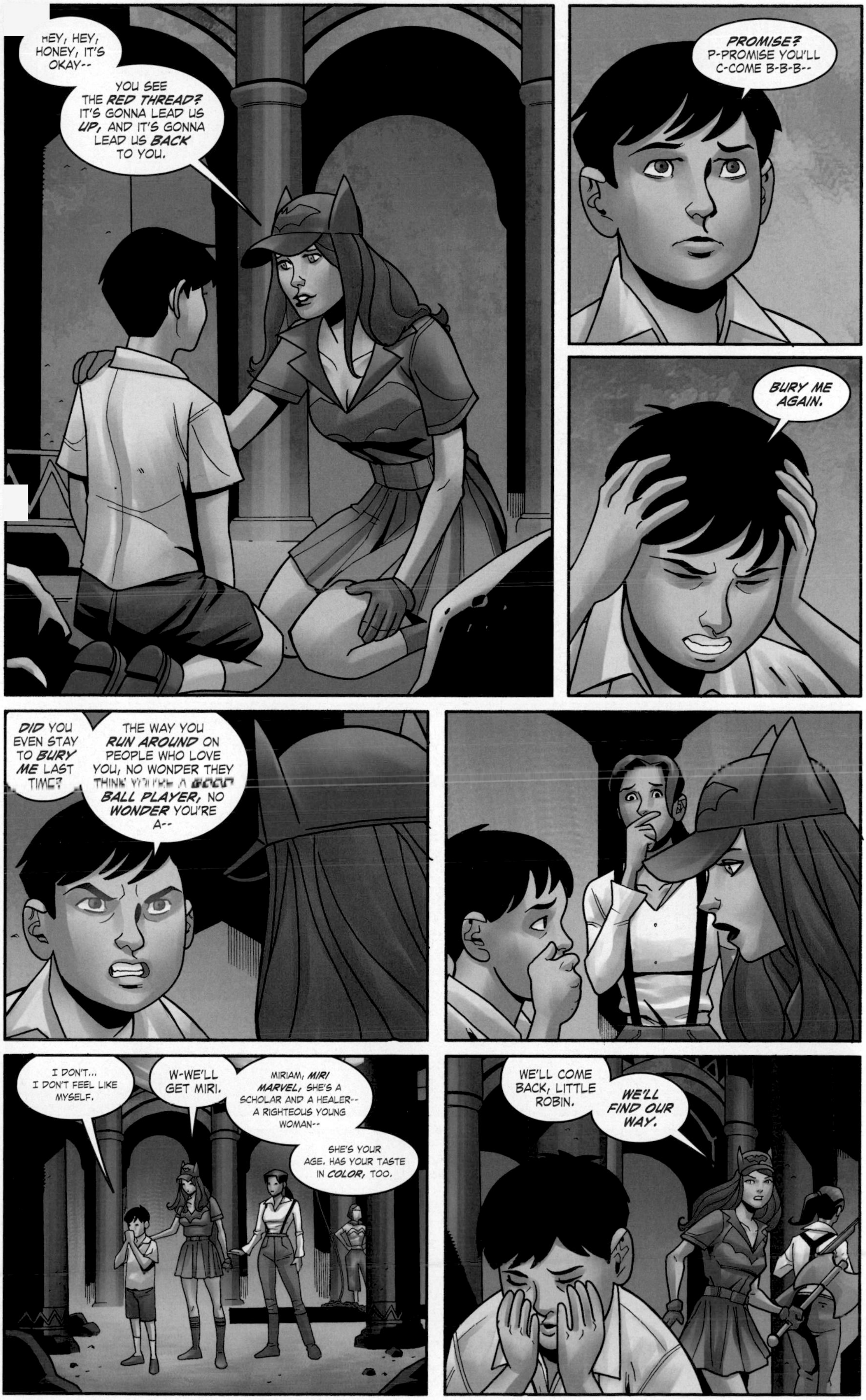
HEY, HEY, HONEY, IT'S OKAY--
YOU SEE THE RED THREAD? IT'S GONNA LEAD US UP, AND IT'S GONNA LEAD US BACK TO YOU.
PROMISE? P-PROMISE YOU'LL C-COME B-B-B--
BURY ME AGAIN.
DID YOU EVEN STAY TO BURY ME LAST TIME?
THE WAY YOU RUN AROUND ON PEOPLE WHO LOVE YOU, NO WONDER THEY THINK YOU'RE A GOOD BALL PLAYER, NO WONDER YOU'RE A--
I DON'T... I DON'T FEEL LIKE MYSELF.
W-WE'LL GET MIRI.
MIRIAM, MIRI MARVEL, SHE'S A SCHOLAR AND A HEALER-- A RIGHTEOUS YOUNG WOMAN--
SHE'S YOUR AGE. HAS YOUR TASTE IN COLOR, TOO.
WE'LL COME BACK, LITTLE ROBIN.
WE'LL FIND OUR WAY.

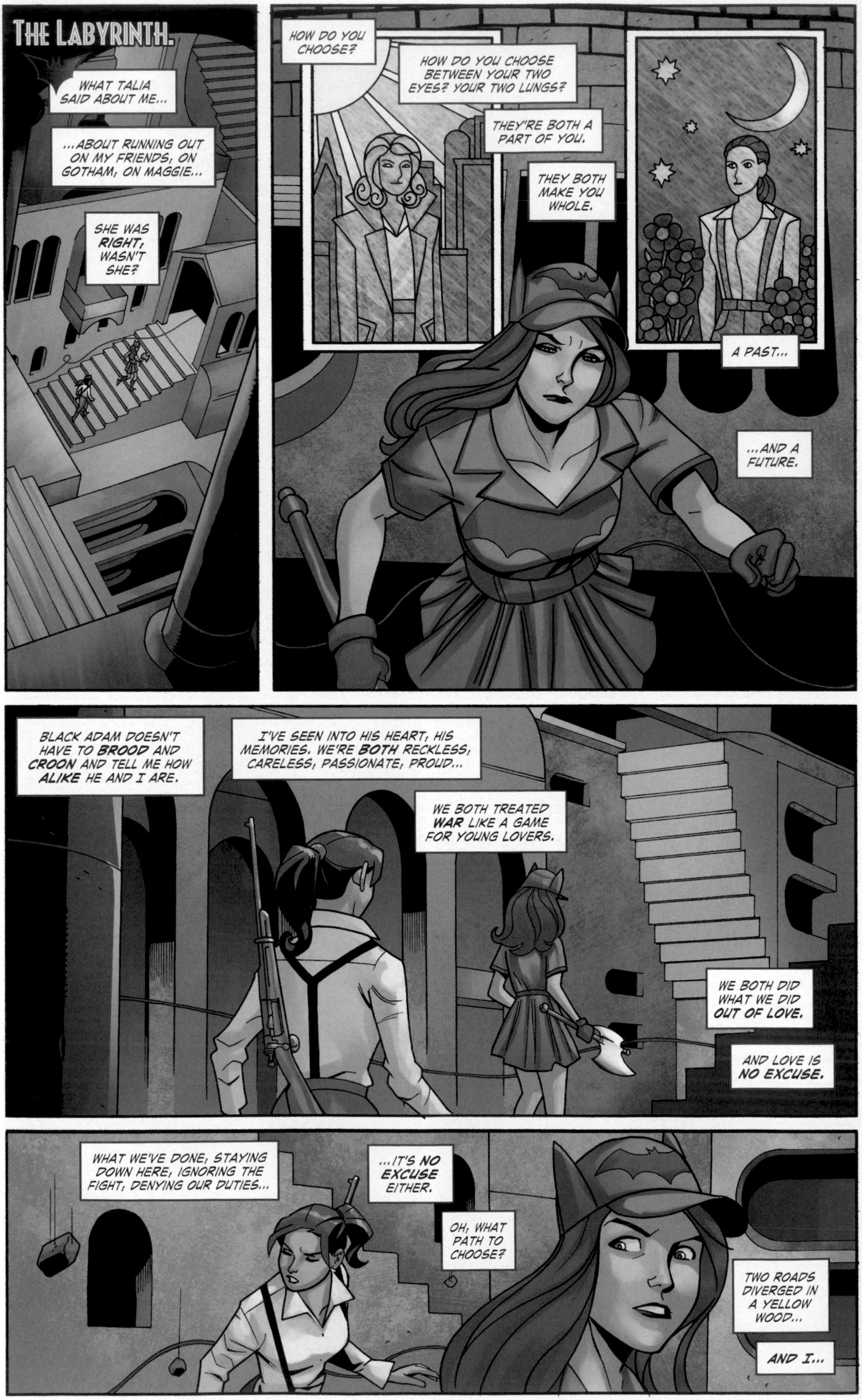
THE LABYRINTH.
WHAT TALIA SAID ABOUT ME...
...ABOUT RUNNING OUT ON MY FRIENDS, ON GOTHAM, ON MAGGIE...
SHE WAS RIGHT, WASN'T SHE?
HOW DO YOU CHOOSE?
HOW DO YOU CHOOSE BETWEEN YOUR TWO EYES? YOUR TWO LUNGS?
THEY'RE BOTH A PART OF YOU.
THEY BOTH MAKE YOU WHOLE.
A PAST...
...AND A FUTURE.
BLACK ADAM DOESN'T HAVE TO BROOD AND CROON AND TELL ME HOW ALIKE HE AND I ARE.
I'VE SEEN INTO HIS HEART, HIS MEMORIES. WE'RE BOTH RECKLESS, CARELESS, PASSIONATE, PROUD...
WE BOTH TREATED WAR LIKE A GAME FOR YOUNG LOVERS.
WE BOTH DID WHAT WE DID OUT OF LOVE.
AND LOVE IS NO EXCUSE.
WHAT WE'VE DONE, STAYING DOWN HERE, IGNORING THE FIGHT, DENYING OUR DUTIES...
...IT'S NO EXCUSE EITHER.
OH, WHAT PATH TO CHOOSE?
TWO ROADS DIVERGED IN A YELLOW WOOD...
AND I...

...I TOOK THE ONE WITH THE GIANT, BLOODTHIRSTY BULL MONSTER AT THE END.

I'LL GIVE YOU THIS, SON--

CRK!

YOU KNOW HOW TO MAKE AN ENTRANCE IN A VERY LITERAL SENSE.

FORTUNATELY, KATE AND I--

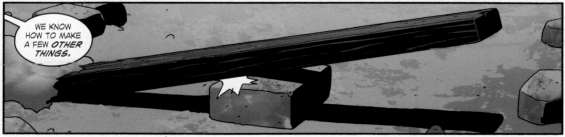

WE KNOW HOW TO MAKE A FEW OTHER THINGS.

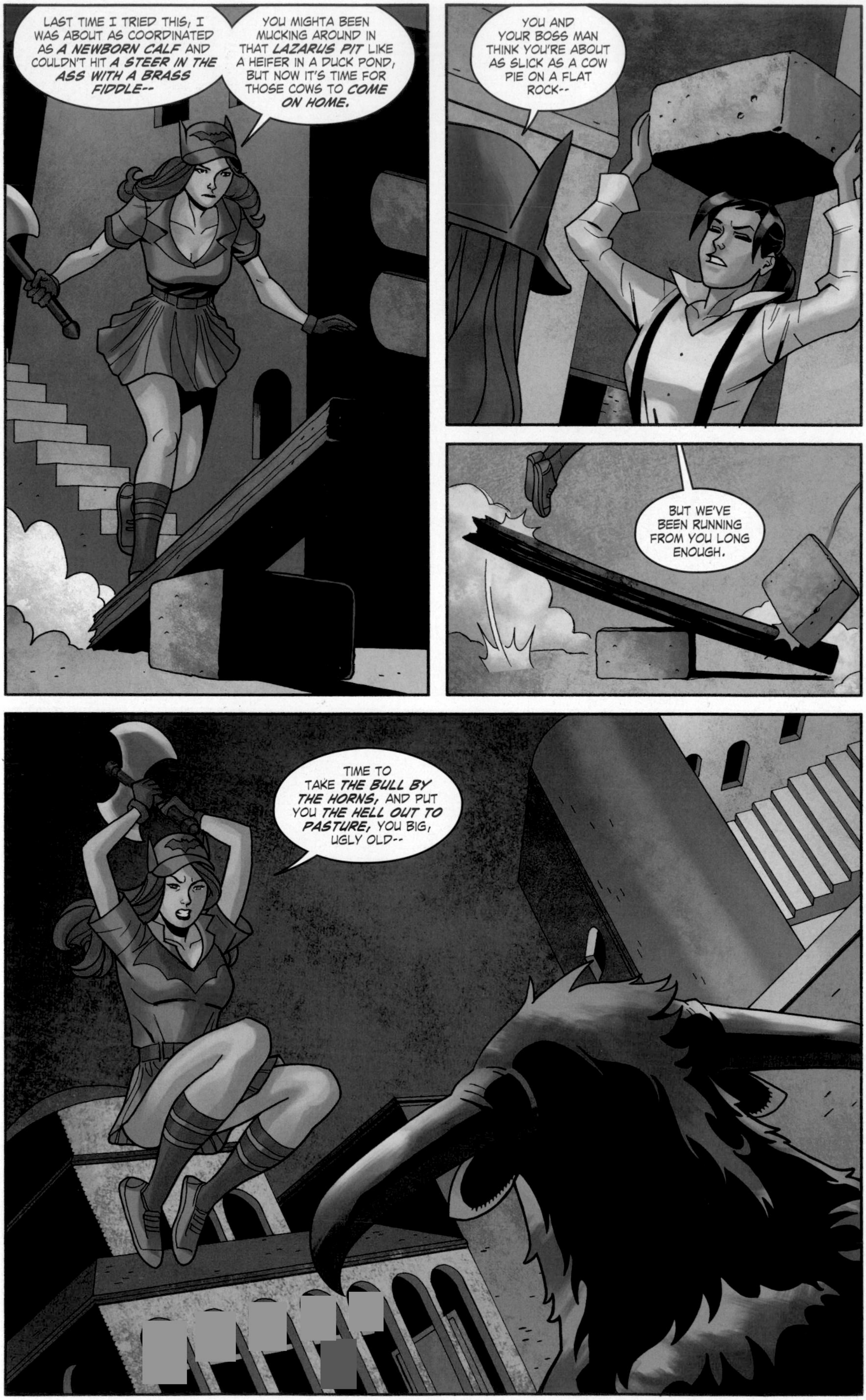
LAST TIME I TRIED THIS, I WAS ABOUT AS COORDINATED AS A NEWBORN CALF AND COULDN'T HIT A STEER IN THE ASS WITH A BRASS FIDDLE--
YOU MIGHTA BEEN MUCKING AROUND IN THAT LAZARUS PIT LIKE A HEIFER IN A DUCK POND, BUT NOW IT'S TIME FOR THOSE COWS TO COME ON HOME.
YOU AND YOUR BOSS MAN THINK YOU'RE ABOUT AS SLICK AS A COW PIE ON A FLAT ROCK--
BUT WE'VE BEEN RUNNING FROM YOU LONG ENOUGH.
TIME TO TAKE THE BULL BY THE HORNS, AND PUT YOU THE HELL OUT TO PASTURE, YOU BIG, UGLY OLD--

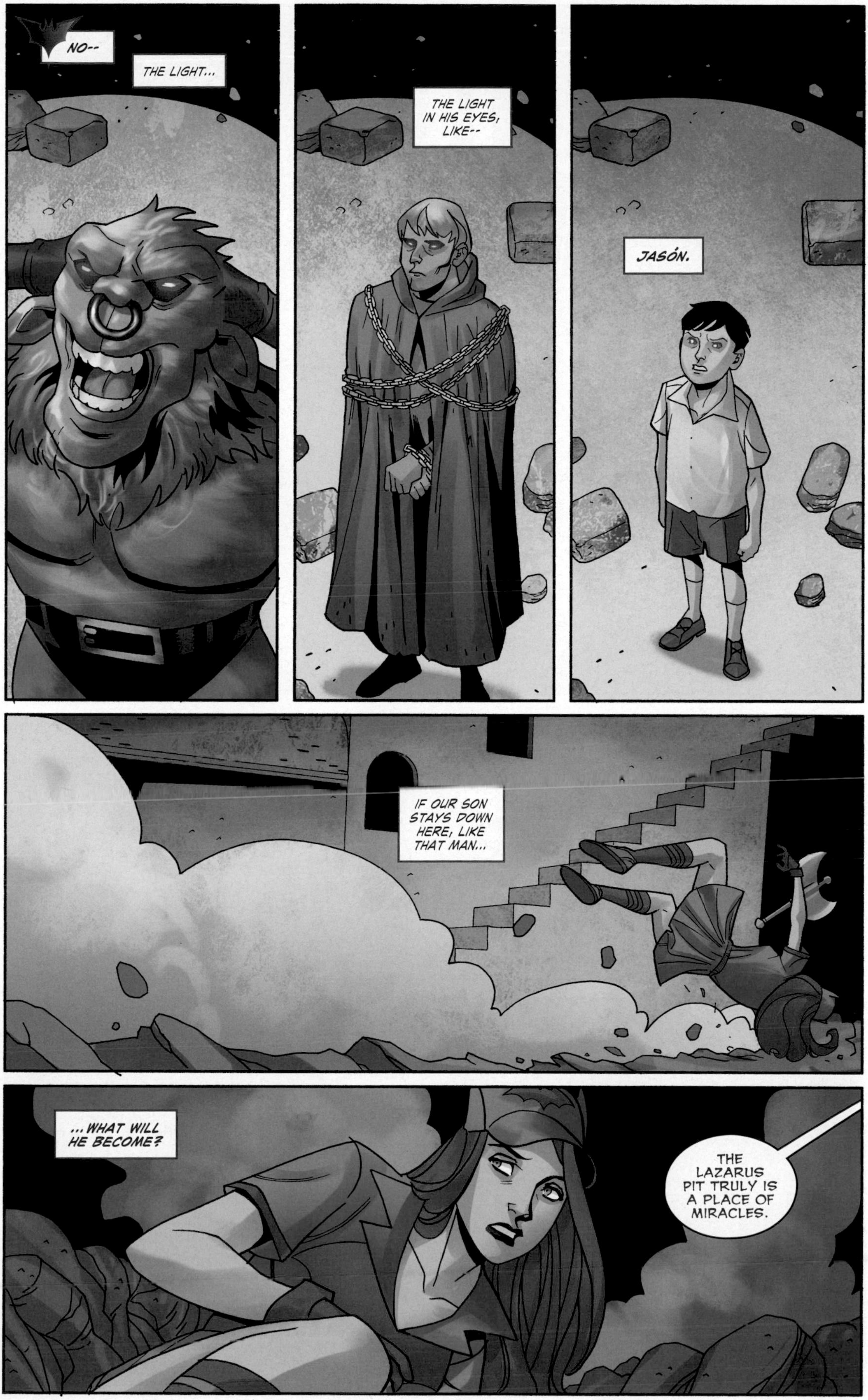
NO--
THE LIGHT...
THE LIGHT IN HIS EYES, LIKE--
JASÓN.
IF OUR SON STAYS DOWN HERE, LIKE THAT MAN...
...WHAT WILL HE BECOME?
THE LAZARUS PIT TRULY IS A PLACE OF MIRACLES.

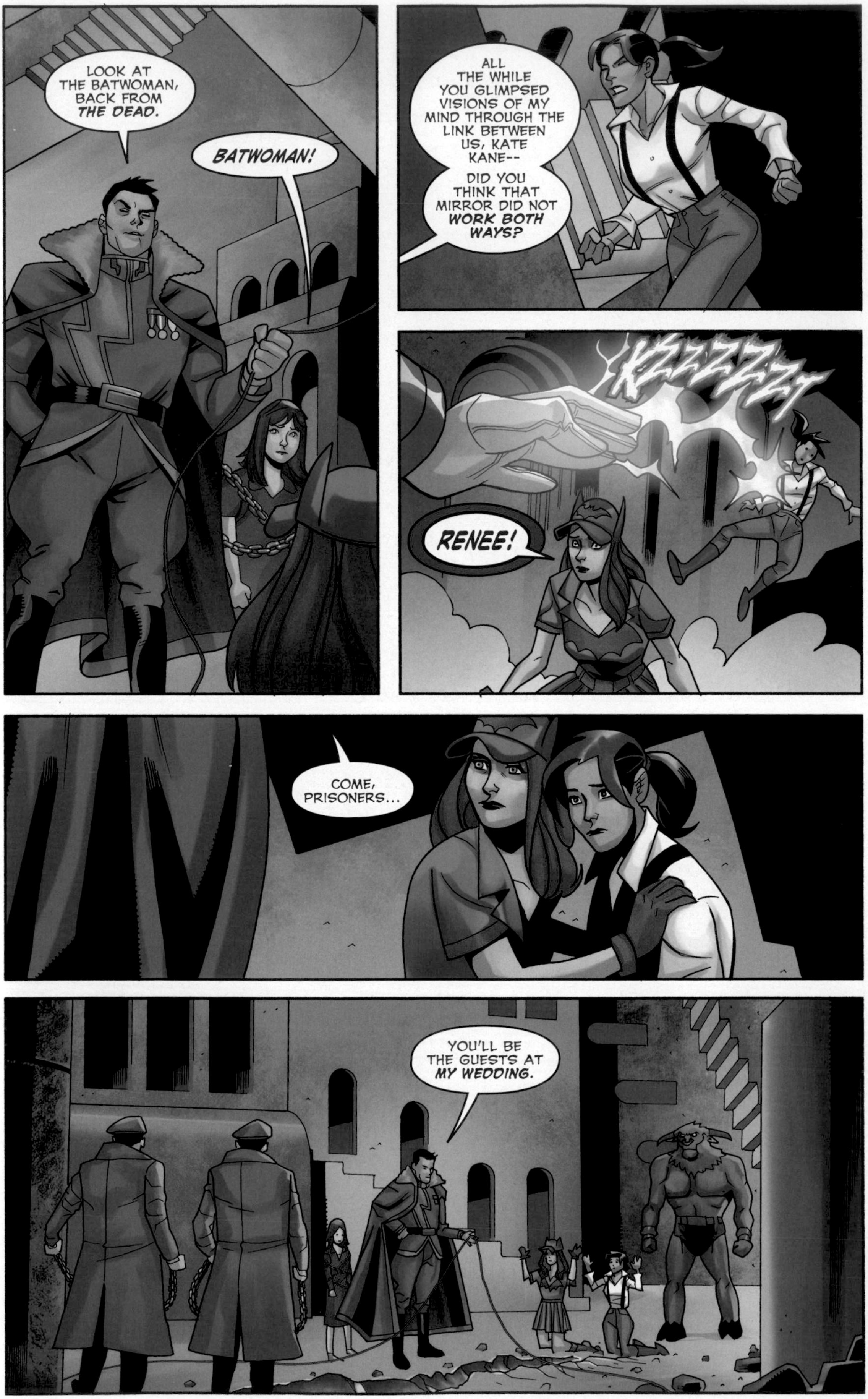
LOOK AT THE BATWOMAN, BACK FROM THE DEAD.
BATWOMAN!
ALL THE WHILE YOU GLIMPSED VISIONS OF MY MIND THROUGH THE LINK BETWEEN US, KATE KANE--
DID YOU THINK THAT MIRROR DID NOT WORK BOTH WAYS?
KZZZZZZT
RENEE!
COME, PRISONERS...
YOU'LL BE THE GUESTS AT MY WEDDING.

AND THIS IS HOW YOU HAND OFF THE CAT'S CRADLE...

DON'T GET TANGLED, LOST IN TOO MANY CHOICES; JUST CHOOSE, LIKE THIS--

AND THE THREAD, WHERE DOES IT LEAD?

A LOOP--

A RETURN.

CHEETAH--

TAKE JASÓN AND RUN!

MOTHER-- I AM READY TO DO MY DUTY.

THE IMMORTAL WILL NOT LEAVE THIS PLACE ALIVE.

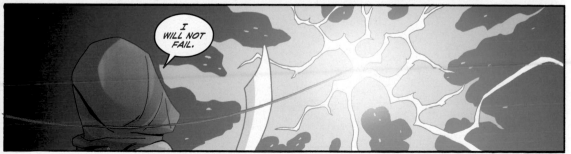

I WILL NOT FAIL.

I *WILL* KILL THEM, PRETTY GUARDIAN.

LOWER YOUR SWORD.

YOUR FACE IS FAMILIAR TO ME...

ARE YOU, PERHAPS, *ANOTHER* IMMORTAL?

I DANCED AND DUELED WITH *A SPY* SO LIKE YOU IN MANNER...

...A SPY NAMED *MELISANDE*.

MY MOTHER.

HEH. SHE TOLD ME A TALE ABOUT *A RED* THREAD, AND HOW IT LEADS YOU TO YOUR *DESTINY*...

AND BEHOLD, SPY'S SCION...

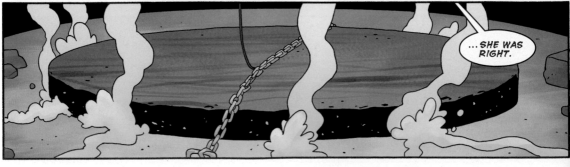

...SHE WAS RIGHT.

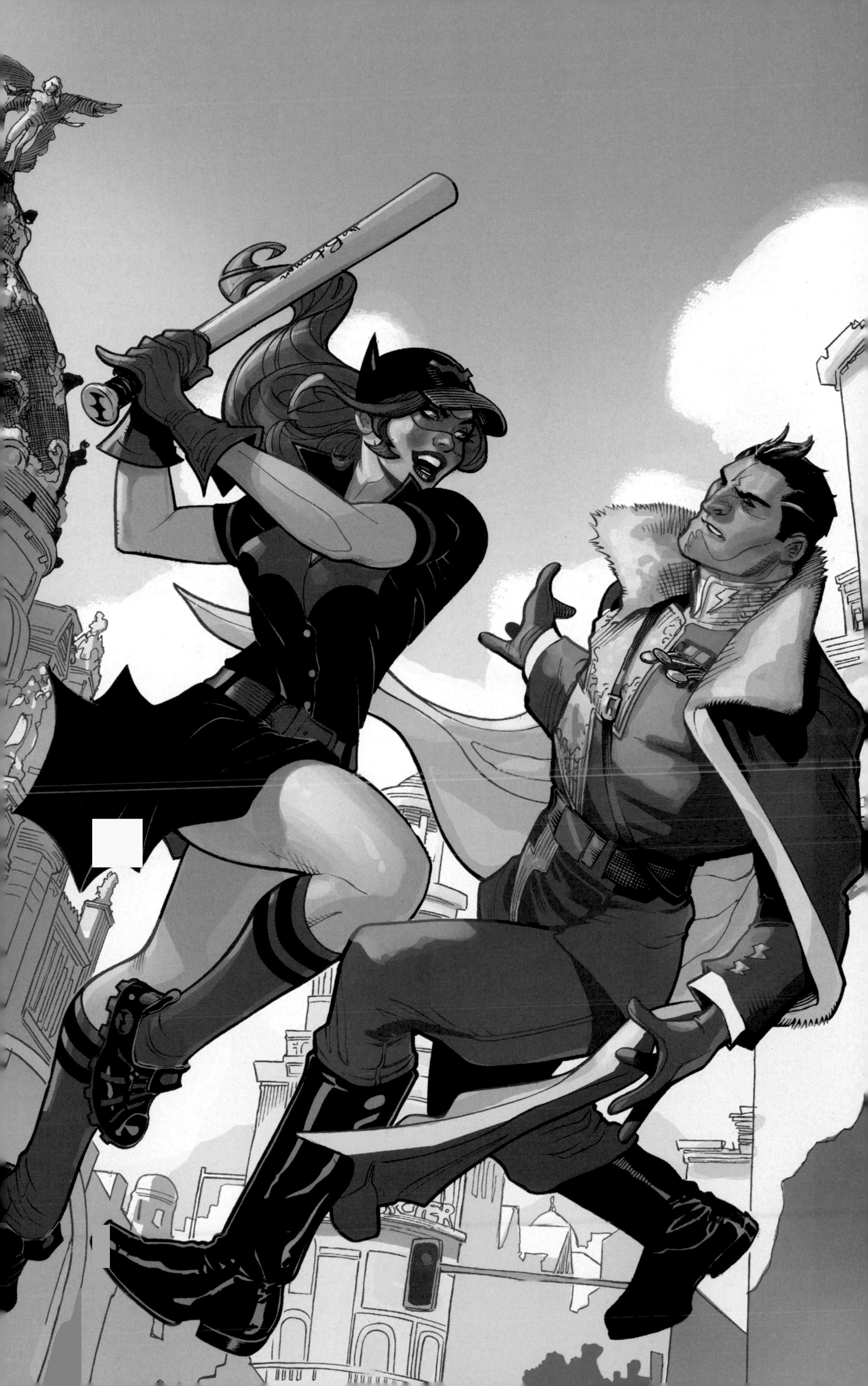

WAR BONDS

PARTS NINE *and* TEN

Written by
MARGUERITE BENNETT

Art by
STEPHEN BYRNE

Colors by
STEPHEN BYRNE

Cover by
TERRY *and* **RACHEL DODSON**

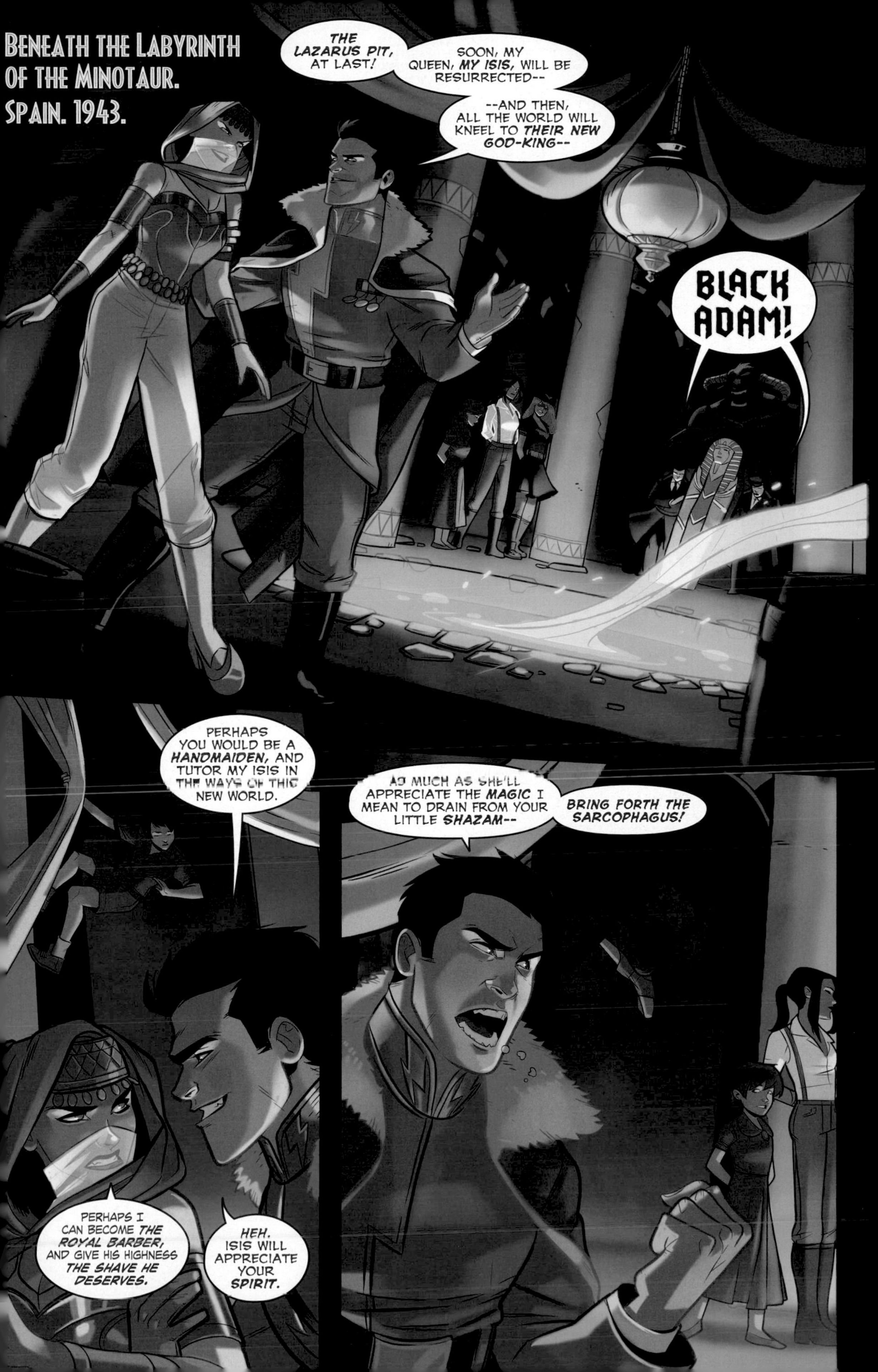

Beneath the Labyrinth of the Minotaur. Spain. 1943.
THE LAZARUS PIT, AT LAST!
SOON, MY QUEEN, MY ISIS, WILL BE RESURRECTED--
--AND THEN, ALL THE WORLD WILL KNEEL TO THEIR NEW GOD-KING--
BLACK ADAM!
PERHAPS YOU WOULD BE A HANDMAIDEN, AND TUTOR MY ISIS IN THE WAYS OF THIS NEW WORLD.
PERHAPS I CAN BECOME THE ROYAL BARBER, AND GIVE HIS HIGHNESS THE SHAVE HE DESERVES.
HEH. ISIS WILL APPRECIATE YOUR SPIRIT.
AS MUCH AS SHE'LL APPRECIATE THE MAGIC I MEAN TO DRAIN FROM YOUR LITTLE SHAZAM--
BRING FORTH THE SARCOPHAGUS!

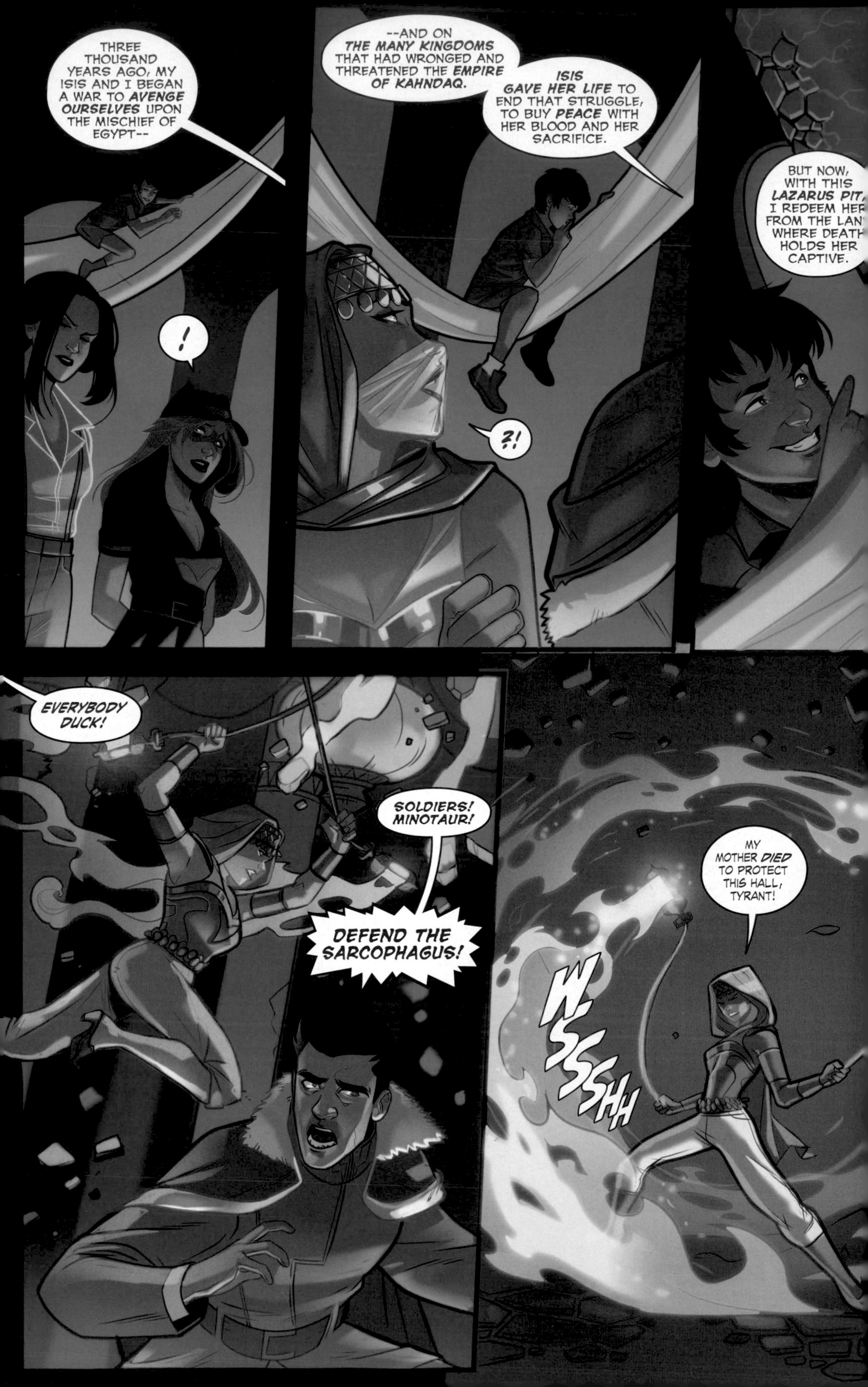

THREE THOUSAND YEARS AGO, MY ISIS AND I BEGAN A WAR TO AVENGE OURSELVES UPON THE MISCHIEF OF EGYPT--
!
--AND ON THE MANY KINGDOMS THAT HAD WRONGED AND THREATENED THE EMPIRE OF KAHNDAQ.
ISIS GAVE HER LIFE TO END THAT STRUGGLE, TO BUY PEACE WITH HER BLOOD AND HER SACRIFICE.
?!
BUT NOW, WITH THIS LAZARUS PIT, I REDEEM HER FROM THE LAN WHERE DEATH HOLDS HER CAPTIVE.
EVERYBODY DUCK!
SOLDIERS! MINOTAUR!
DEFEND THE SARCOPHAGUS!
MY MOTHER DIED TO PROTECT THIS HALL, TYRANT!
WSSSHH

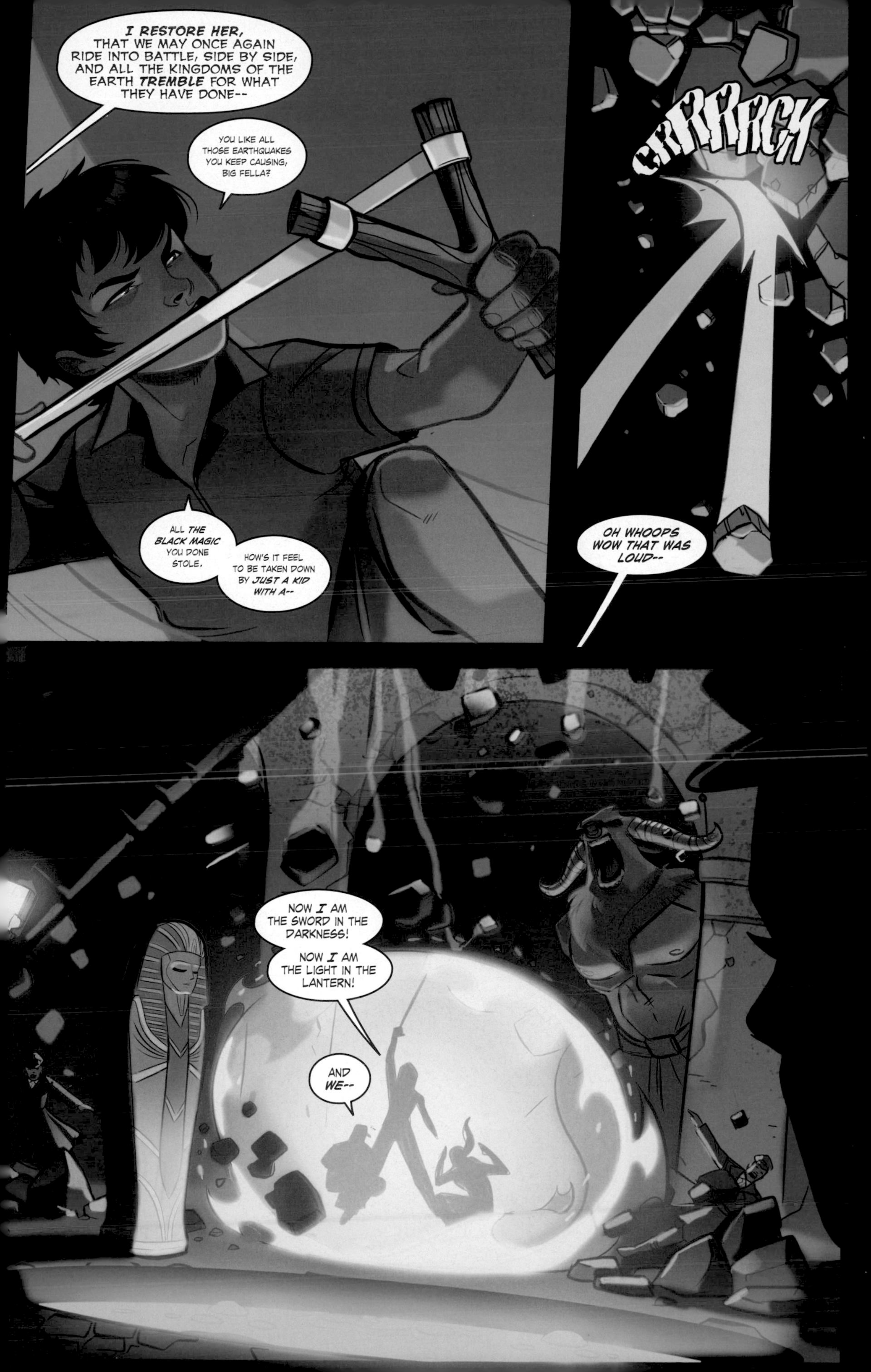
I RESTORE HER, THAT WE MAY ONCE AGAIN RIDE INTO BATTLE, SIDE BY SIDE, AND ALL THE KINGDOMS OF THE EARTH TREMBLE FOR WHAT THEY HAVE DONE--
YOU LIKE ALL THOSE EARTHQUAKES YOU KEEP CAUSING, BIG FELLA?
ALL THE BLACK MAGIC YOU DONE STOLE.
HOW'S IT FEEL TO BE TAKEN DOWN BY JUST A KID WITH A--
CRRRRCK
OH WHOOPS WOW THAT WAS LOUD--
NOW I AM THE SWORD IN THE DARKNESS!
NOW I AM THE LIGHT IN THE LANTERN!
AND WE--

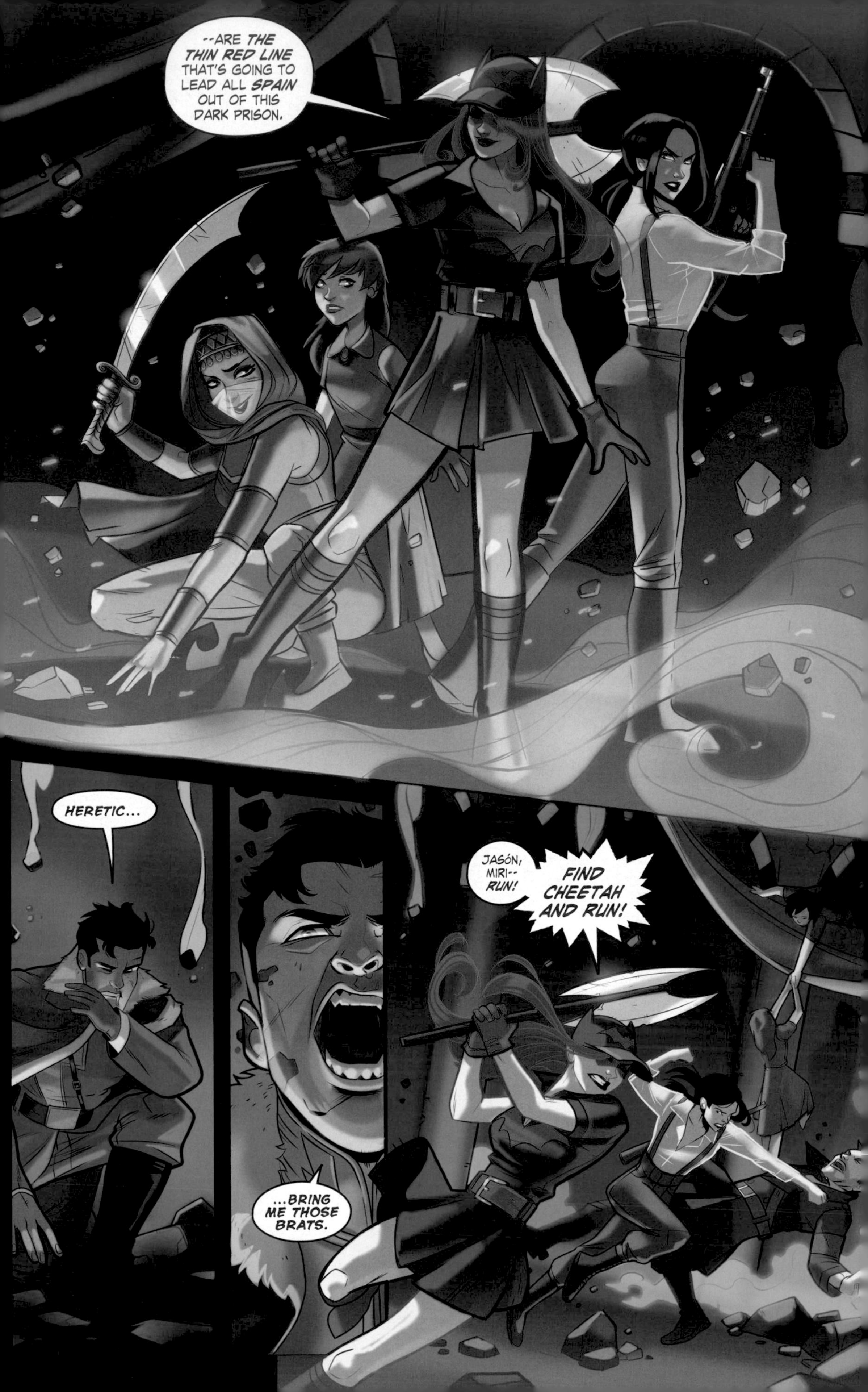
--ARE THE THIN RED LINE THAT'S GOING TO LEAD ALL SPAIN OUT OF THIS DARK PRISON.
HERETIC...
...BRING ME THOSE BRATS.
JASÓN, MIRI-- RUN!
FIND CHEETAH AND RUN!

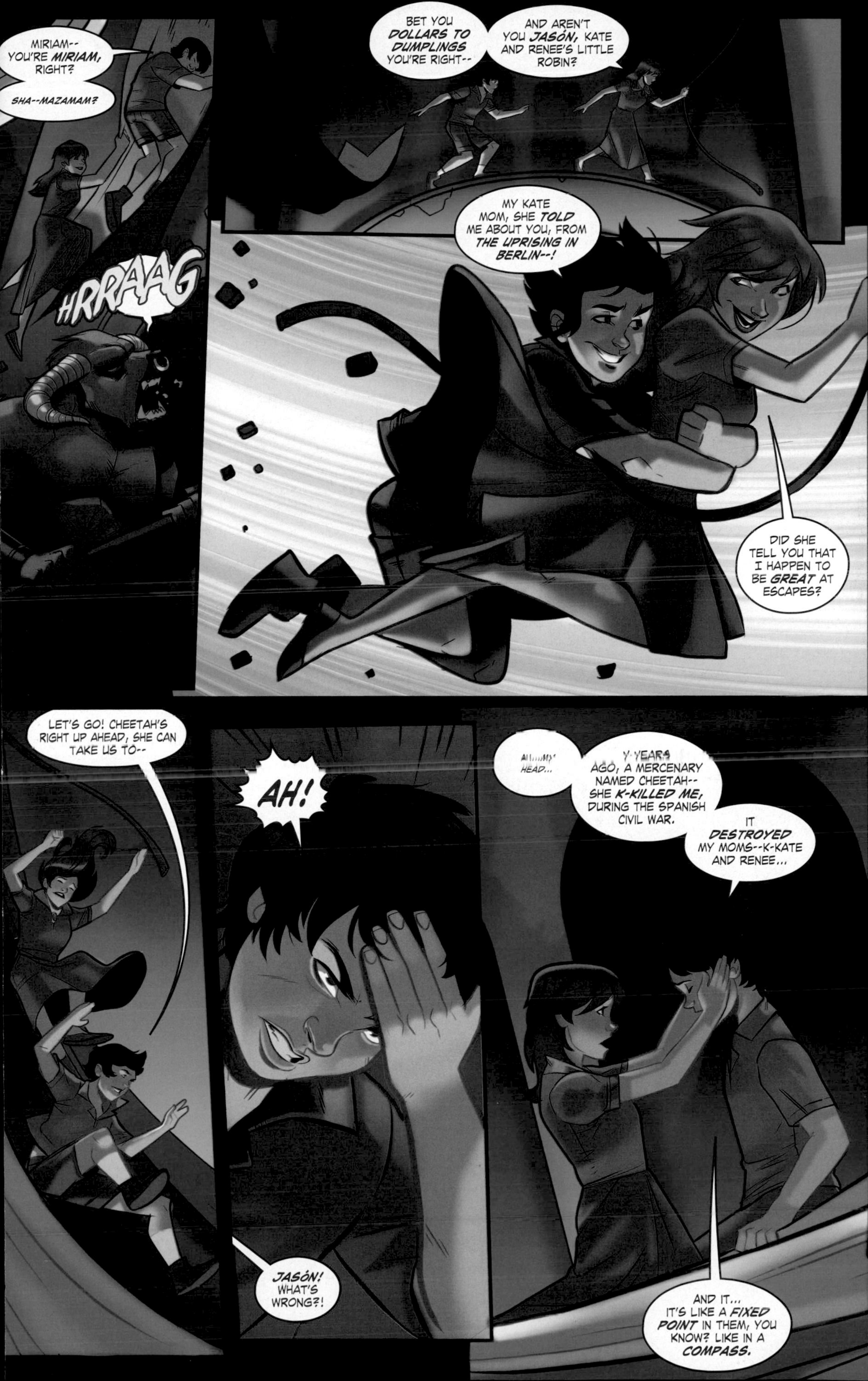
MIRIAM-- YOU'RE MIRIAM, RIGHT?
SHA--MAZAMAM?
HRRAAG
BET YOU DOLLARS TO DUMPLINGS YOU'RE RIGHT--
AND AREN'T YOU JASÓN, KATE AND RENEE'S LITTLE ROBIN?
MY KATE MOM, SHE TOLD ME ABOUT YOU, FROM THE UPRISING IN BERLIN--!
DID SHE TELL YOU THAT I HAPPEN TO BE GREAT AT ESCAPES?
LET'S GO! CHEETAH'S RIGHT UP AHEAD, SHE CAN TAKE US TO--
AH!
JASÓN! WHAT'S WRONG?!
HEAD...
Y-YEARS AGO, A MERCENARY NAMED CHEETAH-- SHE K-KILLED ME, DURING THE SPANISH CIVIL WAR.
IT DESTROYED MY MOMS--K-KATE AND RENEE...
AND IT... IT'S LIKE A FIXED POINT IN THEM, YOU KNOW? LIKE IN A COMPASS.

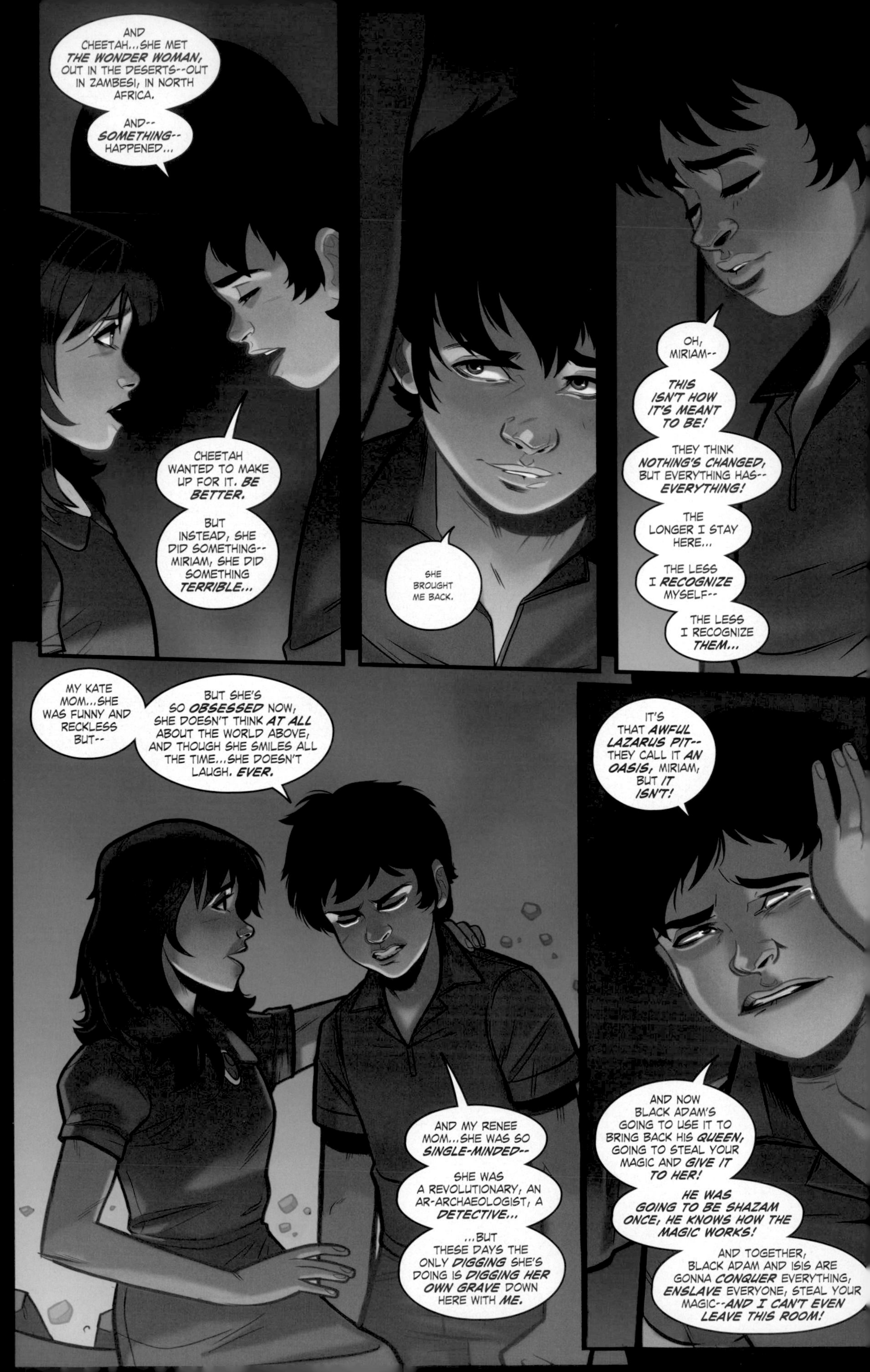
AND CHEETAH...SHE MET THE WONDER WOMAN, OUT IN THE DESERTS--OUT IN ZAMBESI, IN NORTH AFRICA.
AND--SOMETHING--HAPPENED...
CHEETAH WANTED TO MAKE UP FOR IT. BE BETTER.
BUT INSTEAD, SHE DID SOMETHING--MIRIAM, SHE DID SOMETHING TERRIBLE...
SHE BROUGHT ME BACK.
OH, MIRIAM--
THIS ISN'T HOW IT'S MEANT TO BE!
THEY THINK NOTHING'S CHANGED, BUT EVERYTHING HAS--EVERYTHING!
THE LONGER I STAY HERE...
THE LESS I RECOGNIZE MYSELF--
THE LESS I RECOGNIZE THEM...
MY KATE MOM...SHE WAS FUNNY AND RECKLESS BUT--
BUT SHE'S SO OBSESSED NOW, SHE DOESN'T THINK AT ALL ABOUT THE WORLD ABOVE, AND THOUGH SHE SMILES ALL THE TIME...SHE DOESN'T LAUGH. EVER.
AND MY RENEE MOM...SHE WAS SO SINGLE-MINDED--
SHE WAS A REVOLUTIONARY, AN AR-ARCHAEOLOGIST, A DETECTIVE...
...BUT THESE DAYS THE ONLY DIGGING SHE'S DOING IS DIGGING HER OWN GRAVE DOWN HERE WITH ME.
IT'S THAT AWFUL LAZARUS PIT--THEY CALL IT AN OASIS, MIRIAM, BUT IT ISN'T!
AND NOW BLACK ADAM'S GOING TO USE IT TO BRING BACK HIS QUEEN, GOING TO STEAL YOUR MAGIC AND GIVE IT TO HER!
HE WAS GOING TO BE SHAZAM ONCE, HE KNOWS HOW THE MAGIC WORKS!
AND TOGETHER, BLACK ADAM AND ISIS ARE GONNA CONQUER EVERYTHING, ENSLAVE EVERYONE, STEAL YOUR MAGIC--AND I CAN'T EVEN LEAVE THIS ROOM!

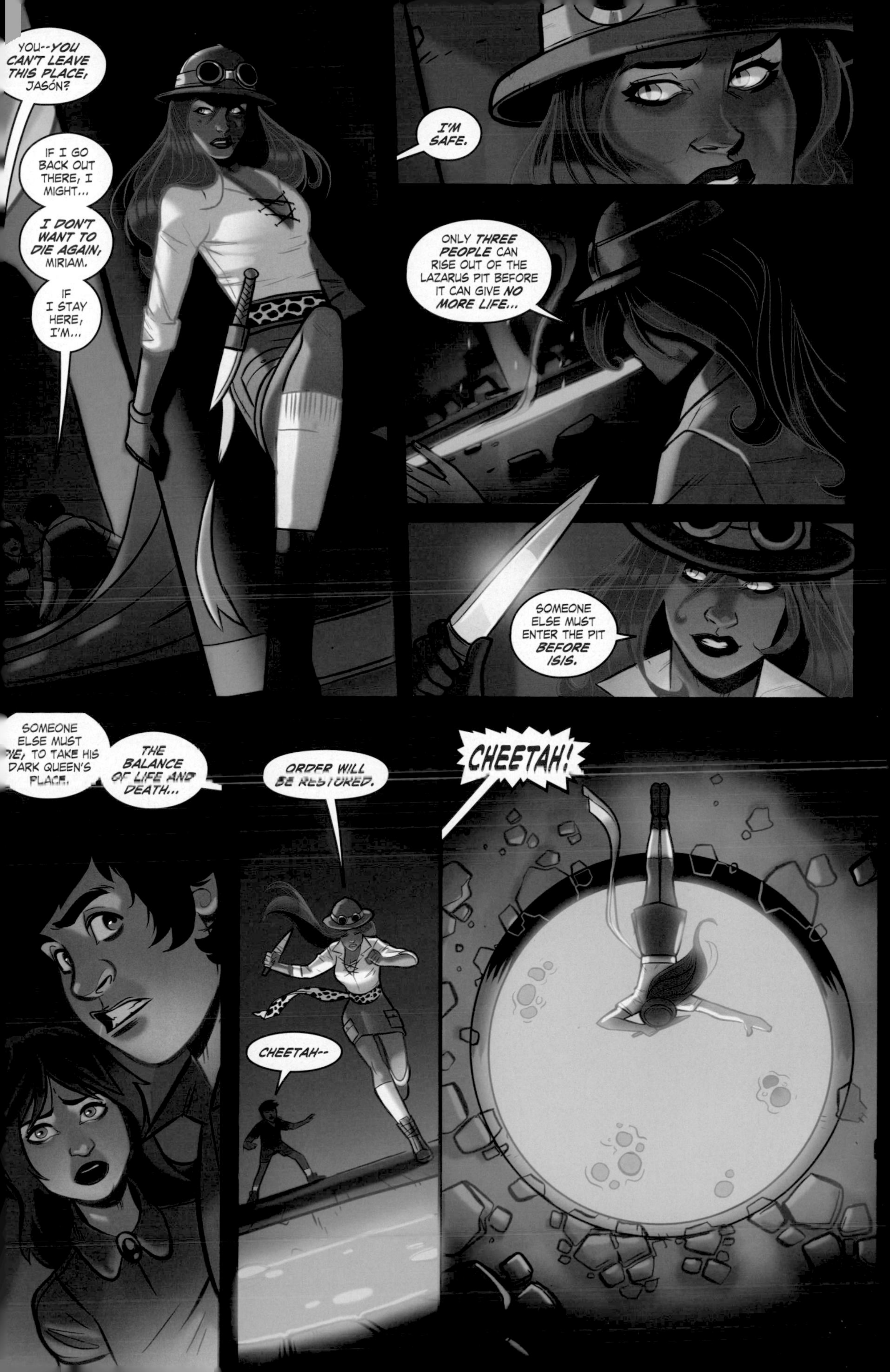

YOU--YOU CAN'T LEAVE THIS PLACE, JASÓN?
IF I GO BACK OUT THERE, I MIGHT...
I DON'T WANT TO DIE AGAIN, MIRIAM.
IF I STAY HERE, I'M...
I'M SAFE.
ONLY THREE PEOPLE CAN RISE OUT OF THE LAZARUS PIT BEFORE IT CAN GIVE NO MORE LIFE...
SOMEONE ELSE MUST ENTER THE PIT BEFORE ISIS.
SOMEONE ELSE MUST DIE, TO TAKE HIS DARK QUEEN'S PLACE.
THE BALANCE OF LIFE AND DEATH...
ORDER WILL BE RESTORED.
CHEETAH--
CHEETAH!

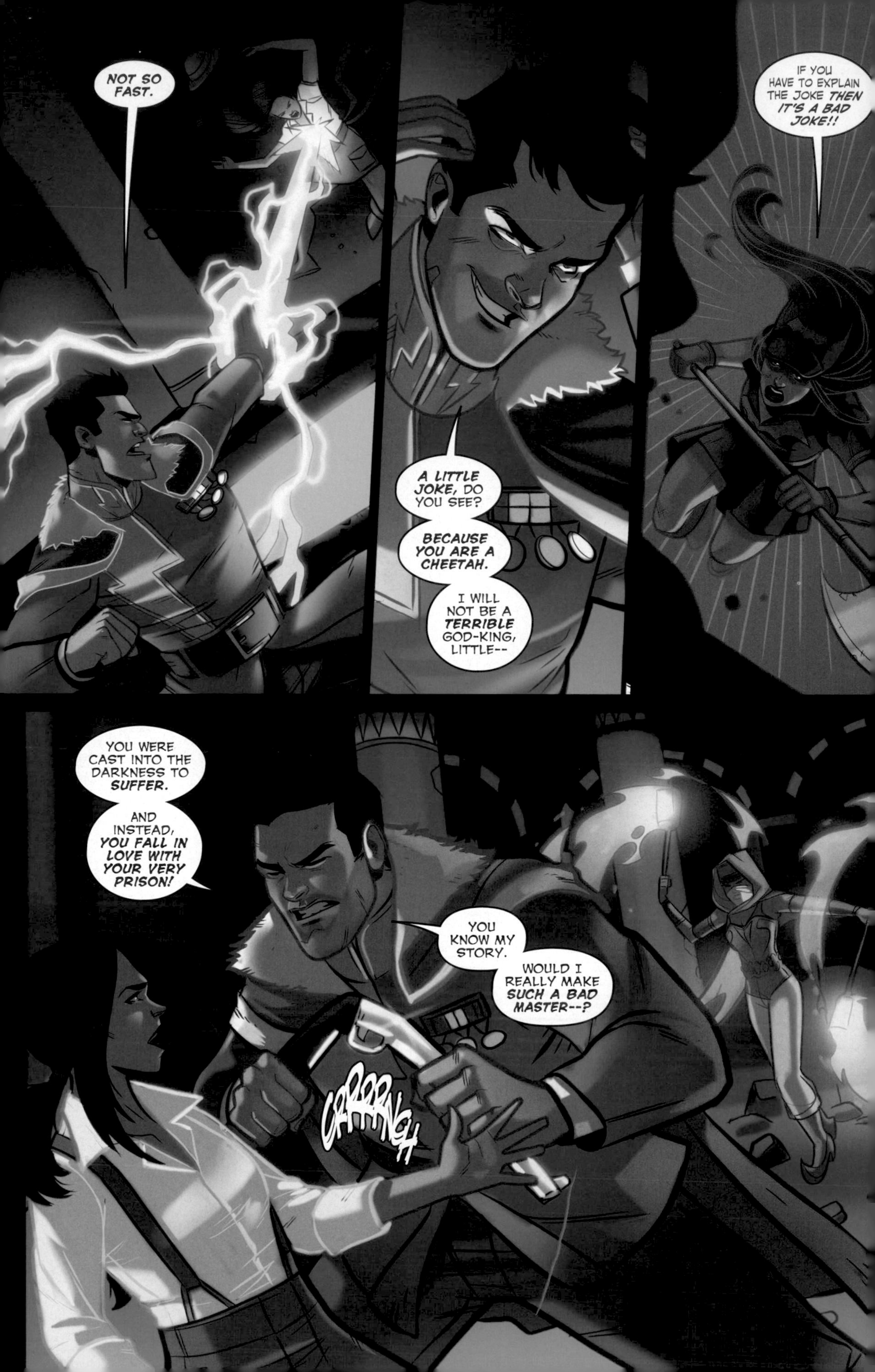
NOT SO FAST.
A LITTLE JOKE, DO YOU SEE?
BECAUSE YOU ARE A CHEETAH.
I WILL NOT BE A TERRIBLE GOD-KING, LITTLE--
IF YOU HAVE TO EXPLAIN THE JOKE THEN IT'S A BAD JOKE!!
YOU WERE CAST INTO THE DARKNESS TO SUFFER.
AND INSTEAD, YOU FALL IN LOVE WITH YOUR VERY PRISON!
YOU KNOW MY STORY.
WOULD I REALLY MAKE SUCH A BAD MASTER--?
CRRRRNGH

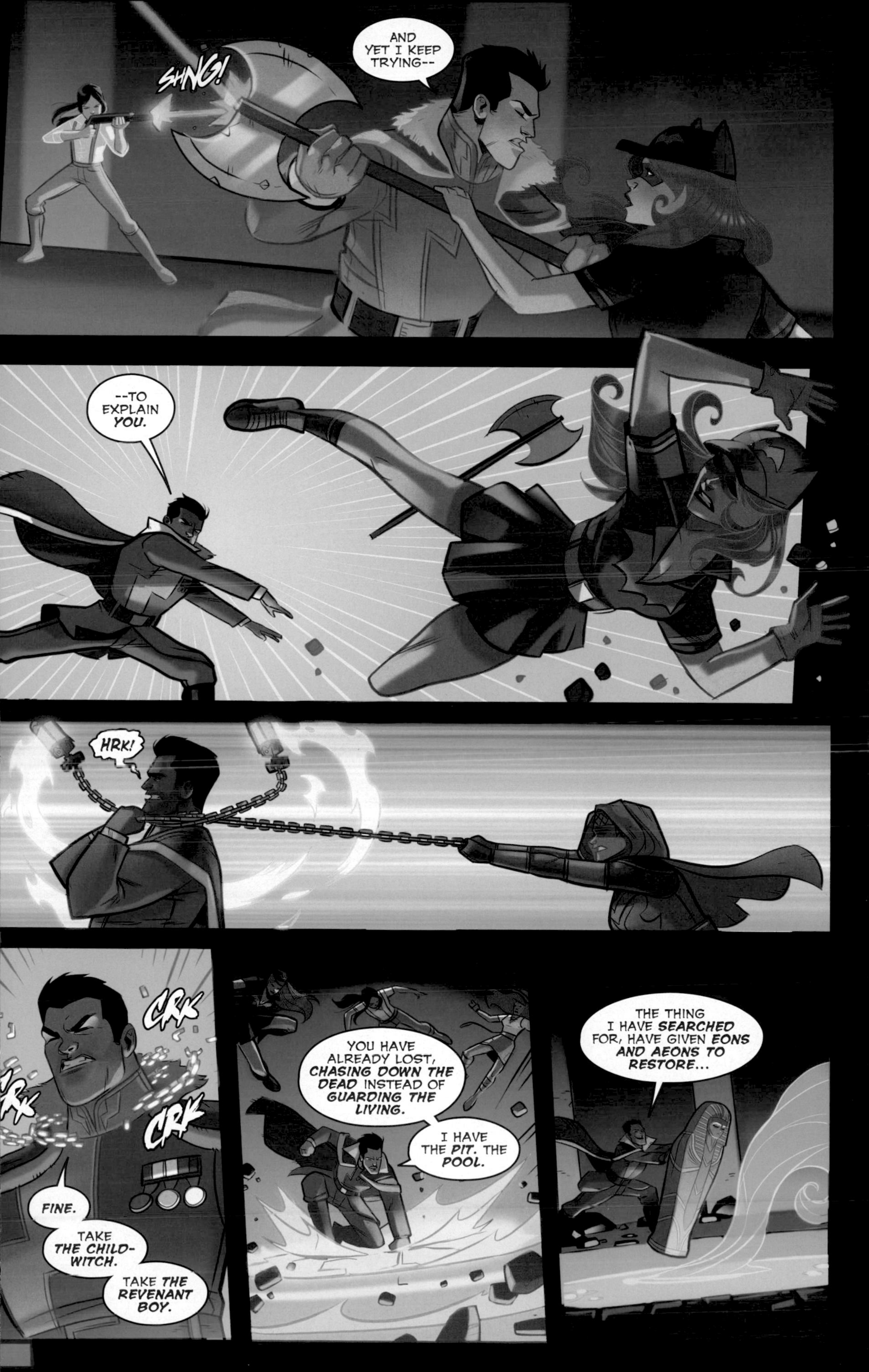
AND YET I KEEP TRYING--
SHNG!
--TO EXPLAIN YOU.
HRK!
CRK
CRK
FINE.
TAKE THE CHILD-WITCH.
TAKE THE REVENANT BOY.
YOU HAVE ALREADY LOST, CHASING DOWN THE DEAD INSTEAD OF GUARDING THE LIVING.
I HAVE THE PIT. THE POOL.
THE THING I HAVE SEARCHED FOR, HAVE GIVEN EONS AND AEONS TO RESTORE...

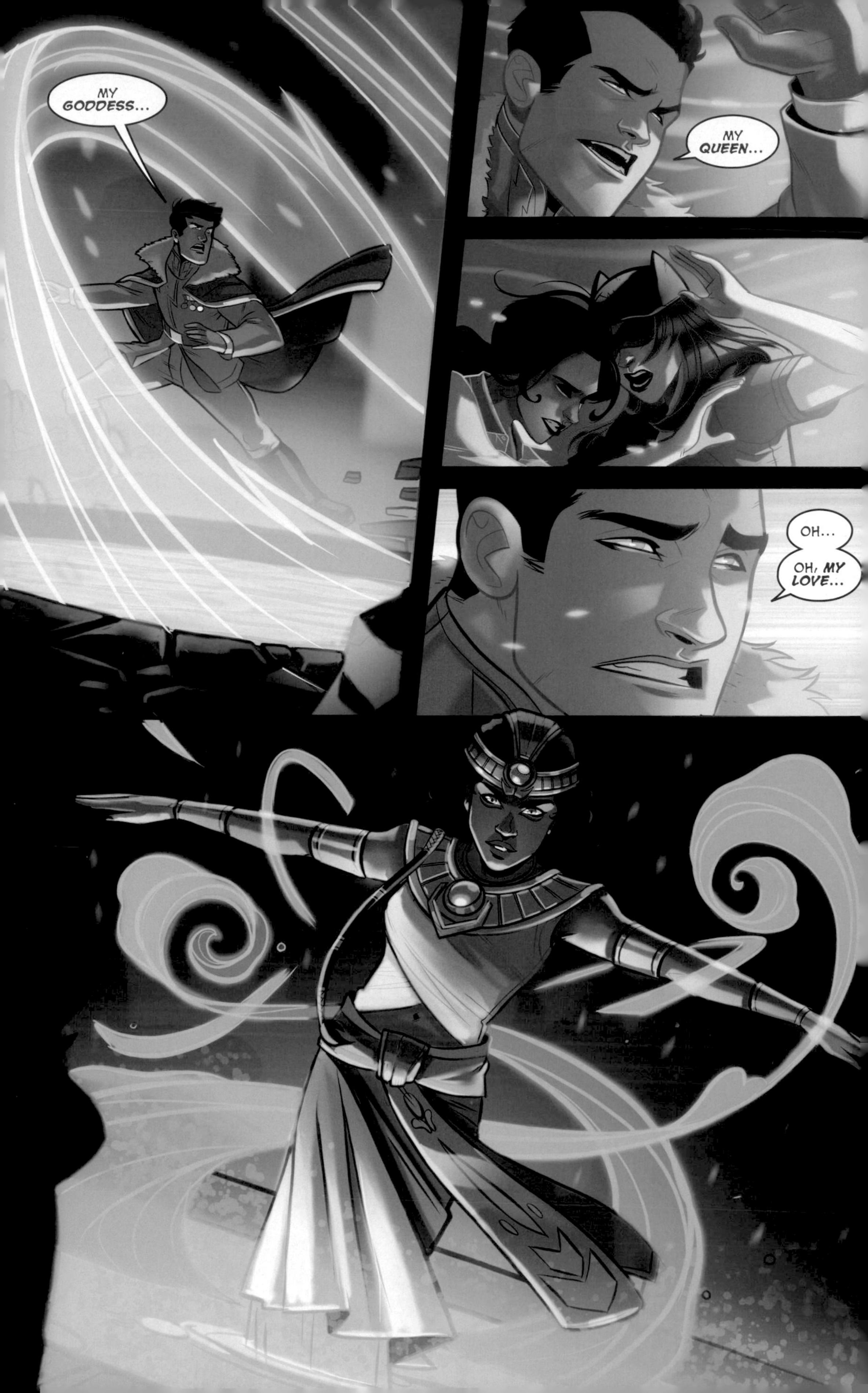
MY GODDESS...
MY QUEEN...
OH...
OH, MY LOVE...

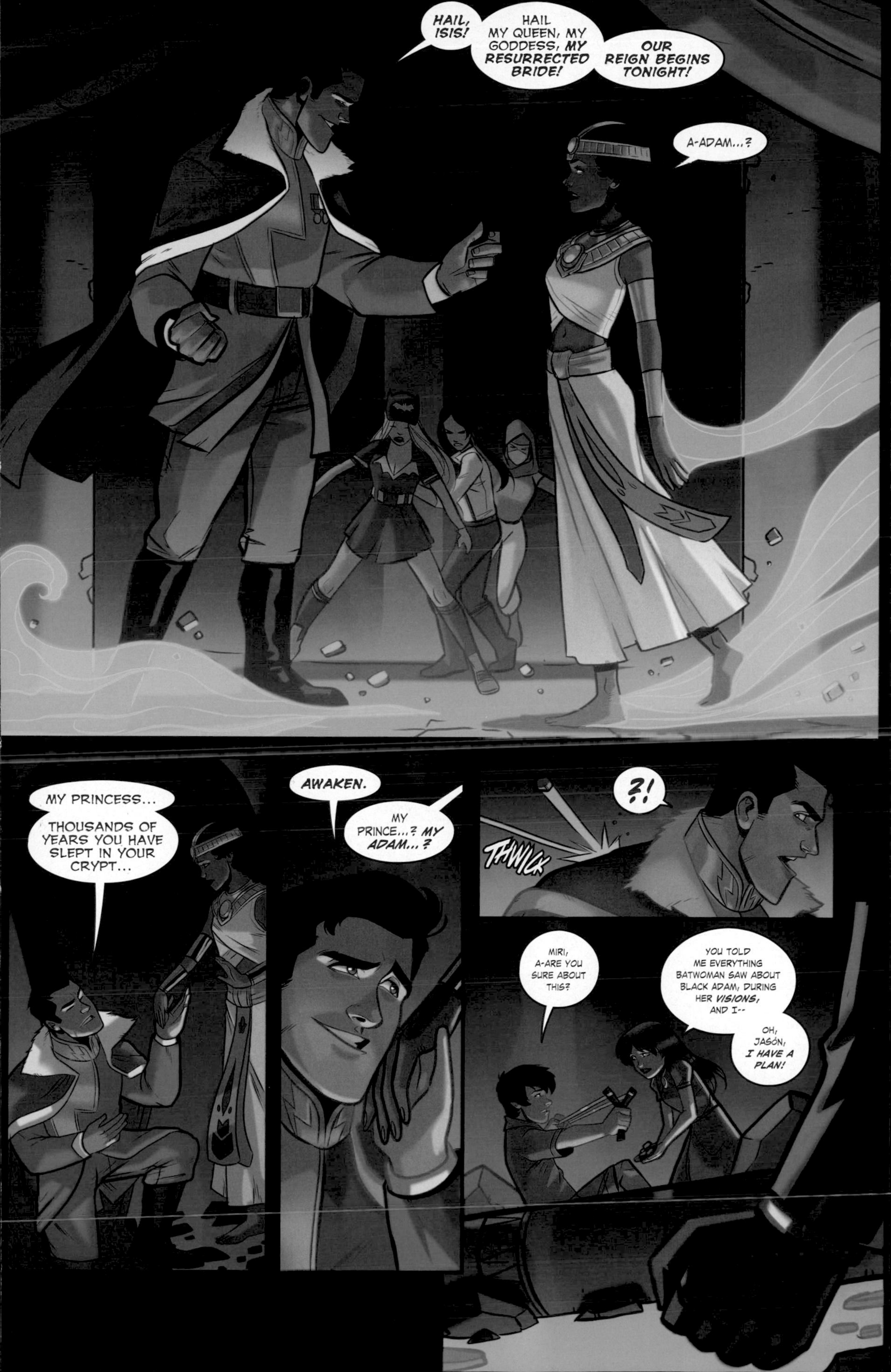
HAIL, ISIS!
HAIL MY QUEEN, MY GODDESS, MY RESURRECTED BRIDE!
OUR REIGN BEGINS TONIGHT!
A-ADAM...?
MY PRINCESS...
THOUSANDS OF YEARS YOU HAVE SLEPT IN YOUR CRYPT...
AWAKEN.
MY PRINCE...? MY ADAM...?
THWICK
?!
MIRI, A-ARE YOU SURE ABOUT THIS?
YOU TOLD ME EVERYTHING BATWOMAN SAW ABOUT BLACK ADAM, DURING HER VISIONS, AND I--
OH, JASÓN, I HAVE A PLAN!

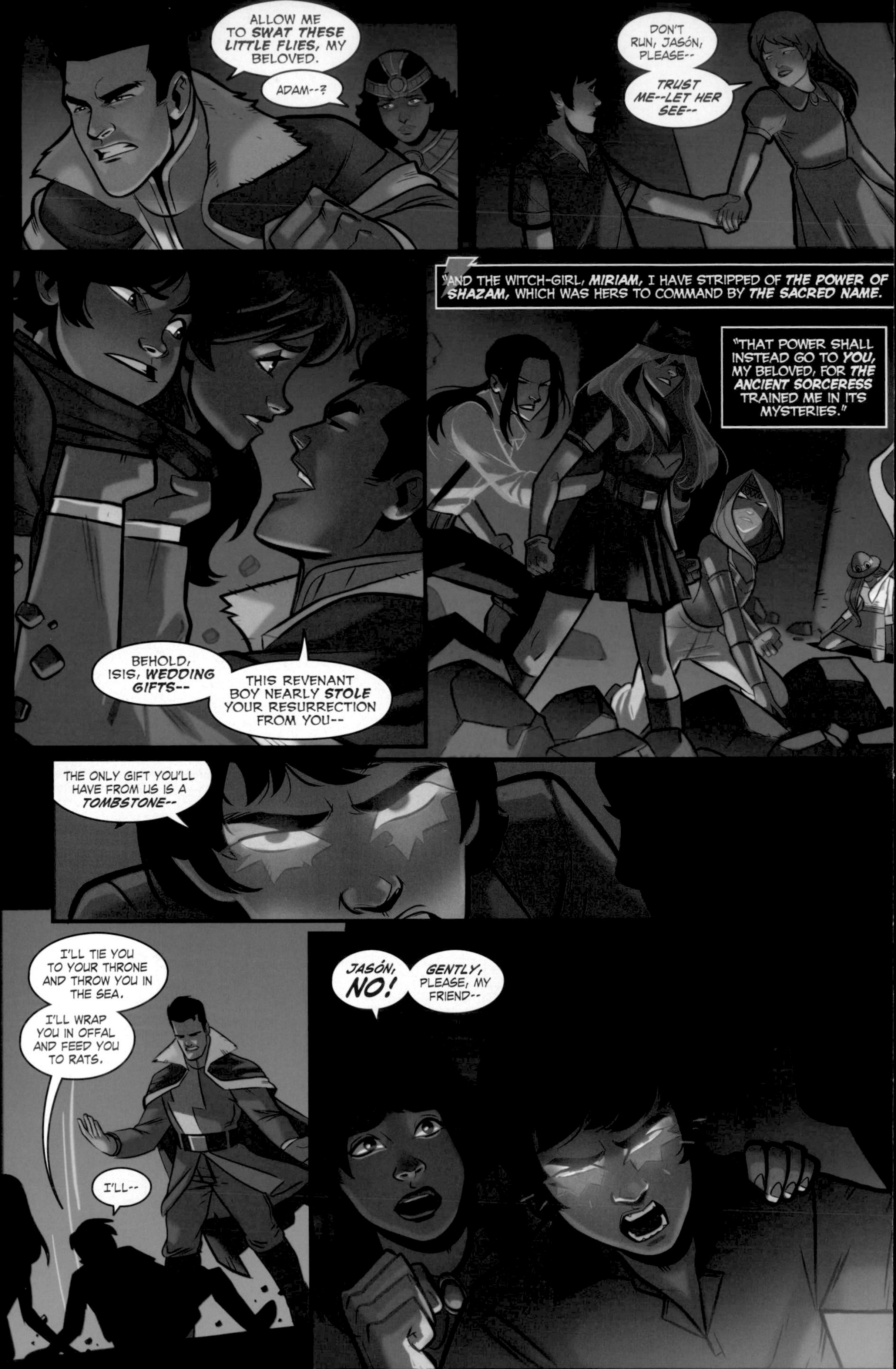
ALLOW ME TO SWAT THESE LITTLE FLIES, MY BELOVED.
ADAM--?
DON'T RUN, JASÓN, PLEASE--
TRUST ME--LET HER SEE--
"AND THE WITCH-GIRL, MIRIAM, I HAVE STRIPPED OF THE POWER OF SHAZAM, WHICH WAS HERS TO COMMAND BY THE SACRED NAME.
"THAT POWER SHALL INSTEAD GO TO YOU, MY BELOVED, FOR THE ANCIENT SORCERESS TRAINED ME IN ITS MYSTERIES."
BEHOLD, ISIS, WEDDING GIFTS--
THIS REVENANT BOY NEARLY STOLE YOUR RESURRECTION FROM YOU--
THE ONLY GIFT YOU'LL HAVE FROM US IS A TOMBSTONE--
I'LL TIE YOU TO YOUR THRONE AND THROW YOU IN THE SEA.
I'LL WRAP YOU IN OFFAL AND FEED YOU TO RATS.
I'LL--
JASÓN, NO!
GENTLY, PLEASE, MY FRIEND--

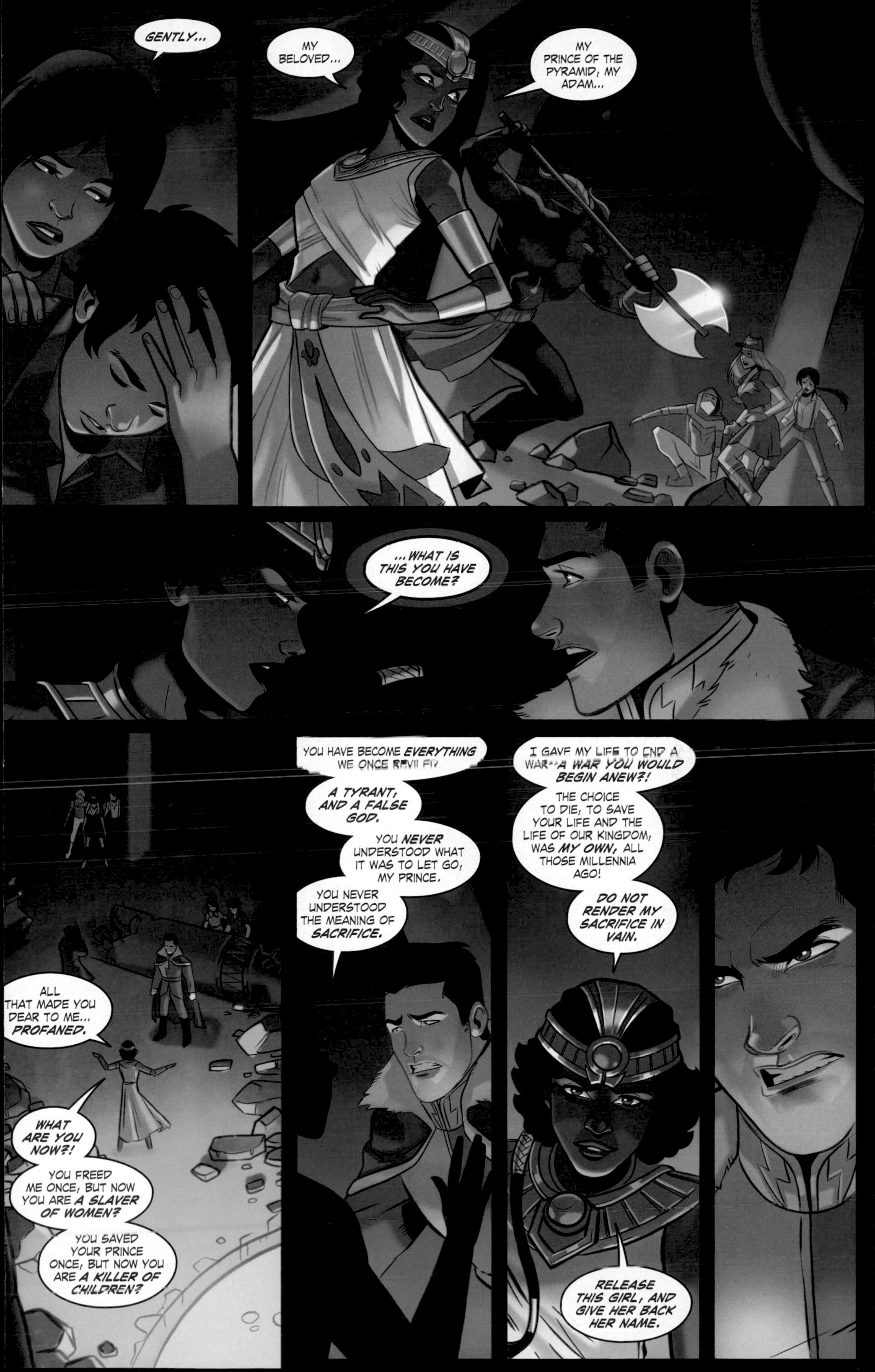
GENTLY...
MY BELOVED...
MY PRINCE OF THE PYRAMID, MY ADAM...
...WHAT IS THIS YOU HAVE BECOME?
ALL THAT MADE YOU DEAR TO ME... PROFANED.
WHAT ARE YOU NOW?!
YOU FREED ME ONCE, BUT NOW YOU ARE A SLAVER OF WOMEN?
YOU SAVED YOUR PRINCE ONCE, BUT NOW YOU ARE A KILLER OF CHILDREN?
YOU HAVE BECOME EVERYTHING WE ONCE REVILED.
A TYRANT, AND A FALSE GOD.
YOU NEVER UNDERSTOOD WHAT IT WAS TO LET GO, MY PRINCE.
YOU NEVER UNDERSTOOD THE MEANING OF SACRIFICE.
I GAVE MY LIFE TO END A WAR--A WAR YOU WOULD BEGIN ANEW?!
THE CHOICE TO DIE, TO SAVE YOUR LIFE AND THE LIFE OF OUR KINGDOM, WAS MY OWN, ALL THOSE MILLENNIA AGO!
DO NOT RENDER MY SACRIFICE IN VAIN.
RELEASE THIS GIRL, AND GIVE HER BACK HER NAME.

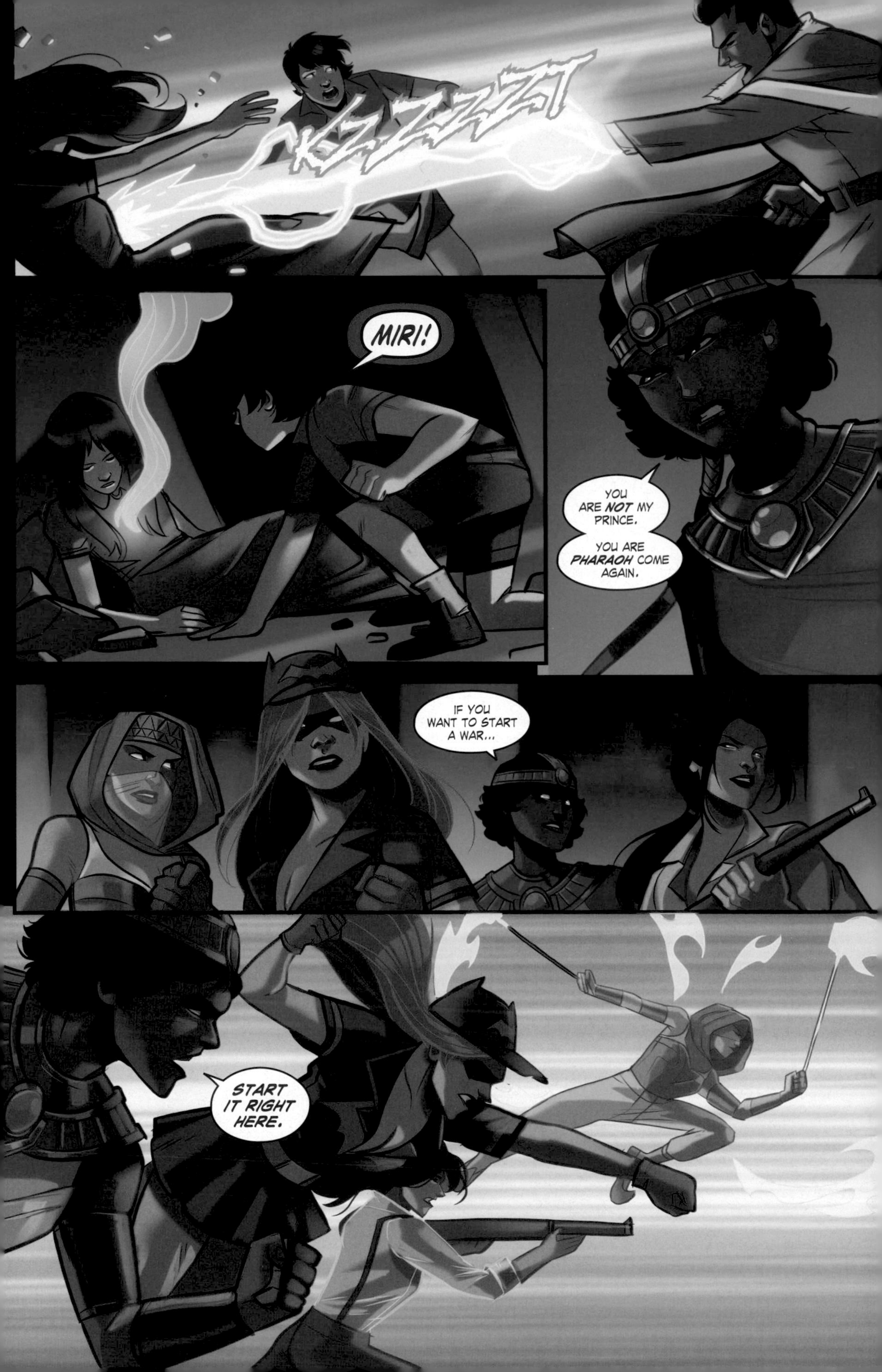
KZZZZT
MIRI!
YOU ARE NOT MY PRINCE.
YOU ARE PHARAOH COME AGAIN.
IF YOU WANT TO START A WAR...
START IT RIGHT HERE.

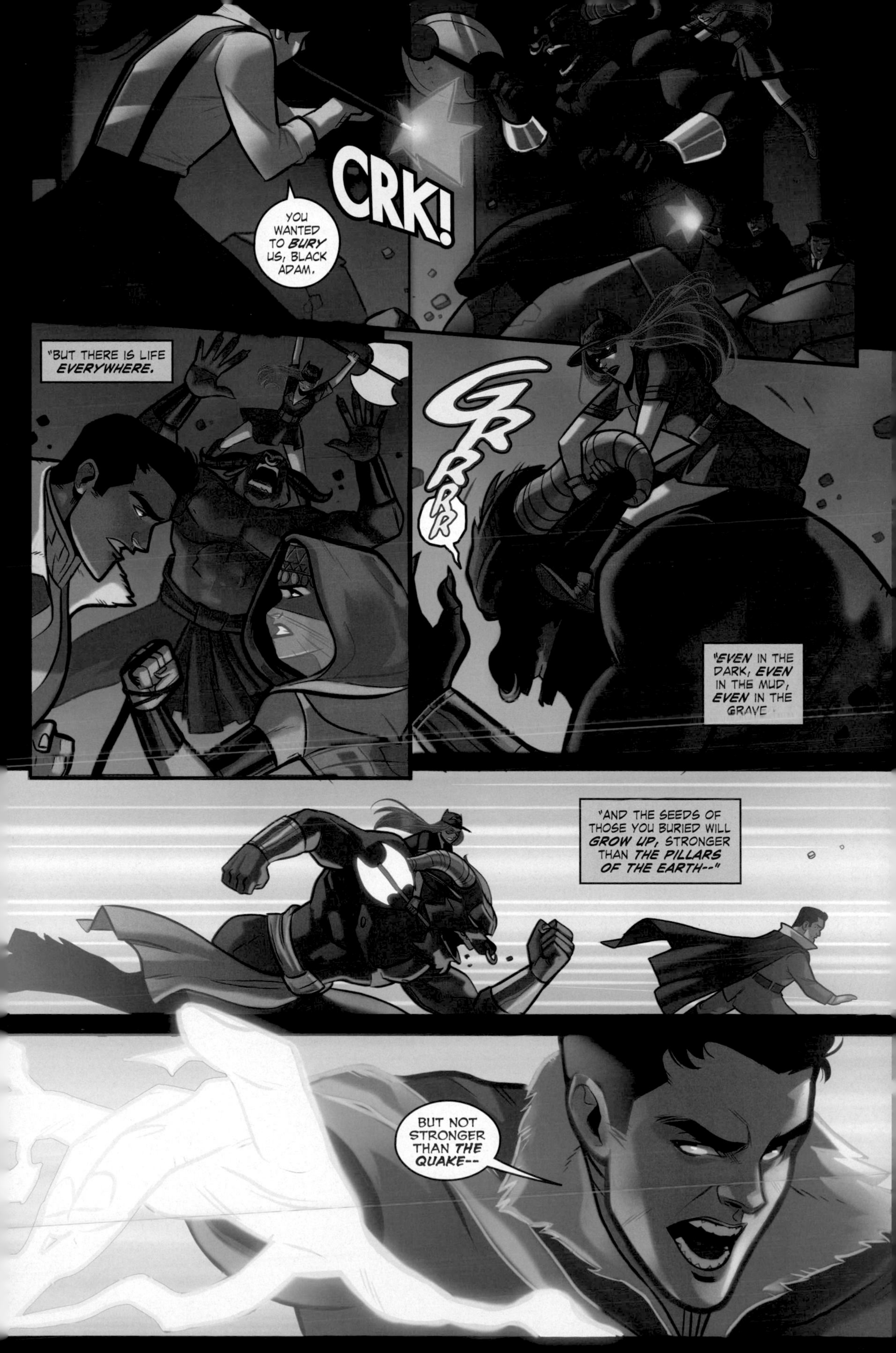
YOU WANTED TO BURY US, BLACK ADAM.
CRK!
"BUT THERE IS LIFE EVERYWHERE.
GRRRRR
"EVEN IN THE DARK, EVEN IN THE MUD, EVEN IN THE GRAVE
"AND THE SEEDS OF THOSE YOU BURIED WILL GROW UP, STRONGER THAN THE PILLARS OF THE EARTH--"
BUT NOT STRONGER THAN THE QUAKE--

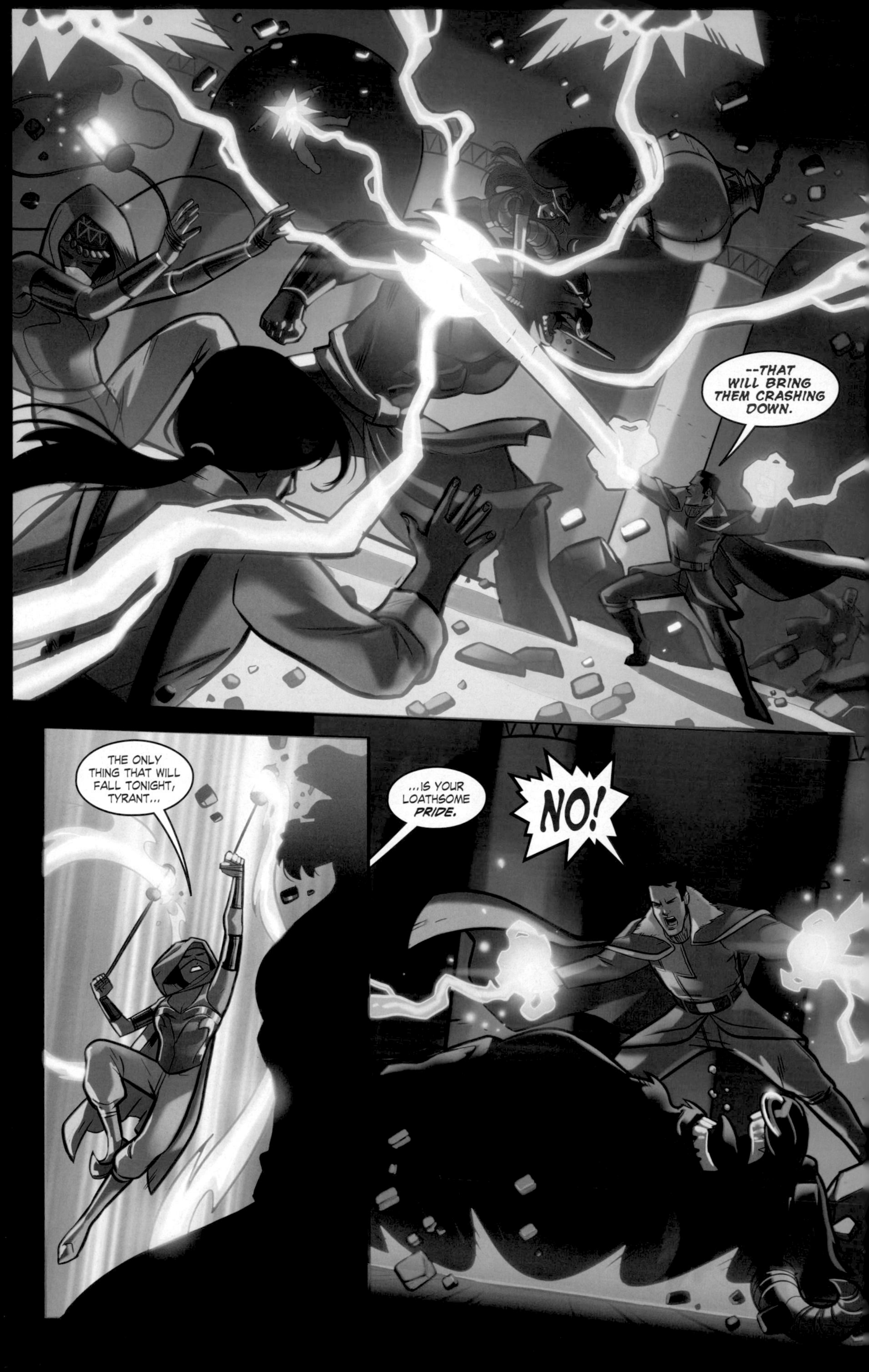
--THAT WILL BRING THEM CRASHING DOWN.
THE ONLY THING THAT WILL FALL TONIGHT, TYRANT...
...IS YOUR LOATHSOME *PRIDE.*
NO!

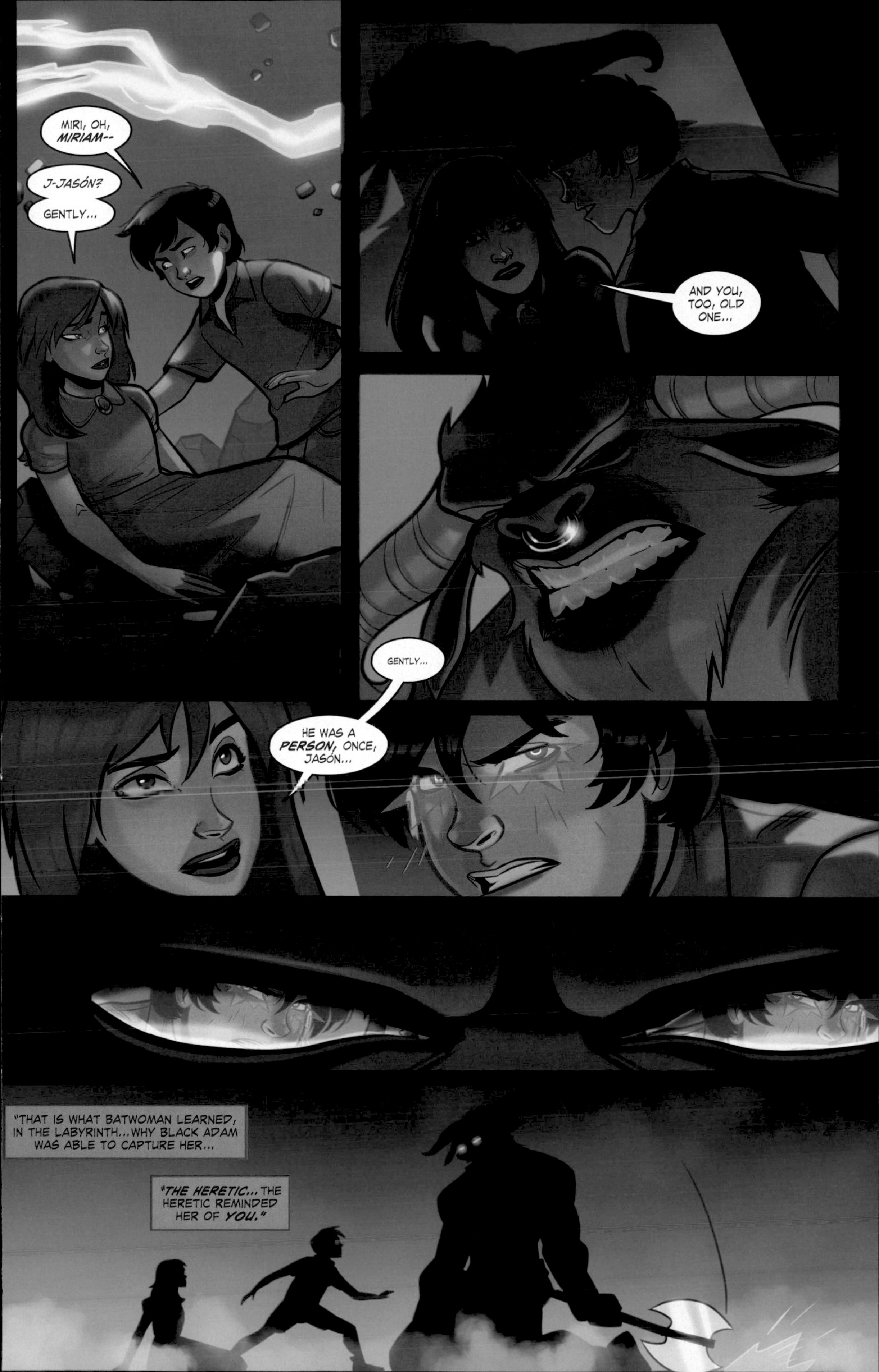

MIRI, OH, *MIRIAM--*
J-JASÓN?
GENTLY...
AND YOU, TOO, OLD ONE...
GENTLY...
HE WAS A *PERSON,* ONCE, JASÓN...
"THAT IS WHAT BATWOMAN LEARNED, IN THE LABYRINTH...WHY BLACK ADAM WAS ABLE TO CAPTURE HER...
"*THE HERETIC...* THE HERETIC REMINDED HER OF *YOU.*"

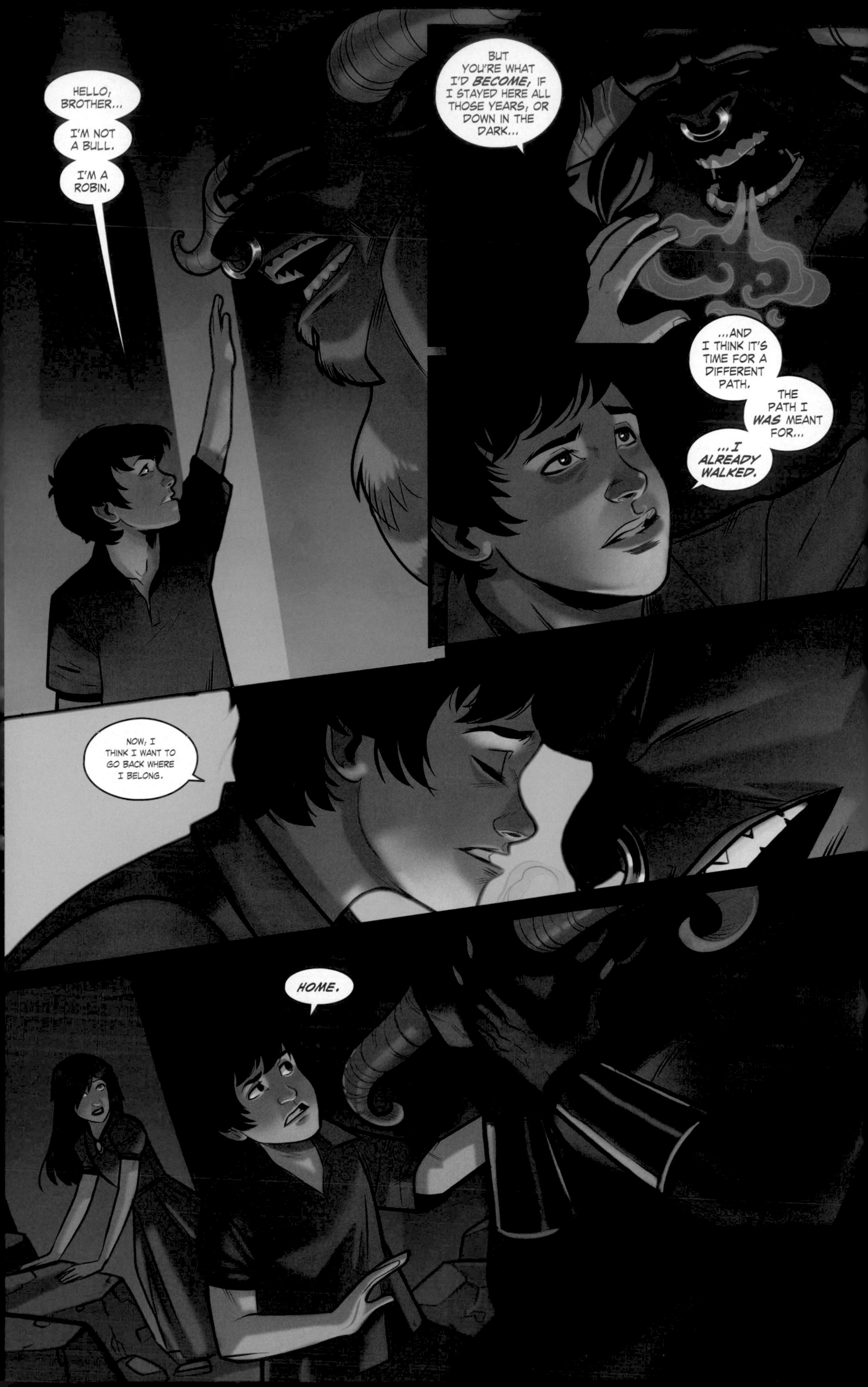
HELLO, BROTHER...
I'M NOT A BULL.
I'M A ROBIN.
BUT YOU'RE WHAT I'D BECOME, IF I STAYED HERE ALL THOSE YEARS, OR DOWN IN THE DARK...
...AND I THINK IT'S TIME FOR A DIFFERENT PATH.
THE PATH I WAS MEANT FOR...
...I ALREADY WALKED.
NOW, I THINK I WANT TO GO BACK WHERE I BELONG.
HOME.

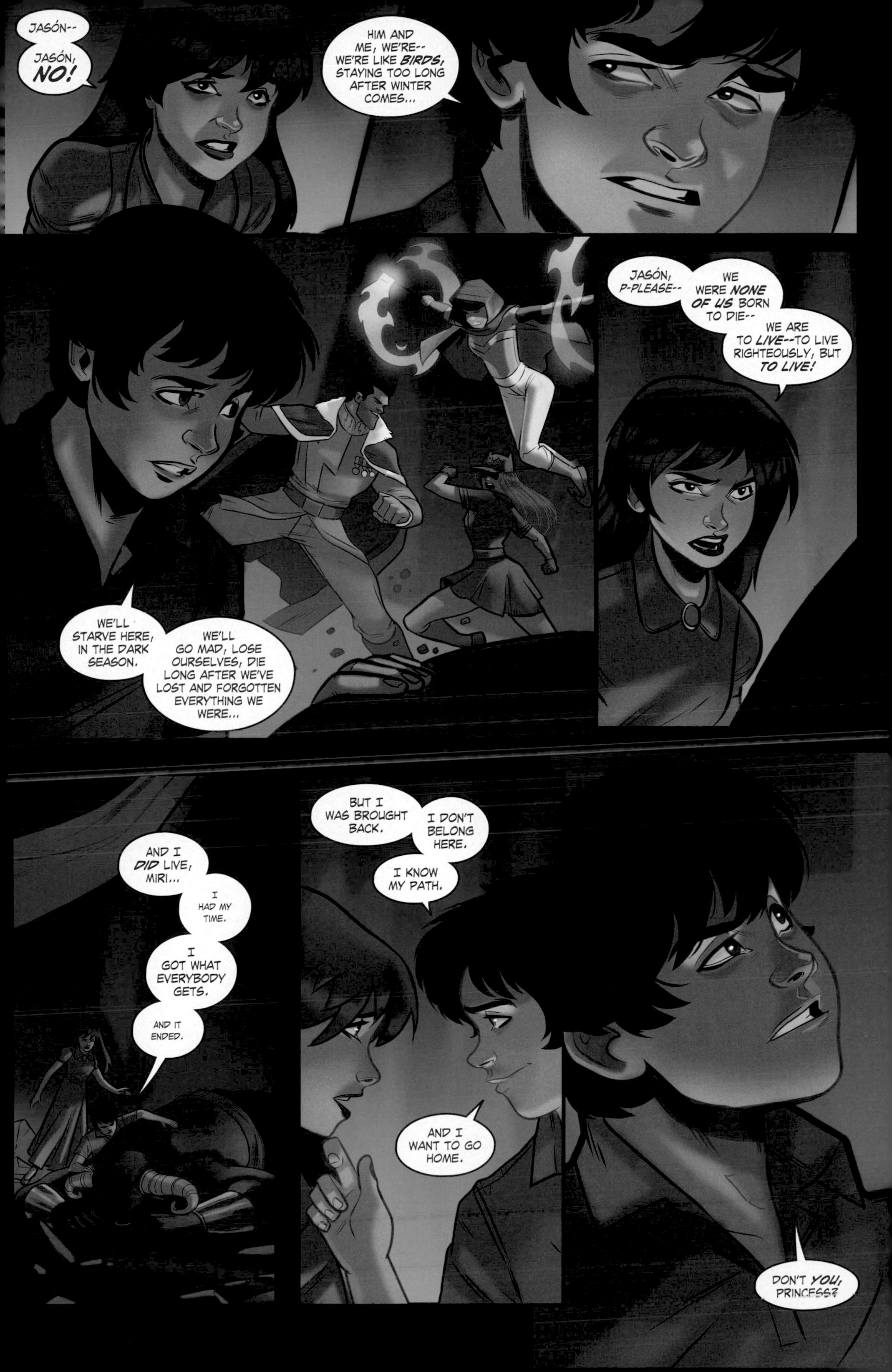
JASÓN--
JASÓN, NO!
HIM AND ME, WE'RE-- WE'RE LIKE BIRDS, STAYING TOO LONG AFTER WINTER COMES...
WE'LL STARVE HERE, IN THE DARK SEASON.
WE'LL GO MAD, LOSE OURSELVES, DIE LONG AFTER WE'VE LOST AND FORGOTTEN EVERYTHING WE WERE...
JASÓN, P-PLEASE--
WE WERE NONE OF US BORN TO DIE--
WE ARE TO LIVE--TO LIVE RIGHTEOUSLY, BUT TO LIVE!
AND I DID LIVE, MIRI...
I HAD MY TIME.
I GOT WHAT EVERYBODY GETS.
AND IT ENDED.
BUT I WAS BROUGHT BACK.
I DON'T BELONG HERE.
I KNOW MY PATH.
AND I WANT TO GO HOME.
DON'T YOU, PRINCESS?

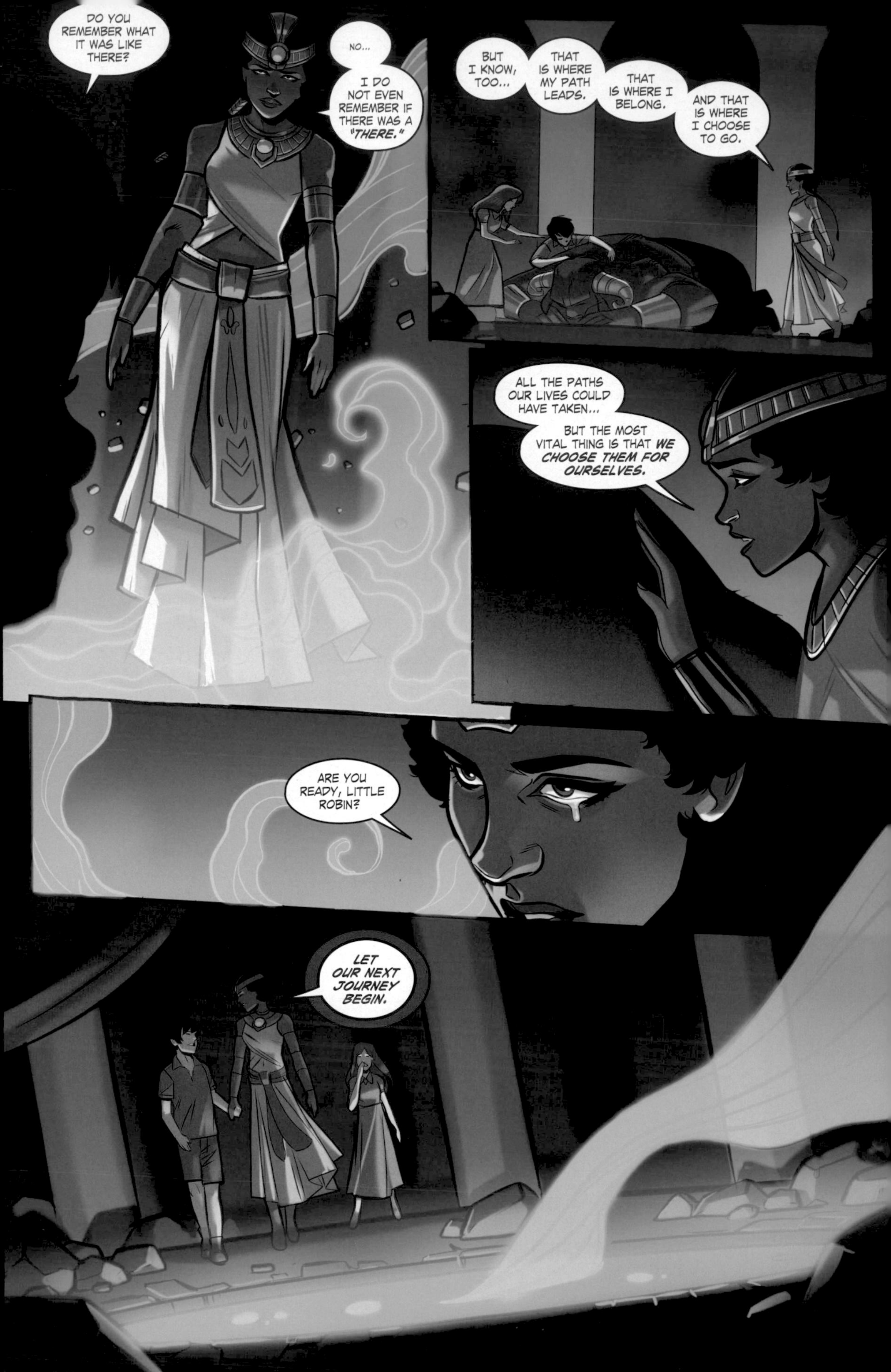
DO YOU REMEMBER WHAT IT WAS LIKE THERE?
NO...
I DO NOT EVEN REMEMBER IF THERE WAS A *"THERE."*
BUT I KNOW, TOO...
THAT IS WHERE MY PATH LEADS.
THAT IS WHERE I BELONG.
AND THAT IS WHERE I CHOOSE TO GO.
ALL THE PATHS OUR LIVES COULD HAVE TAKEN...
BUT THE MOST VITAL THING IS THAT ***WE CHOOSE THEM FOR OURSELVES.***
ARE YOU READY, LITTLE ROBIN?
LET OUR NEXT JOURNEY BEGIN.

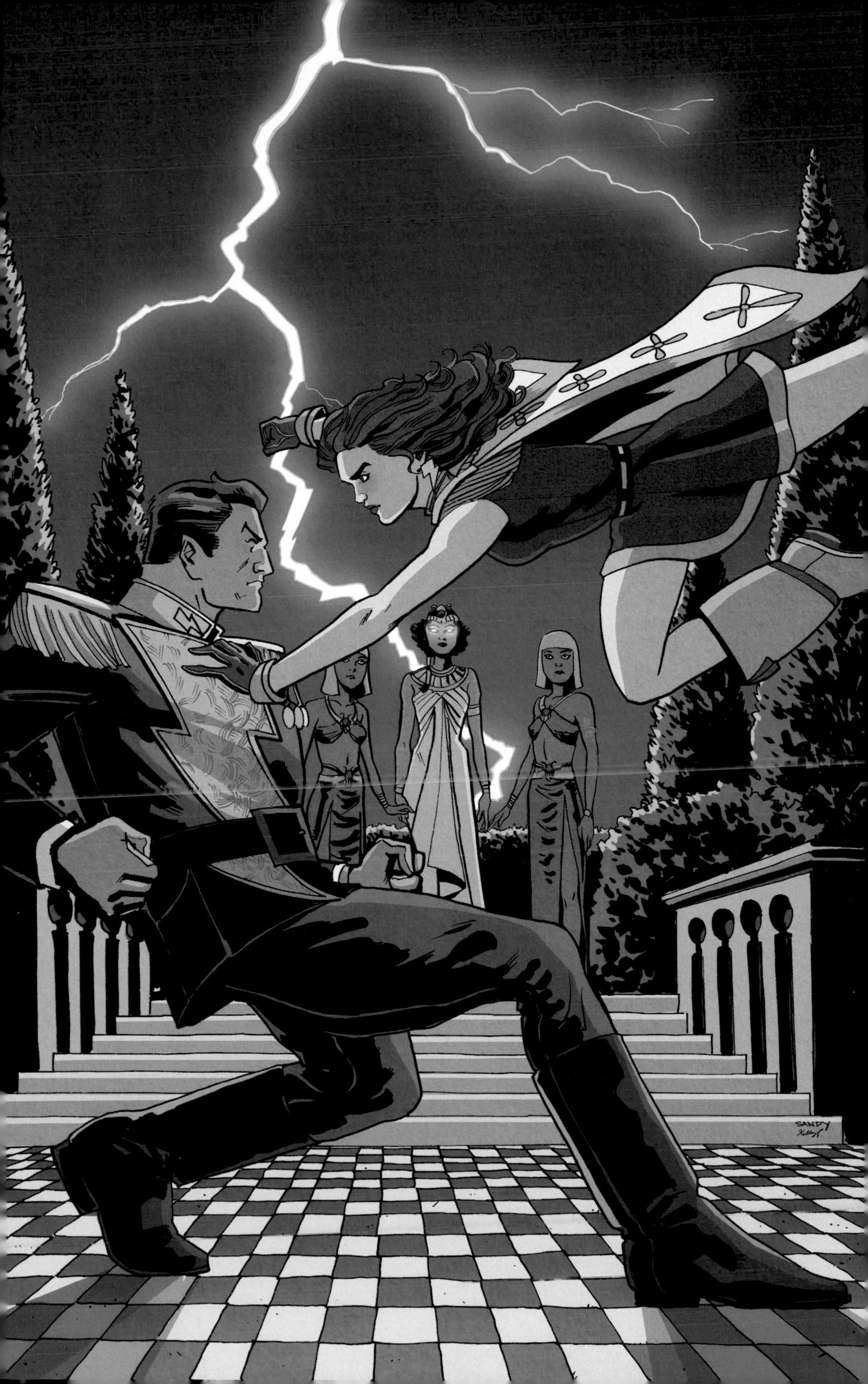
SANDY

WAR BONDS
PARTS ELEVEN *and* TWELVE

Written by
MARGUERITE BENNETT

Art by
SANDY JARRELL

Colors by
KELLY FITZPATRICK

Cover by
SANDY JARRELL
and **KELLY FITZPATRICK**

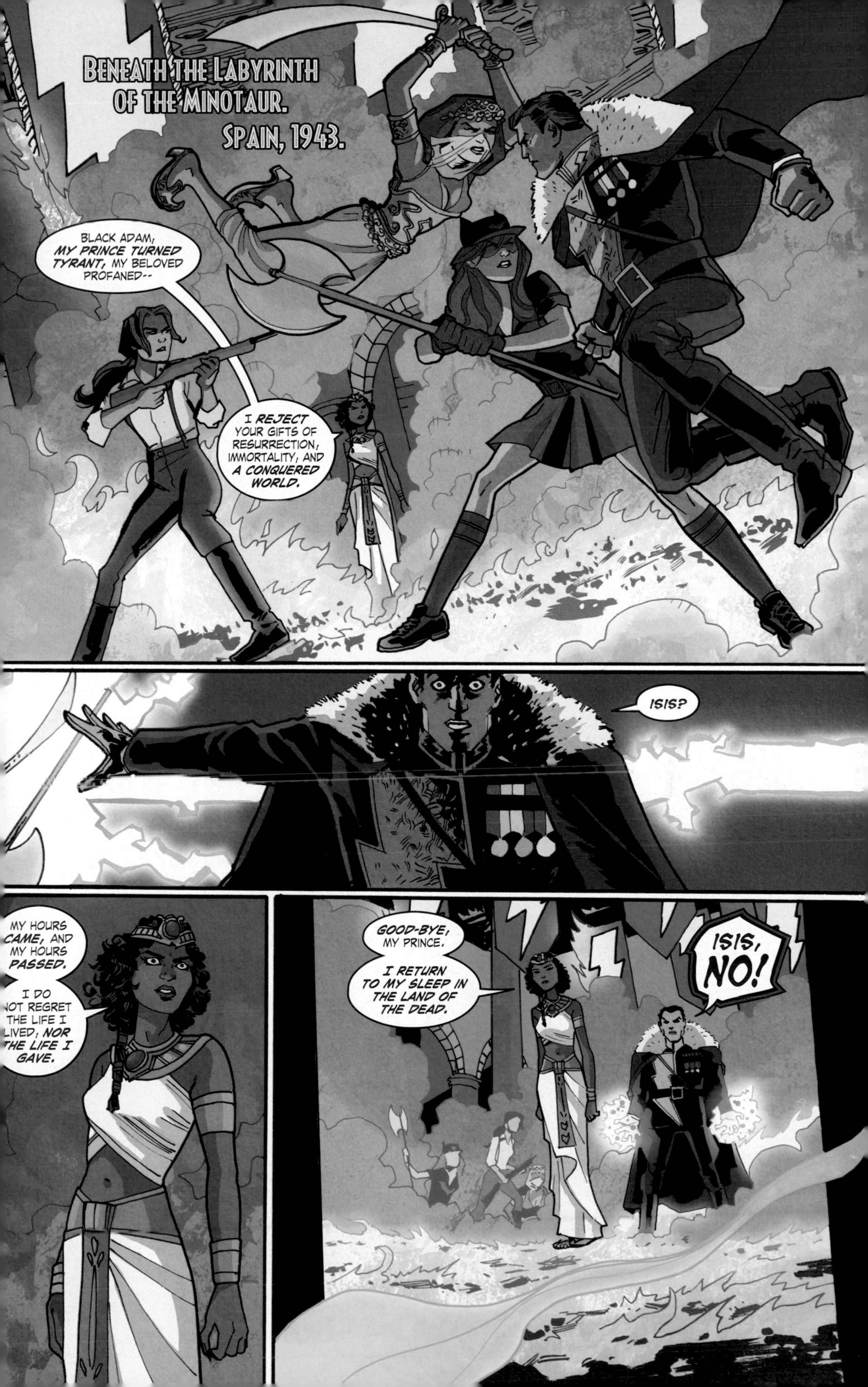

BENEATH THE LABYRINTH OF THE MINOTAUR.
SPAIN, 1943.
BLACK ADAM, MY PRINCE TURNED TYRANT, MY BELOVED PROFANED--
I REJECT YOUR GIFTS OF RESURRECTION, IMMORTALITY, AND A CONQUERED WORLD.
ISIS?
MY HOURS CAME, AND MY HOURS PASSED.
I DO NOT REGRET THE LIFE I LIVED, NOR THE LIFE I GAVE.
GOOD-BYE, MY PRINCE.
I RETURN TO MY SLEEP IN THE LAND OF THE DEAD.
ISIS, NO!

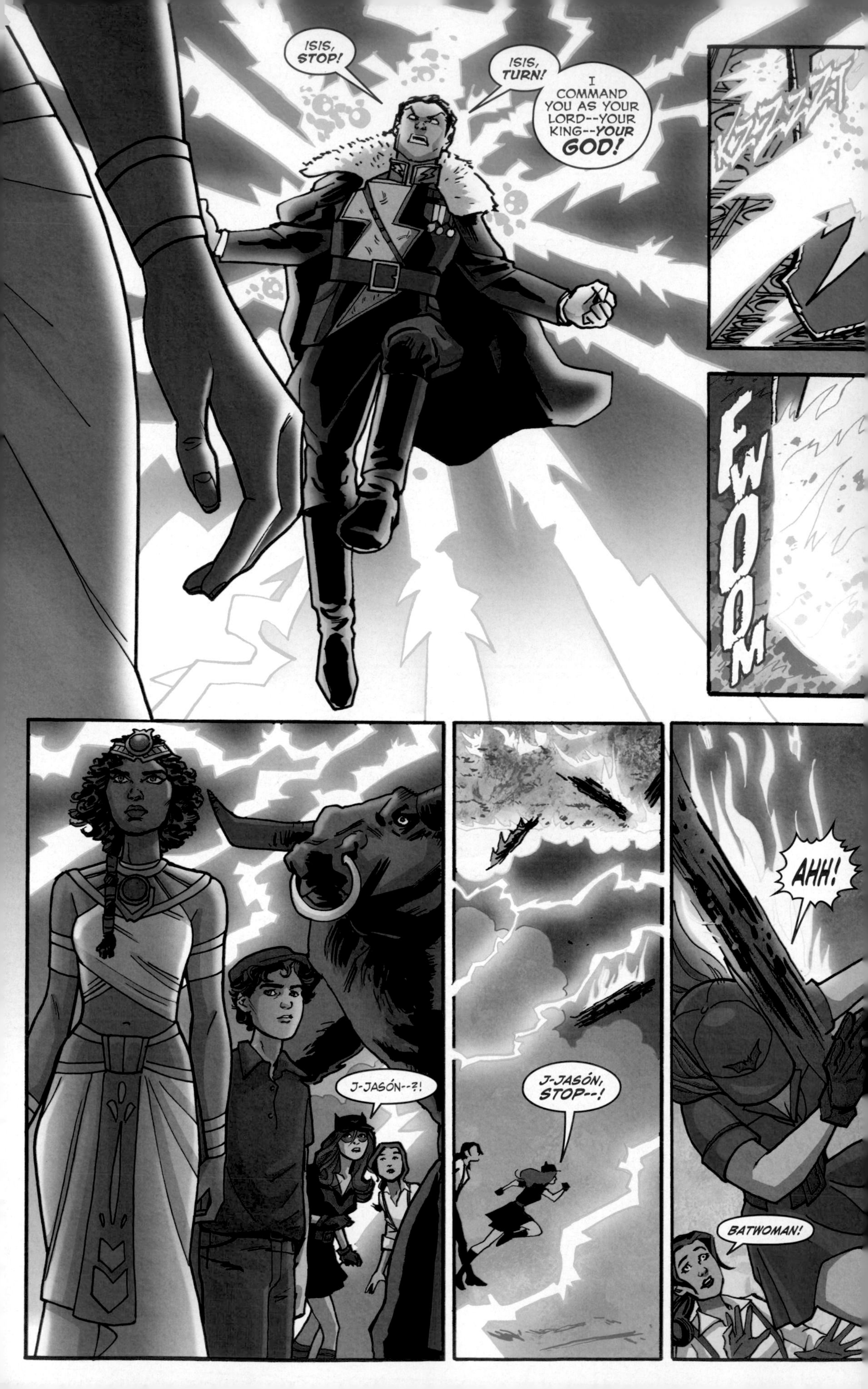
ISIS, STOP!
ISIS, TURN!
I COMMAND YOU AS YOUR LORD--YOUR KING--YOUR GOD!
FWOOM
J-JASÓN--?!
J-JASÓN, STOP--!
AHH!
BATWOMAN!

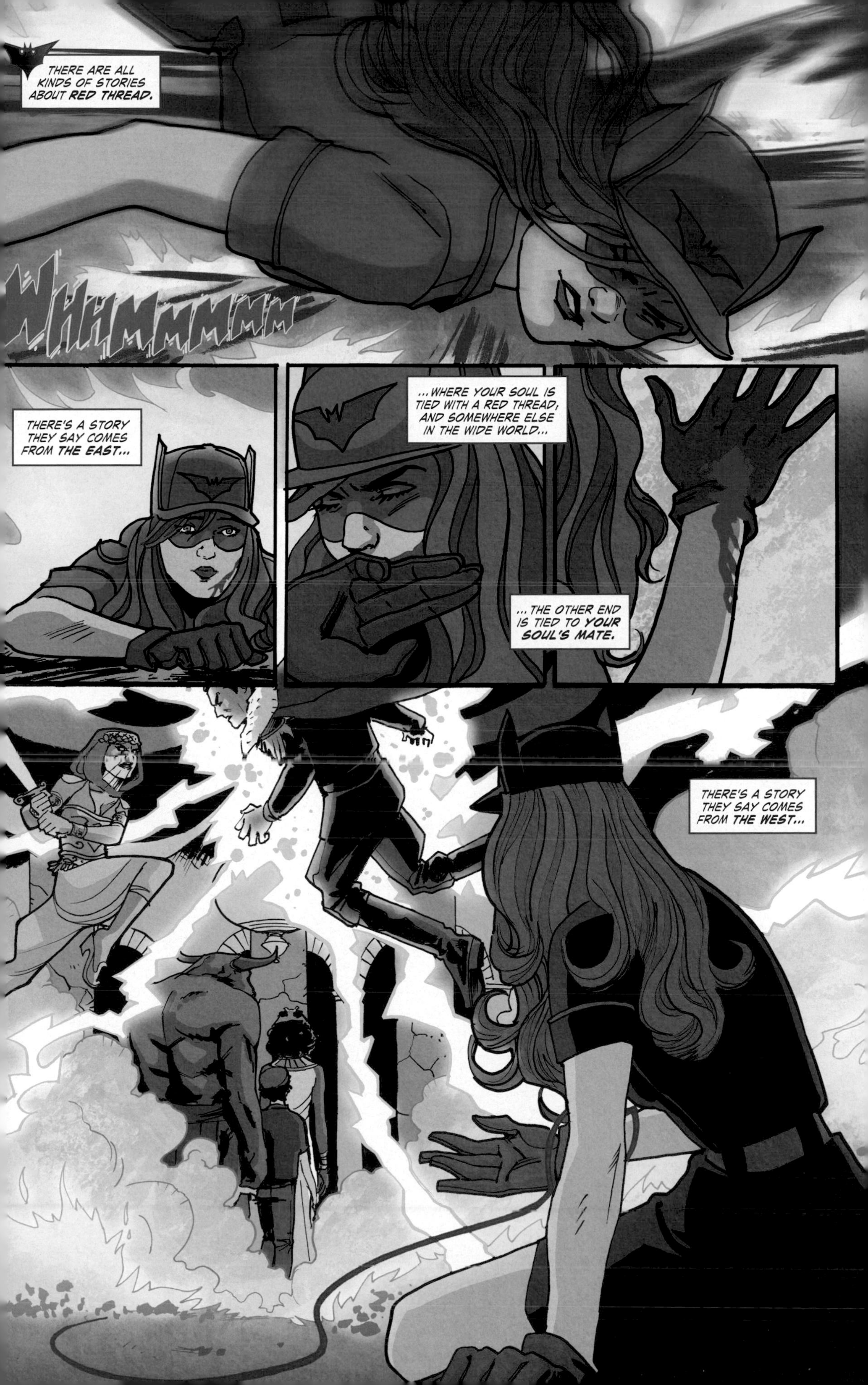
THERE ARE ALL KINDS OF STORIES ABOUT RED THREAD.
WHHMMMMMM
THERE'S A STORY THEY SAY COMES FROM THE EAST...
...WHERE YOUR SOUL IS TIED WITH A RED THREAD, AND SOMEWHERE ELSE IN THE WIDE WORLD...
...THE OTHER END IS TIED TO YOUR SOUL'S MATE.
THERE'S A STORY THEY SAY COMES FROM THE WEST...

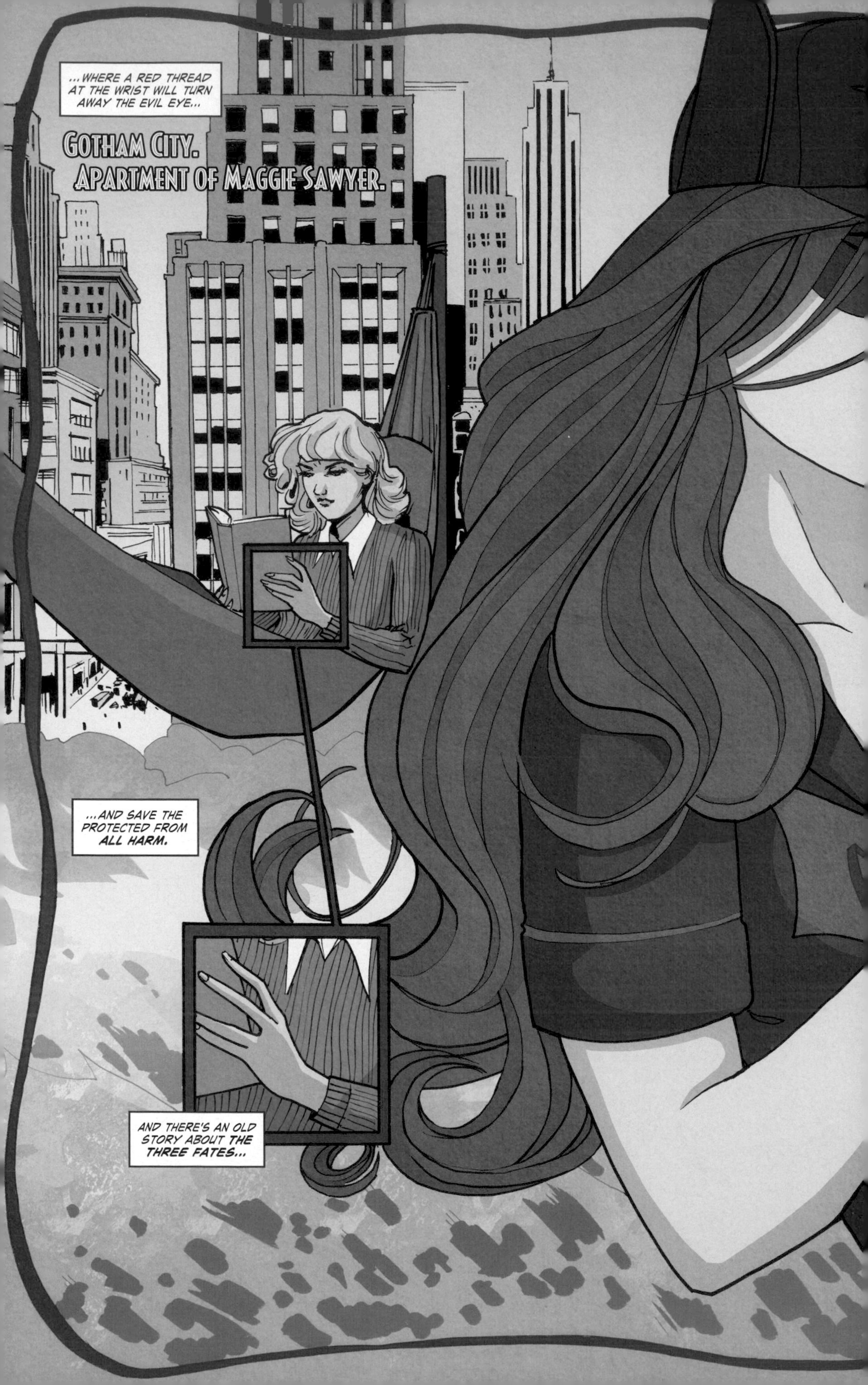
...WHERE A RED THREAD AT THE WRIST WILL TURN AWAY THE EVIL EYE...
GOTHAM CITY. APARTMENT OF MAGGIE SAWYER.
...AND SAVE THE PROTECTED FROM ALL HARM.
AND THERE'S AN OLD STORY ABOUT THE THREE FATES...

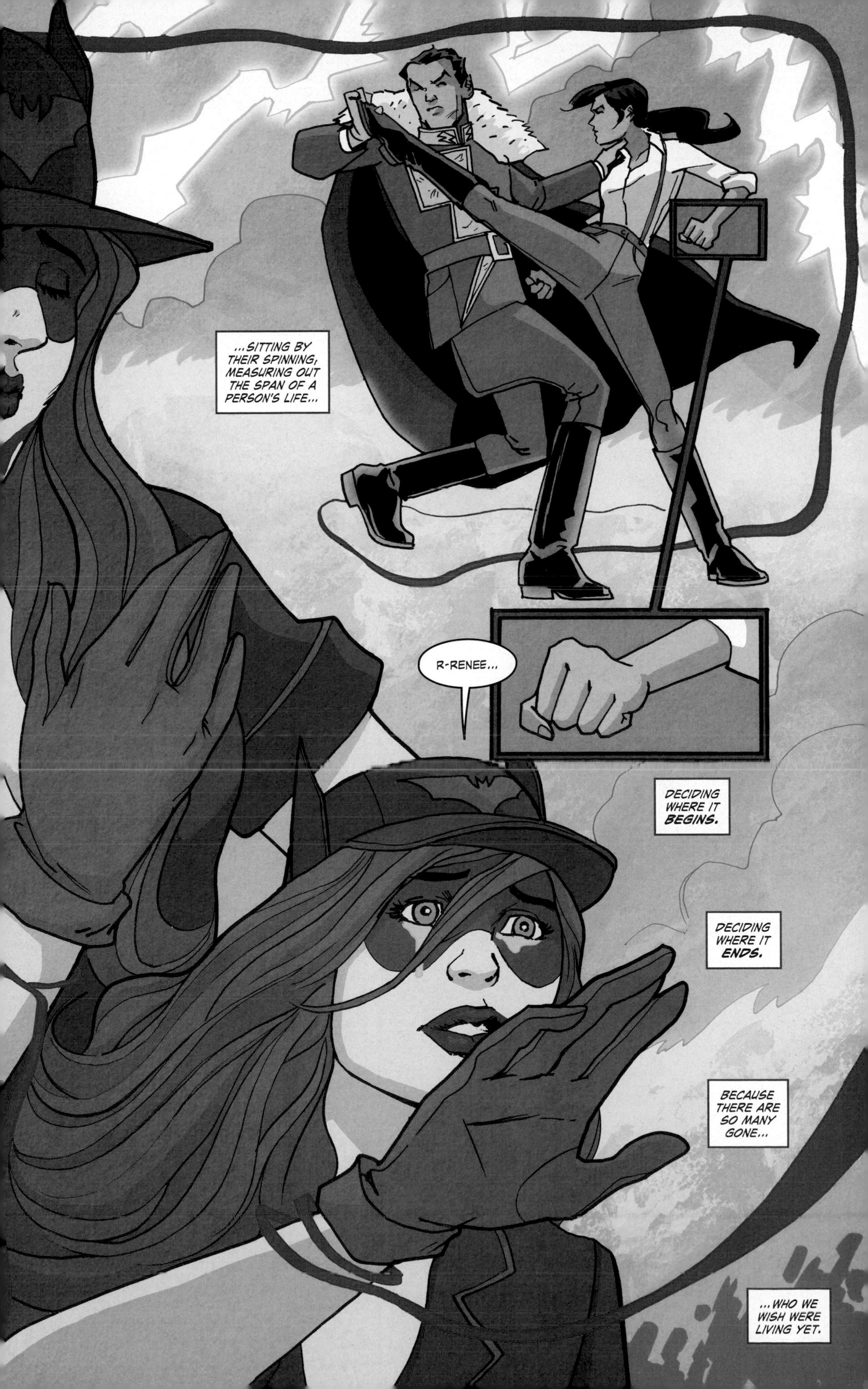
...SITTING BY THEIR SPINNING, MEASURING OUT THE SPAN OF A PERSON'S LIFE...
R-RENEE...
DECIDING WHERE IT **BEGINS.**
DECIDING WHERE IT **ENDS.**
BECAUSE THERE ARE SO MANY GONE...
...WHO WE WISH WERE LIVING YET.

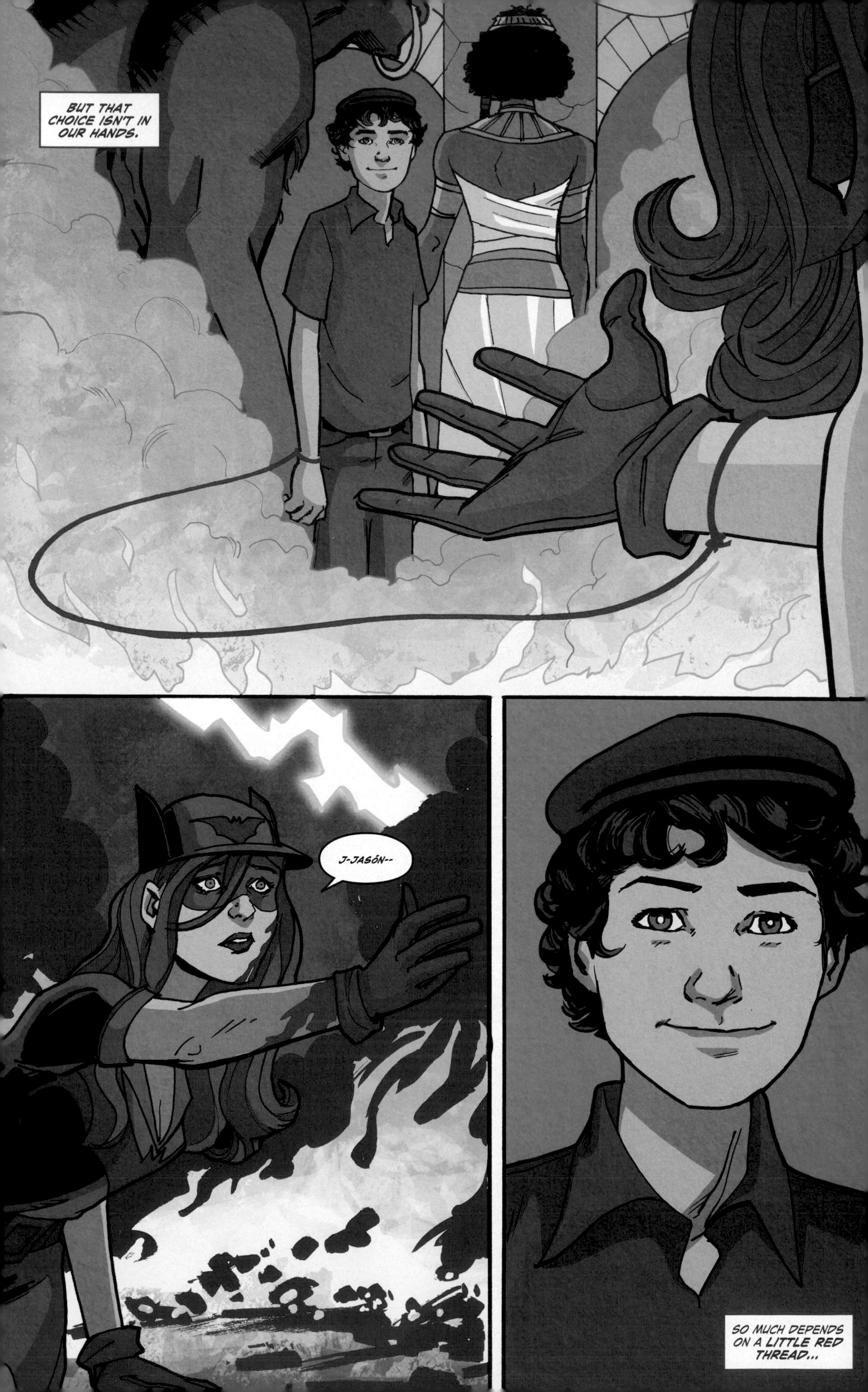
BUT THAT CHOICE ISN'T IN OUR HANDS.
J-JASÓN--
SO MUCH DEPENDS ON A LITTLE RED THREAD...

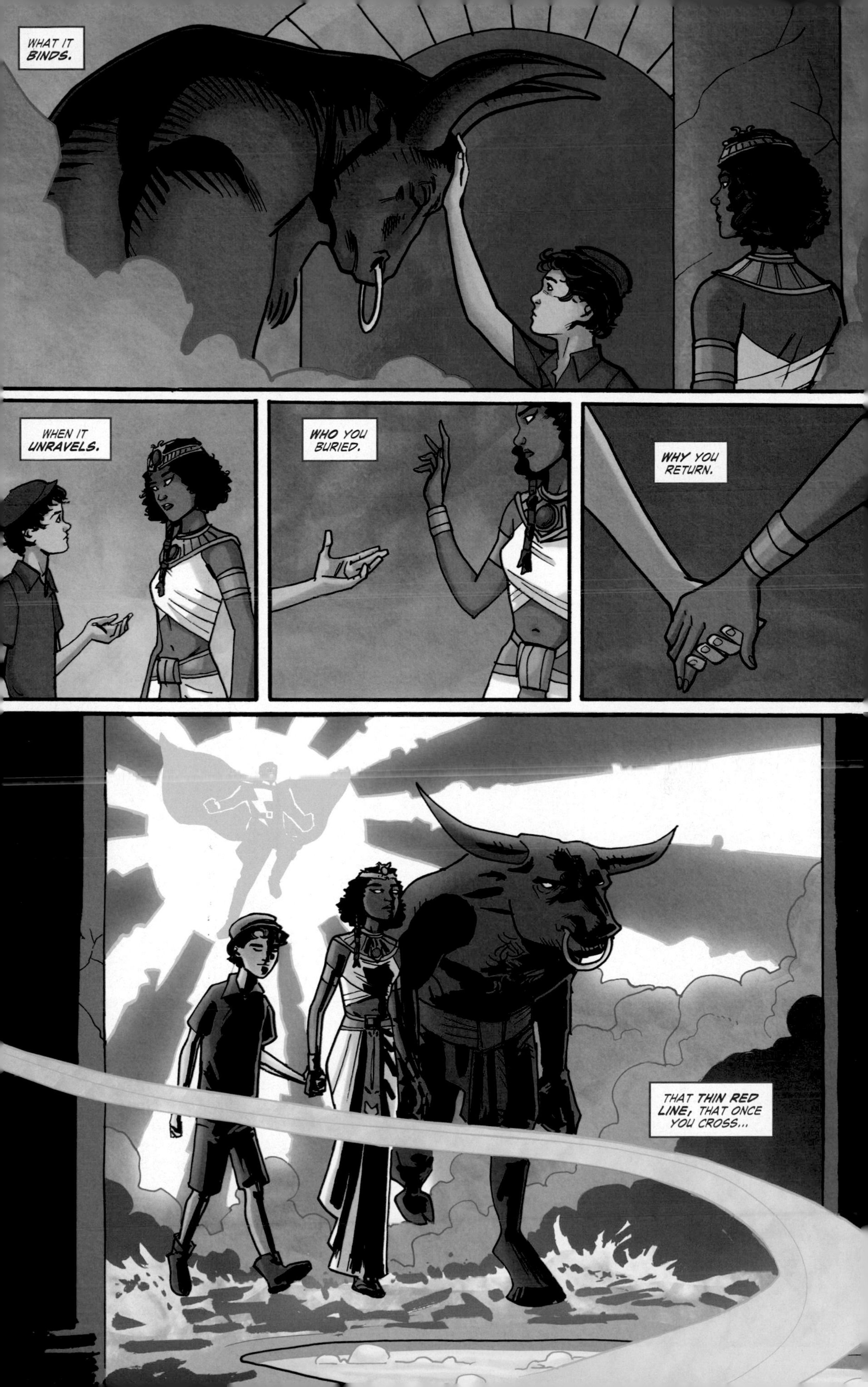
WHAT IT BINDS.
WHEN IT UNRAVELS.
WHO YOU BURIED.
WHY YOU RETURN.
THAT THIN RED LINE, THAT ONCE YOU CROSS...

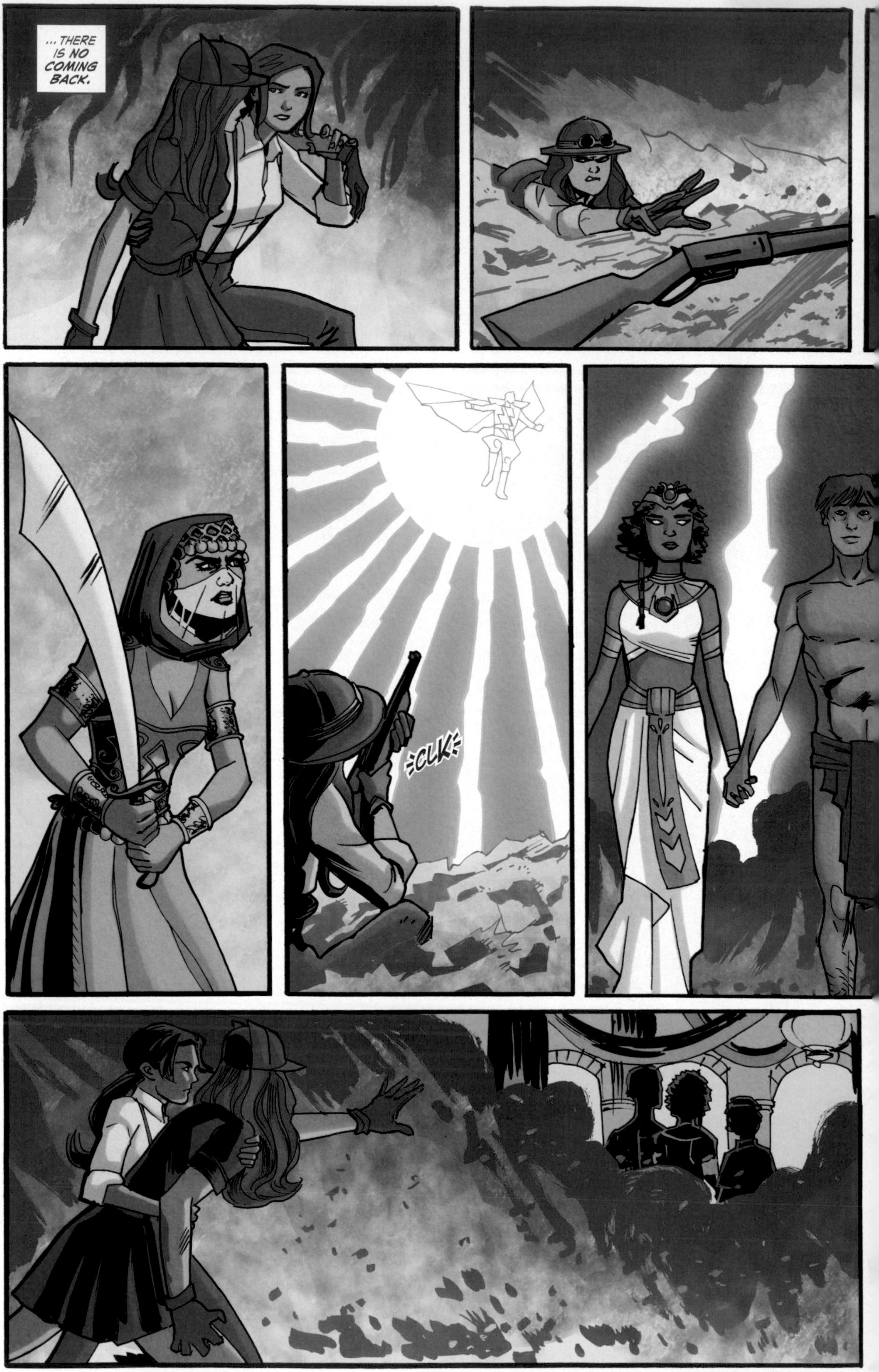
...THERE IS NO COMING BACK.
CLK

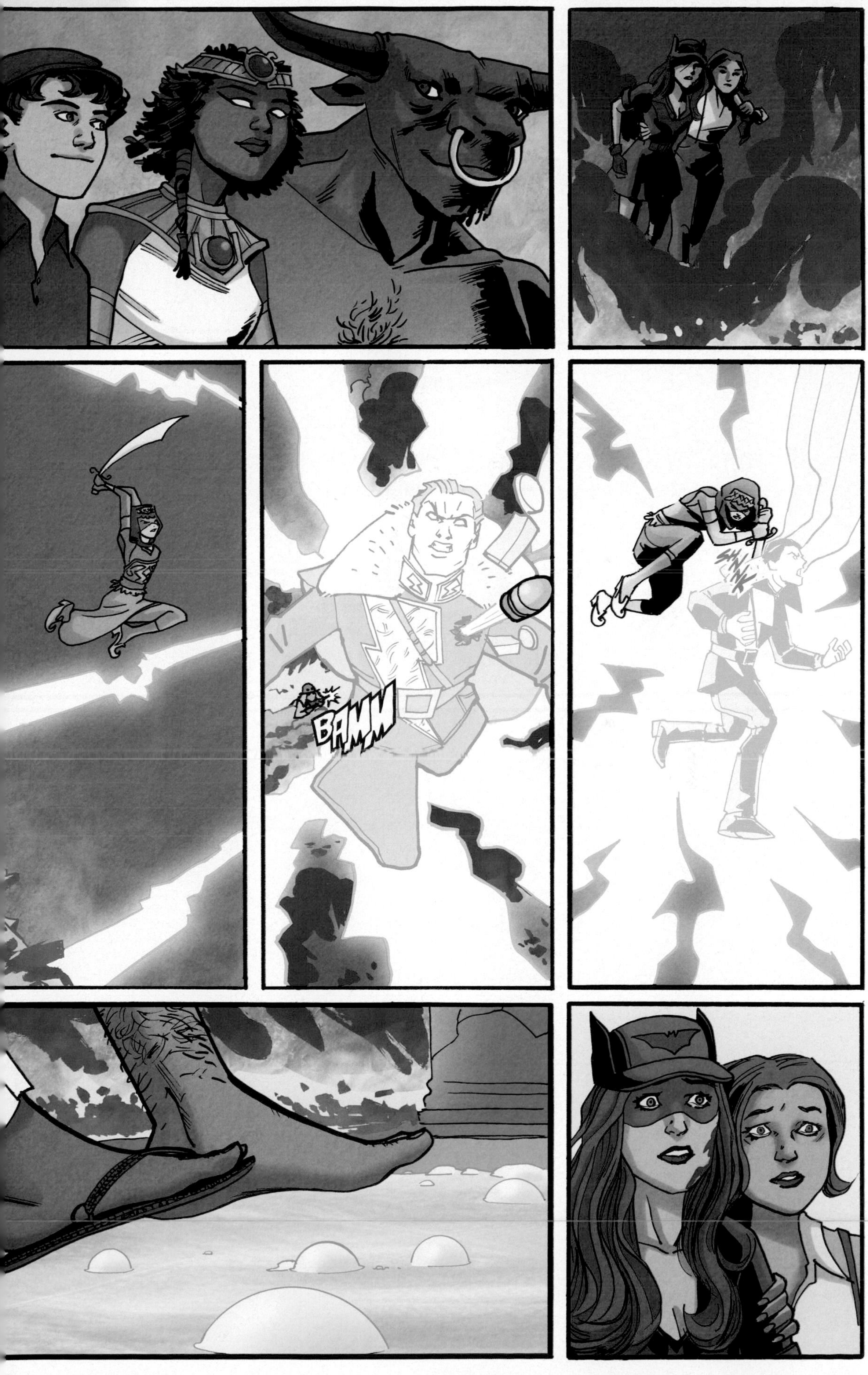
BAMM
SHNNK

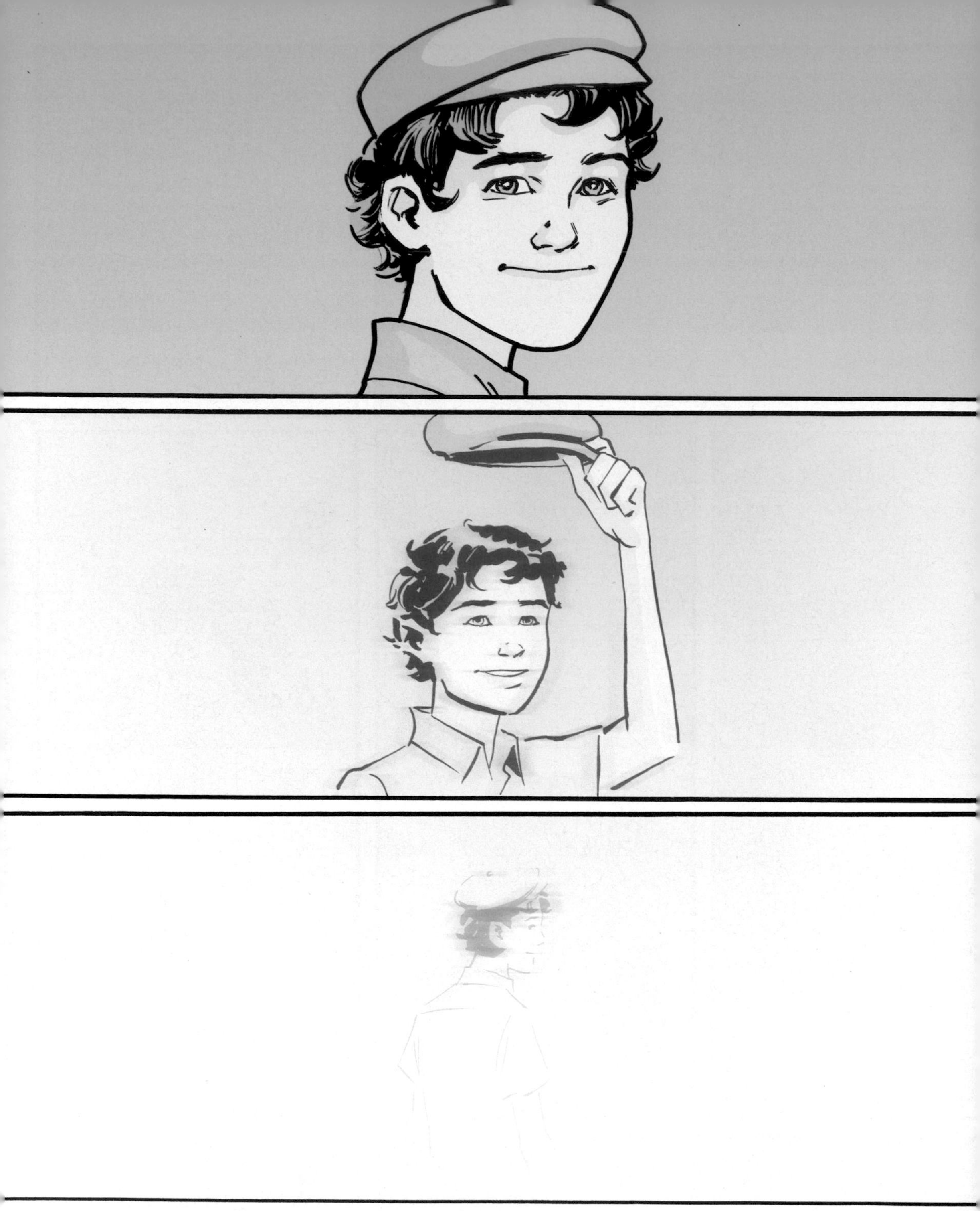

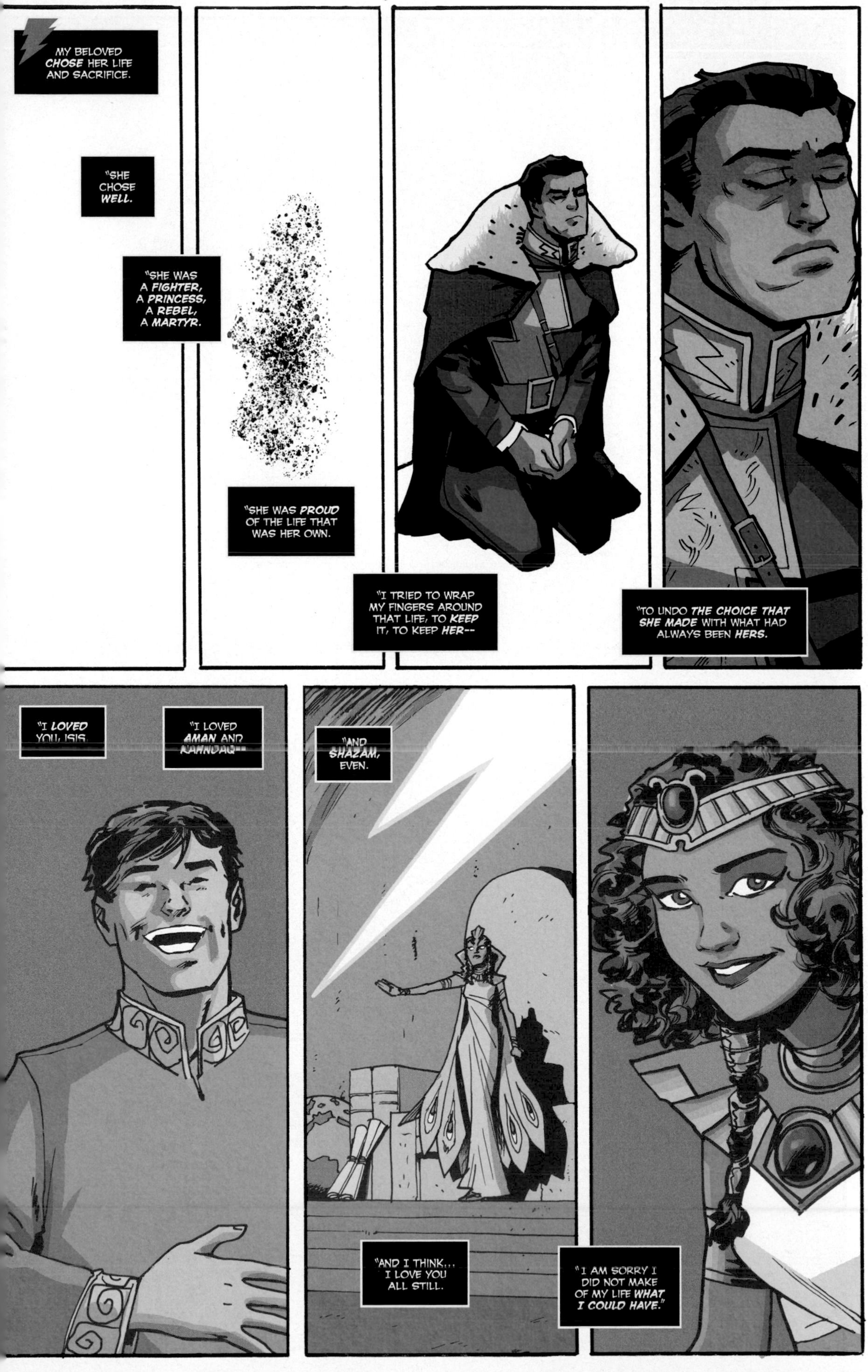
MY BELOVED CHOSE HER LIFE AND SACRIFICE.
"SHE CHOSE WELL.
"SHE WAS A FIGHTER, A PRINCESS, A REBEL, A MARTYR.
"SHE WAS PROUD OF THE LIFE THAT WAS HER OWN.
"I TRIED TO WRAP MY FINGERS AROUND THAT LIFE, TO KEEP IT, TO KEEP HER--
"TO UNDO THE CHOICE THAT SHE MADE WITH WHAT HAD ALWAYS BEEN HERS.
"I LOVED YOU, ISIS.
"I LOVED AMAN AND KAHNDAQ--
"AND SHAZAM, EVEN.
"AND I THINK... I LOVE YOU ALL STILL.
"I AM SORRY I DID NOT MAKE OF MY LIFE WHAT I COULD HAVE."

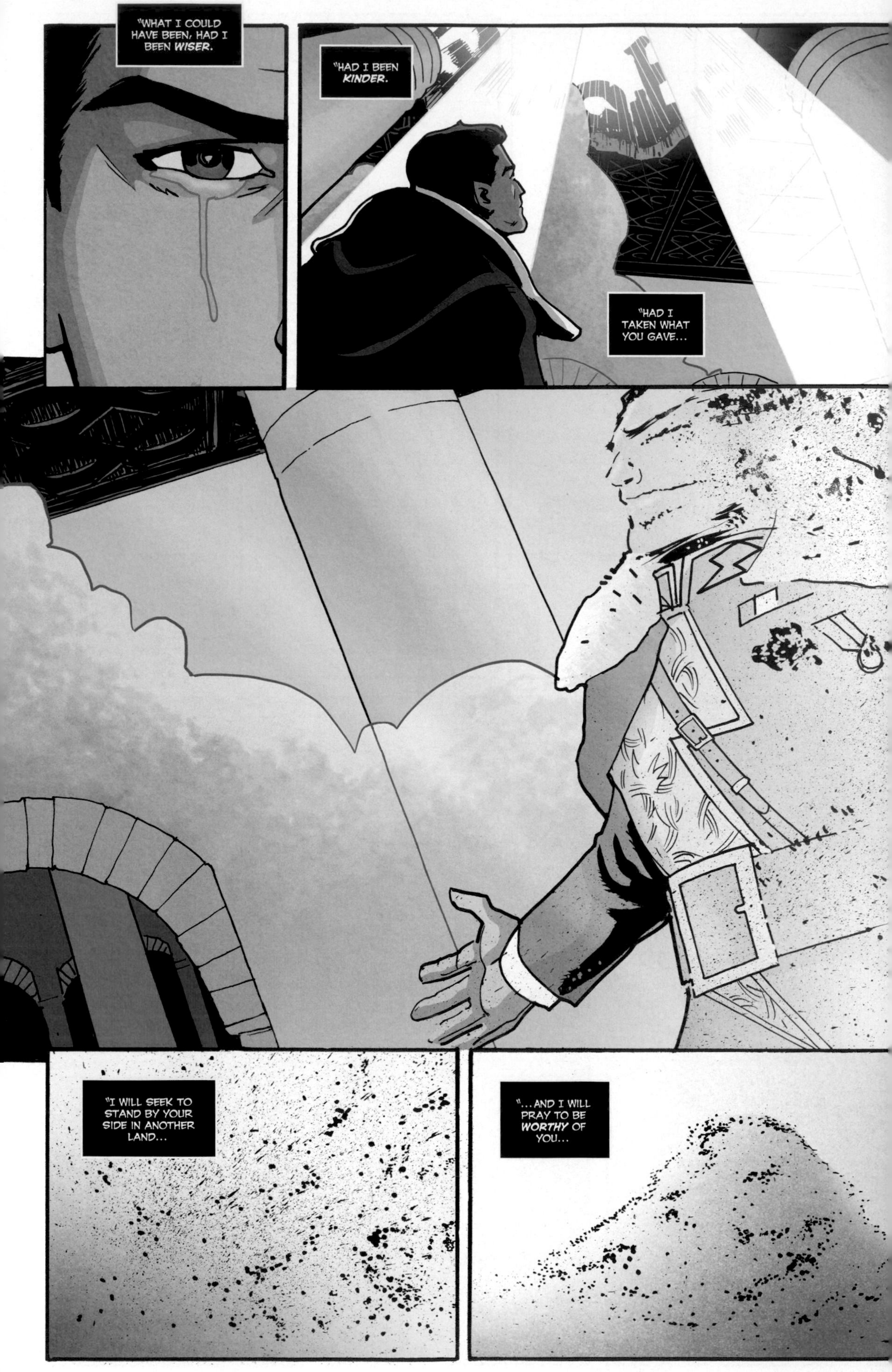
"WHAT I COULD HAVE BEEN, HAD I BEEN *WISER*.
"HAD I BEEN *KINDER*.
"HAD I TAKEN WHAT YOU GAVE...
"I WILL SEEK TO STAND BY YOUR SIDE IN ANOTHER LAND...
"...AND I WILL PRAY TO BE *WORTHY* OF YOU...

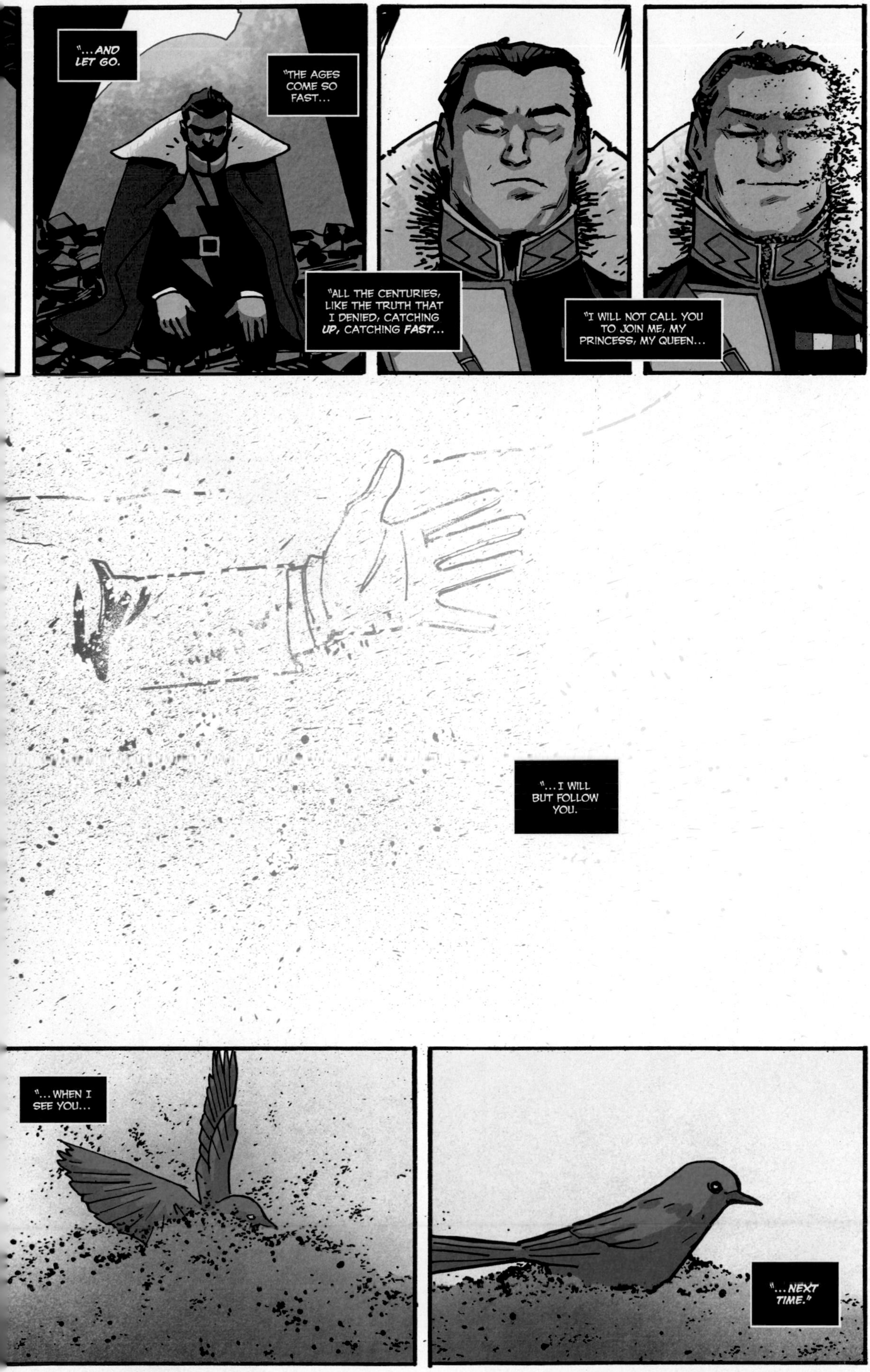
"...AND LET GO.
"THE AGES COME SO FAST...
"ALL THE CENTURIES, LIKE THE TRUTH THAT I DENIED, CATCHING UP, CATCHING FAST...
"I WILL NOT CALL YOU TO JOIN ME, MY PRINCESS, MY QUEEN...
"...I WILL BUT FOLLOW YOU.
"...WHEN I SEE YOU...
"...NEXT TIME."

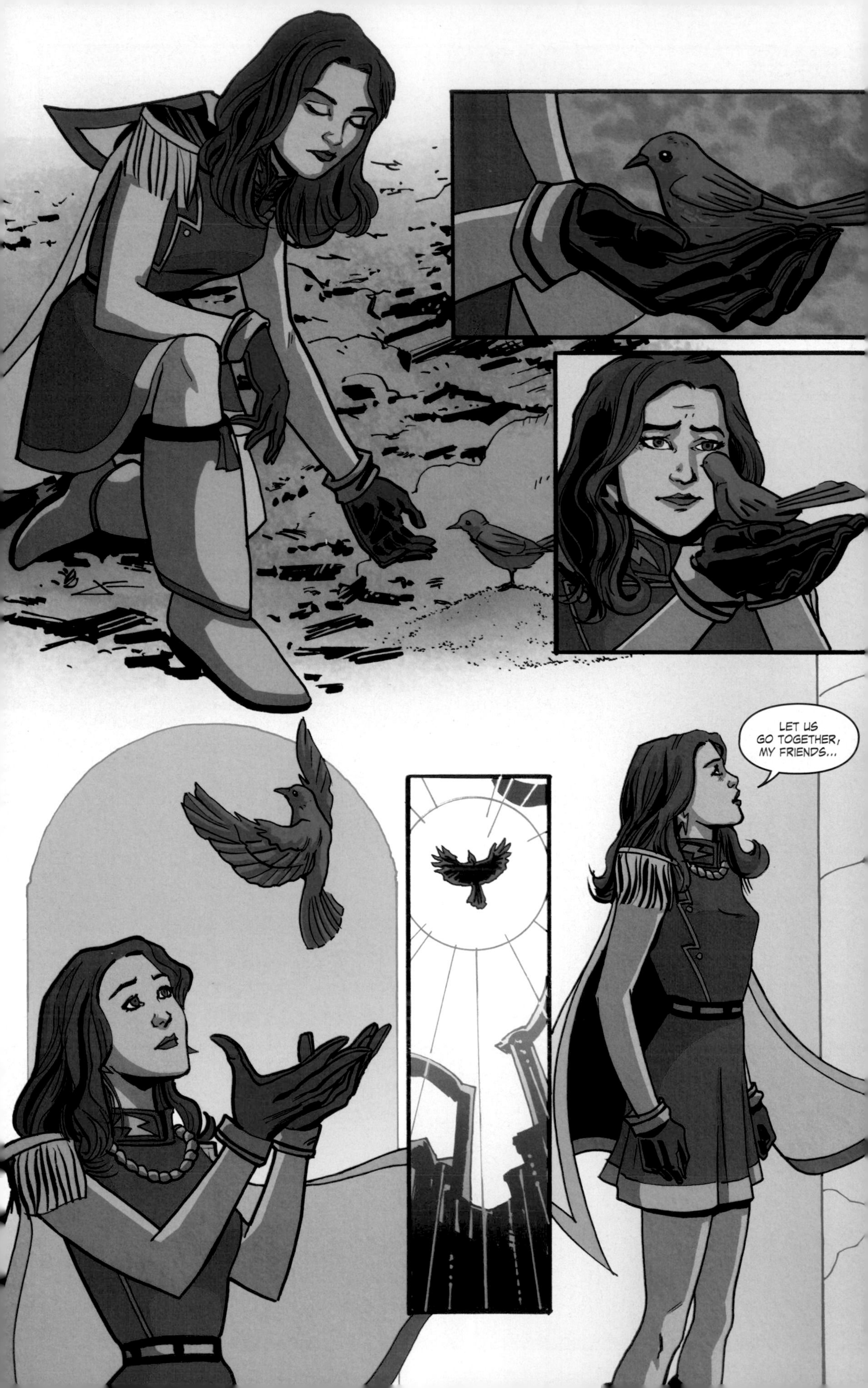
LET US GO TOGETHER, MY FRIENDS...

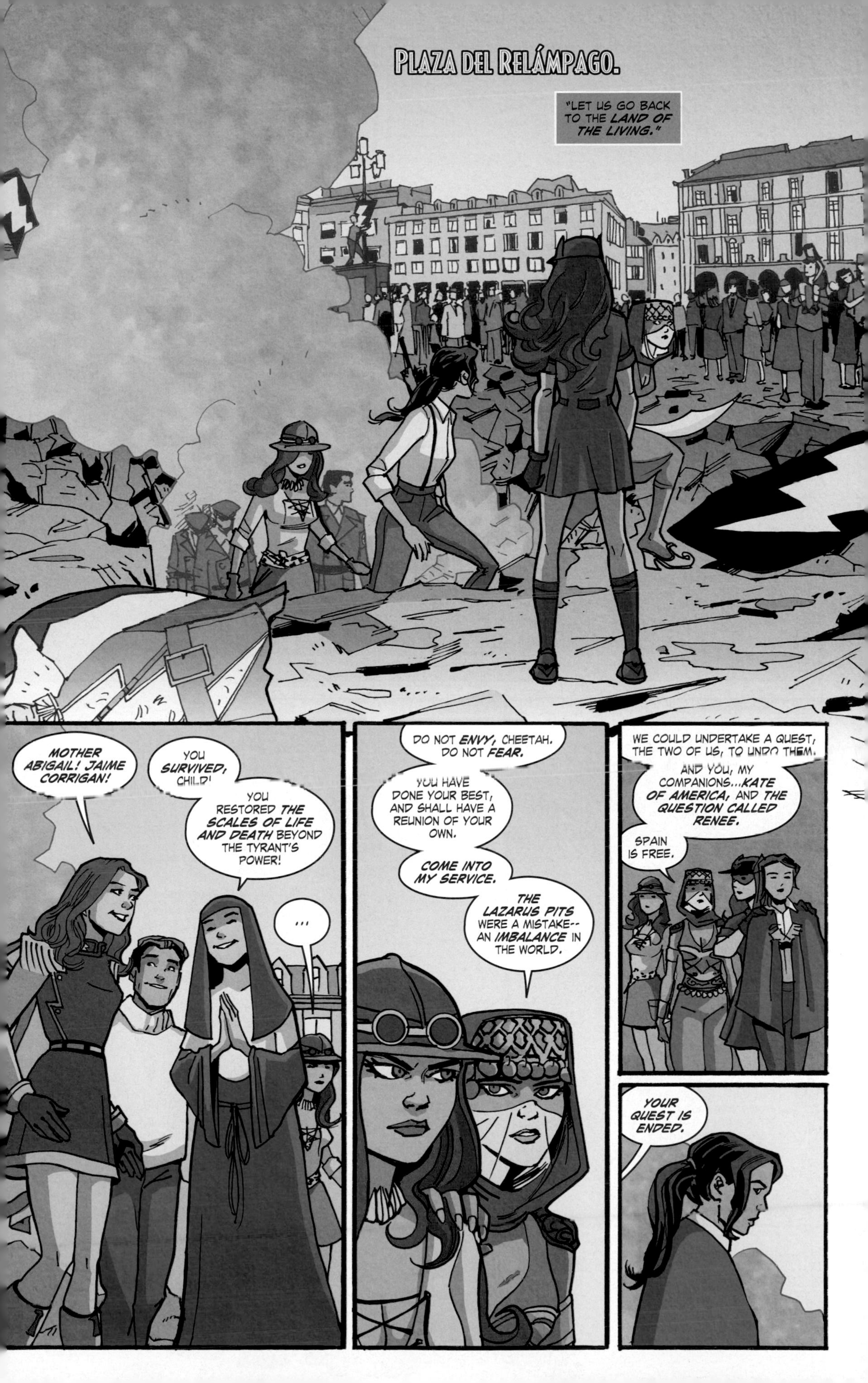
PLAZA DEL RELÁMPAGO.
"LET US GO BACK TO THE LAND OF THE LIVING."
MOTHER ABIGAIL! JAIME CORRIGAN!
YOU SURVIVED, CHILD!
YOU RESTORED THE SCALES OF LIFE AND DEATH BEYOND THE TYRANT'S POWER!
...
DO NOT ENVY, CHEETAH. DO NOT FEAR.
YOU HAVE DONE YOUR BEST, AND SHALL HAVE A REUNION OF YOUR OWN.
COME INTO MY SERVICE.
THE LAZARUS PITS WERE A MISTAKE-- AN IMBALANCE IN THE WORLD.
WE COULD UNDERTAKE A QUEST, THE TWO OF US, TO UNDO THEM.
AND YOU, MY COMPANIONS...KATE OF AMERICA, AND THE QUESTION CALLED RENEE.
SPAIN IS FREE.
YOUR QUEST IS ENDED.

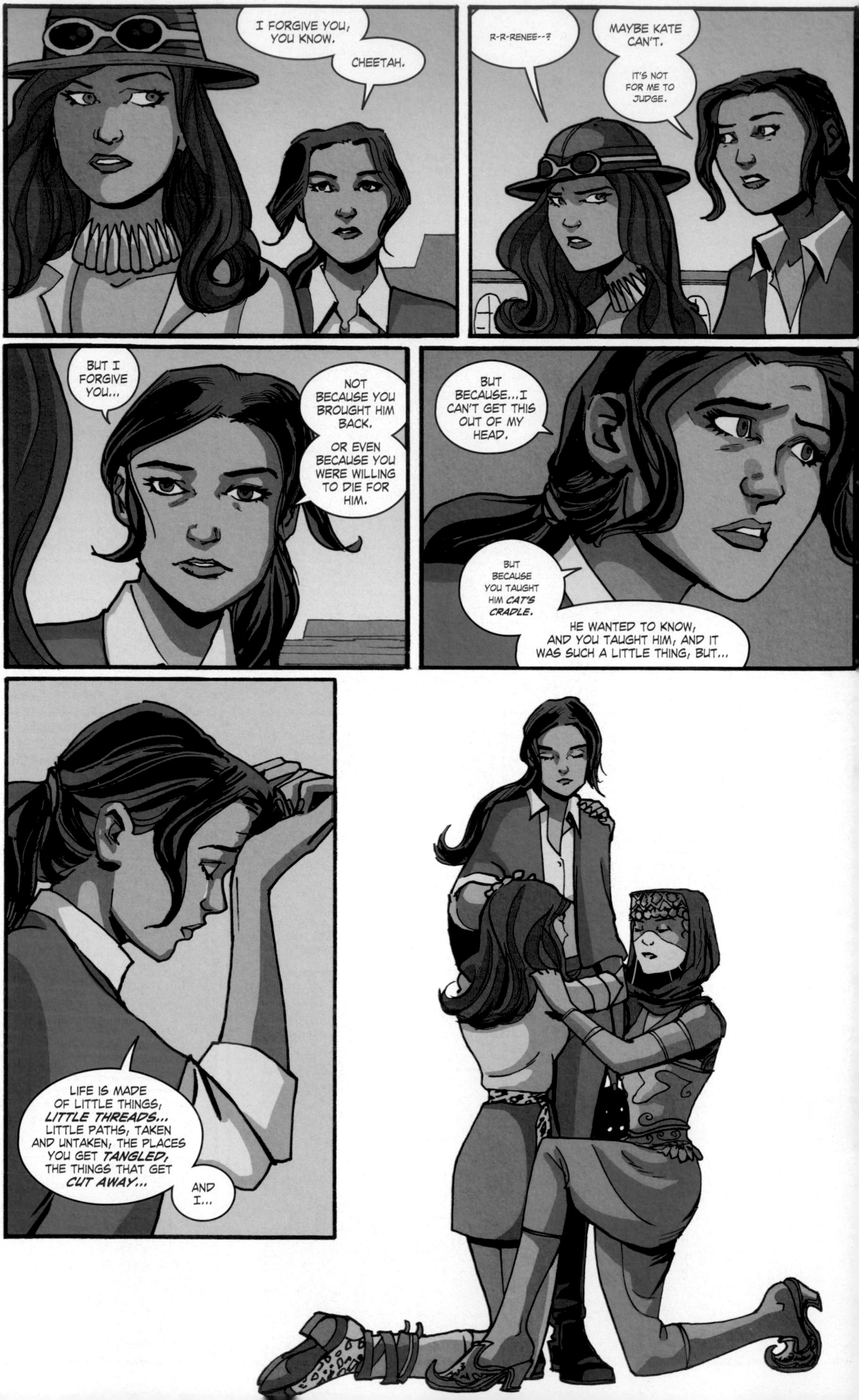
I FORGIVE YOU, YOU KNOW.
CHEETAH.
R-R-RENEE--?
MAYBE KATE CAN'T.
IT'S NOT FOR ME TO JUDGE.
BUT I FORGIVE YOU...
NOT BECAUSE YOU BROUGHT HIM BACK.
OR EVEN BECAUSE YOU WERE WILLING TO DIE FOR HIM.
BUT BECAUSE...I CAN'T GET THIS OUT OF MY HEAD.
BUT BECAUSE YOU TAUGHT HIM *CAT'S CRADLE.*
HE WANTED TO KNOW, AND YOU TAUGHT HIM, AND IT WAS SUCH A LITTLE THING, BUT...
LIFE IS MADE OF LITTLE THINGS, *LITTLE THREADS...* LITTLE PATHS, TAKEN AND UNTAKEN, THE PLACES YOU GET *TANGLED,* THE THINGS THAT GET *CUT AWAY...*
AND I...

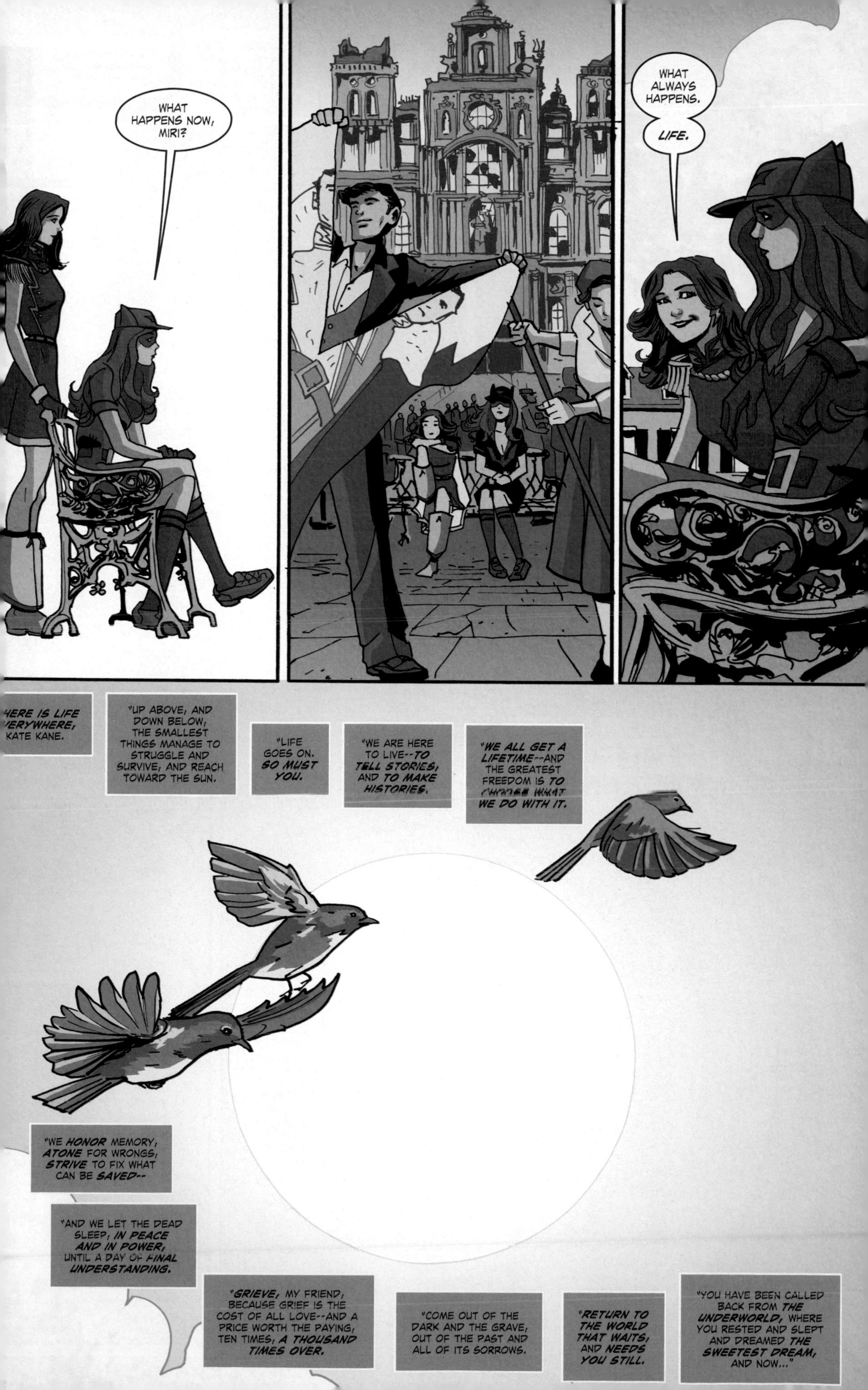
WHAT HAPPENS NOW, MIRI?
WHAT ALWAYS HAPPENS.
LIFE.
HERE IS LIFE EVERYWHERE, KATE KANE.
"UP ABOVE, AND DOWN BELOW, THE SMALLEST THINGS MANAGE TO STRUGGLE AND SURVIVE, AND REACH TOWARD THE SUN.
"LIFE GOES ON. SO MUST YOU.
"WE ARE HERE TO LIVE--TO TELL STORIES, AND TO MAKE HISTORIES.
"WE ALL GET A LIFETIME--AND THE GREATEST FREEDOM IS TO CHOOSE WHAT WE DO WITH IT.
"WE HONOR MEMORY, ATONE FOR WRONGS, STRIVE TO FIX WHAT CAN BE SAVED--
"AND WE LET THE DEAD SLEEP, IN PEACE AND IN POWER, UNTIL A DAY OF FINAL UNDERSTANDING.
"GRIEVE, MY FRIEND, BECAUSE GRIEF IS THE COST OF ALL LOVE--AND A PRICE WORTH THE PAYING, TEN TIMES, A THOUSAND TIMES OVER.
"COME OUT OF THE DARK AND THE GRAVE, OUT OF THE PAST AND ALL OF ITS SORROWS.
"RETURN TO THE WORLD THAT WAITS, AND NEEDS YOU STILL.
"YOU HAVE BEEN CALLED BACK FROM THE UNDERWORLD, WHERE YOU RESTED AND SLEPT AND DREAMED THE SWEETEST DREAM, AND NOW..."

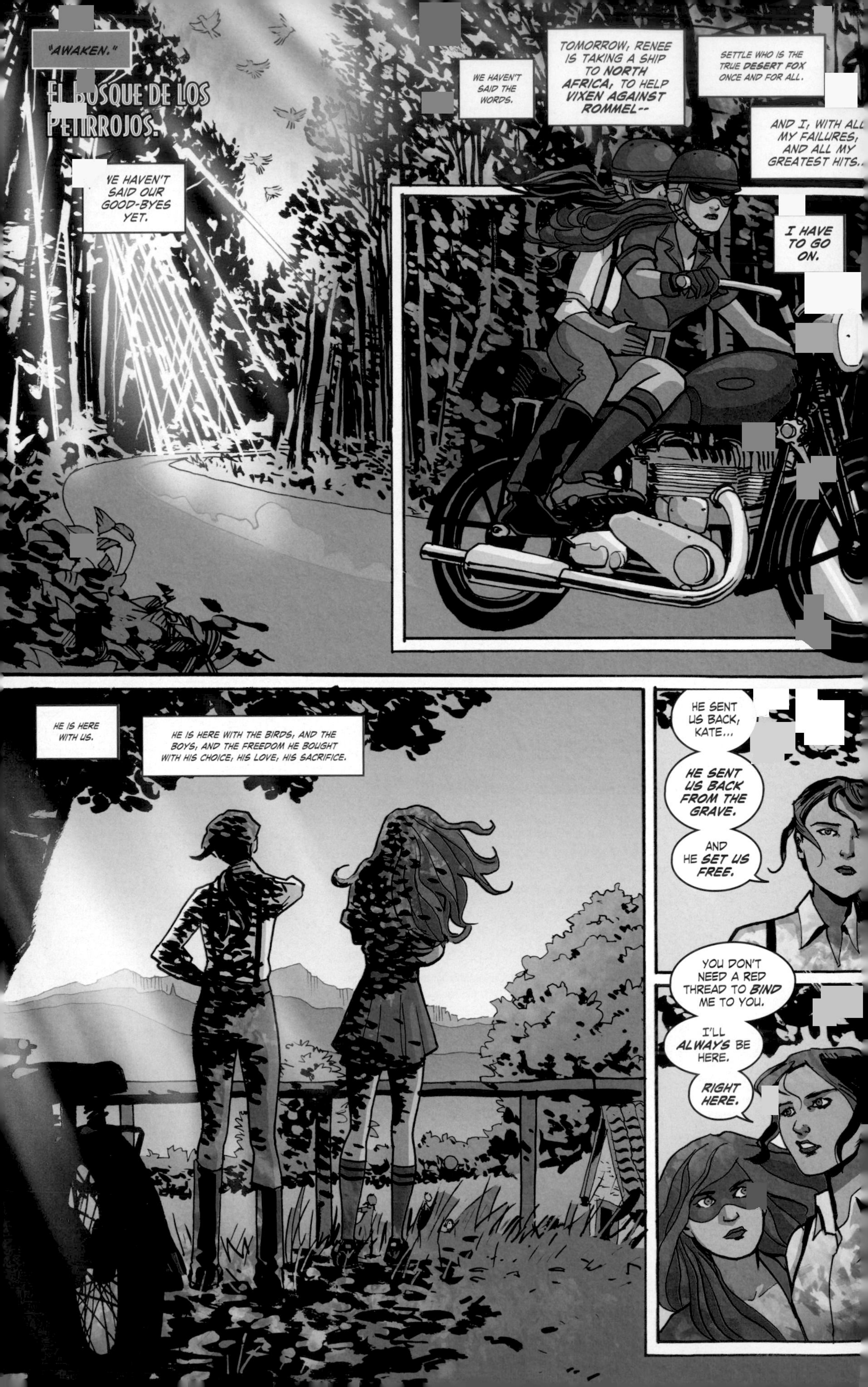
"AWAKEN."
El Bosque de los Petirrojos.
WE HAVEN'T SAID OUR GOOD-BYES YET.
WE HAVEN'T SAID THE WORDS.
TOMORROW, RENEE IS TAKING A SHIP TO NORTH AFRICA, TO HELP VIXEN AGAINST ROMMEL--
SETTLE WHO IS THE TRUE DESERT FOX ONCE AND FOR ALL.
AND I, WITH ALL MY FAILURES, AND ALL MY GREATEST HITS...
I HAVE TO GO ON.
HE IS HERE WITH US.
HE IS HERE WITH THE BIRDS, AND THE BOYS, AND THE FREEDOM HE BOUGHT WITH HIS CHOICE, HIS LOVE, HIS SACRIFICE.
HE SENT US BACK, KATE...
HE SENT US BACK FROM THE GRAVE.
AND HE SET US FREE.
YOU DON'T NEED A RED THREAD TO BIND ME TO YOU.
I'LL ALWAYS BE HERE.
RIGHT HERE.

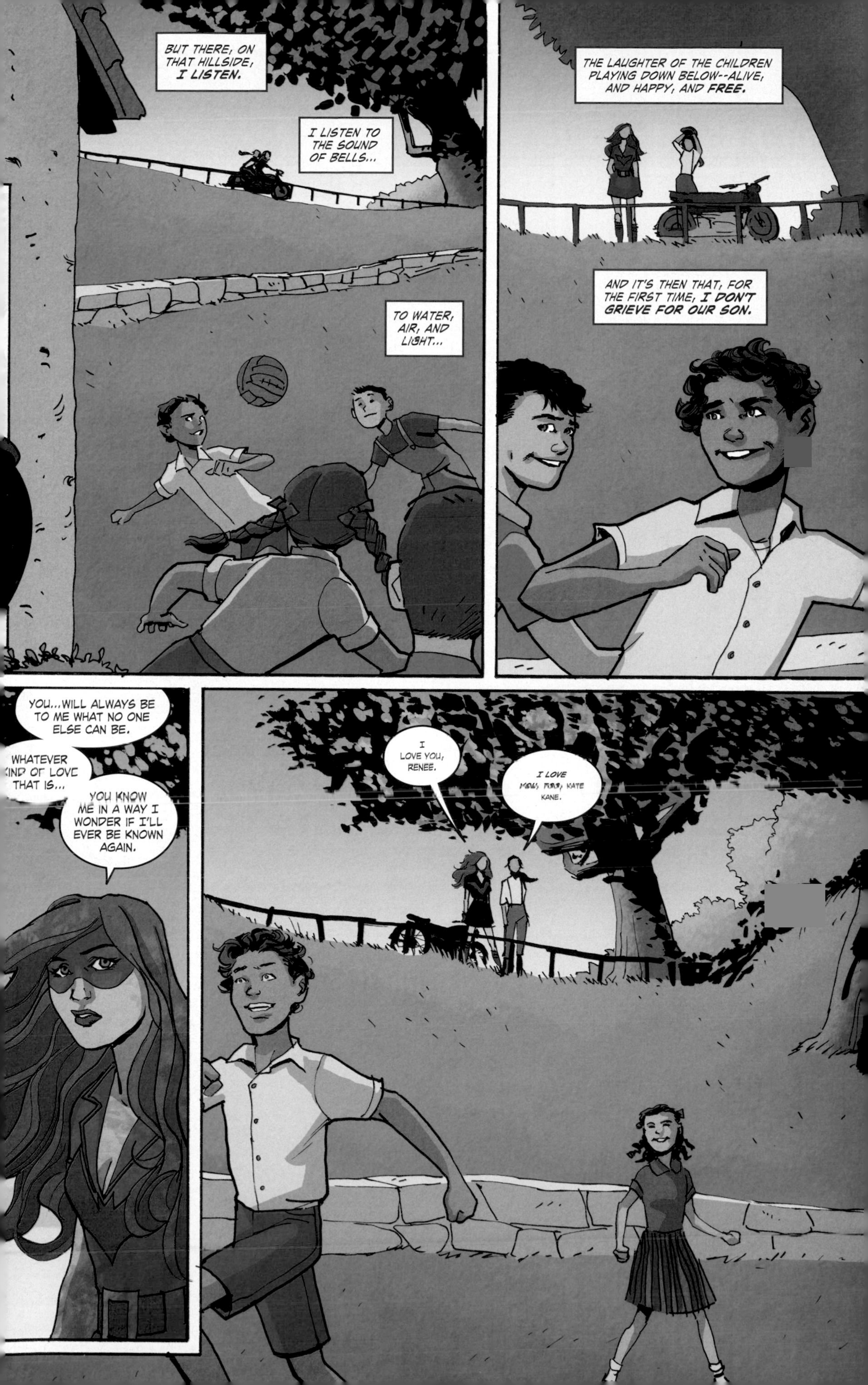

BUT THERE, ON THAT HILLSIDE, I LISTEN.
I LISTEN TO THE SOUND OF BELLS...
TO WATER, AIR, AND LIGHT...
THE LAUGHTER OF THE CHILDREN PLAYING DOWN BELOW--ALIVE, AND HAPPY, AND FREE.
AND IT'S THEN THAT, FOR THE FIRST TIME, I DON'T GRIEVE FOR OUR SON.
YOU...WILL ALWAYS BE TO ME WHAT NO ONE ELSE CAN BE.
WHATEVER KIND OF LOVE THAT IS...
YOU KNOW ME IN A WAY I WONDER IF I'LL EVER BE KNOWN AGAIN.
I LOVE YOU, RENEE.
I LOVE
KATE KANE.

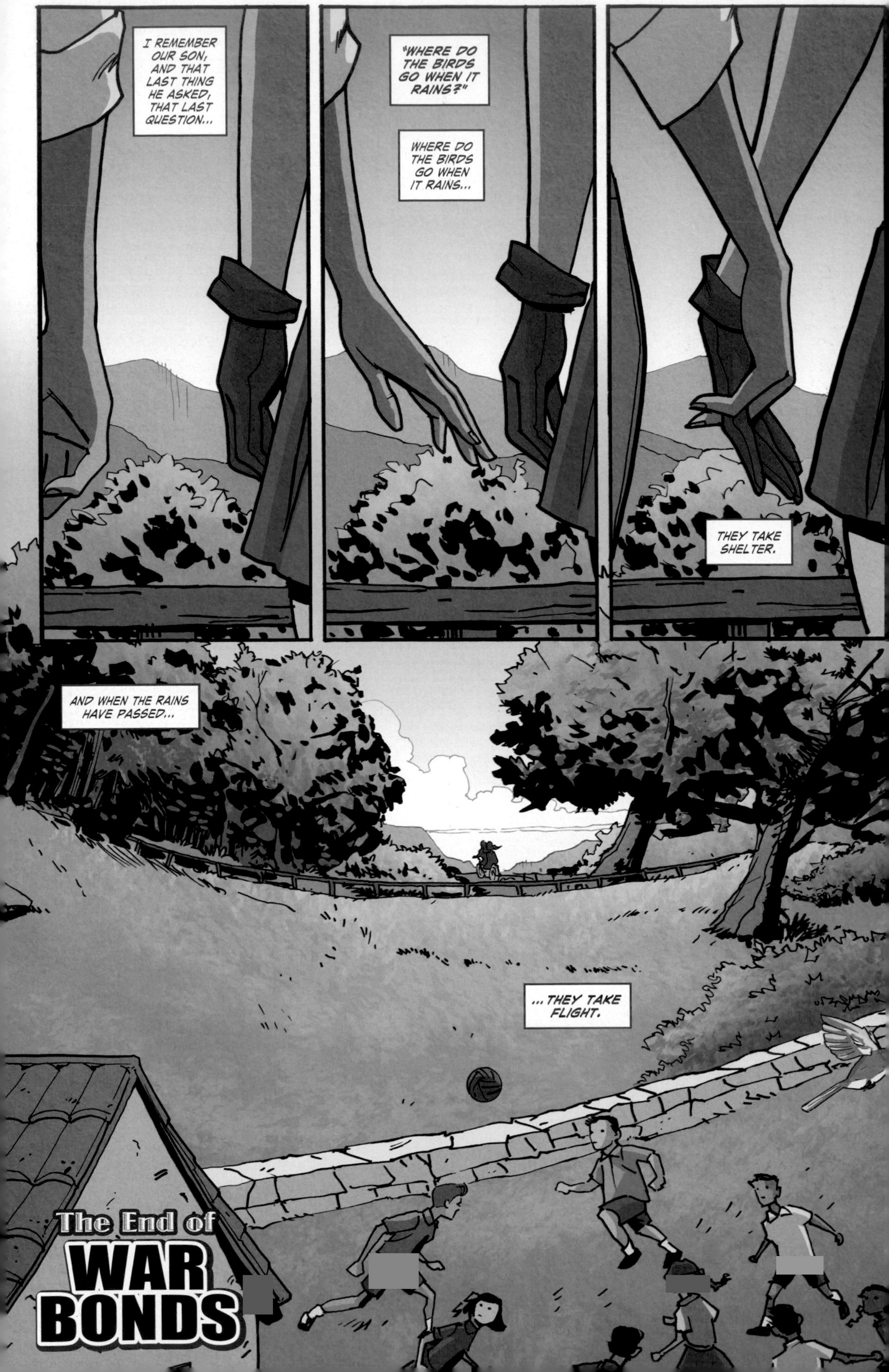
I REMEMBER OUR SON, AND THAT LAST THING HE ASKED, THAT LAST QUESTION...
"WHERE DO THE BIRDS GO WHEN IT RAINS?"
WHERE DO THE BIRDS GO WHEN IT RAINS...
THEY TAKE SHELTER.
AND WHEN THE RAINS HAVE PASSED...
...THEY TAKE FLIGHT.
The End of WAR BONDS

ISIS and SHAZAM concept sketches by SIYA OUM

BOMBSHELLS: UNITED #7 cover sketches by EMANUELA LUPACCHINO

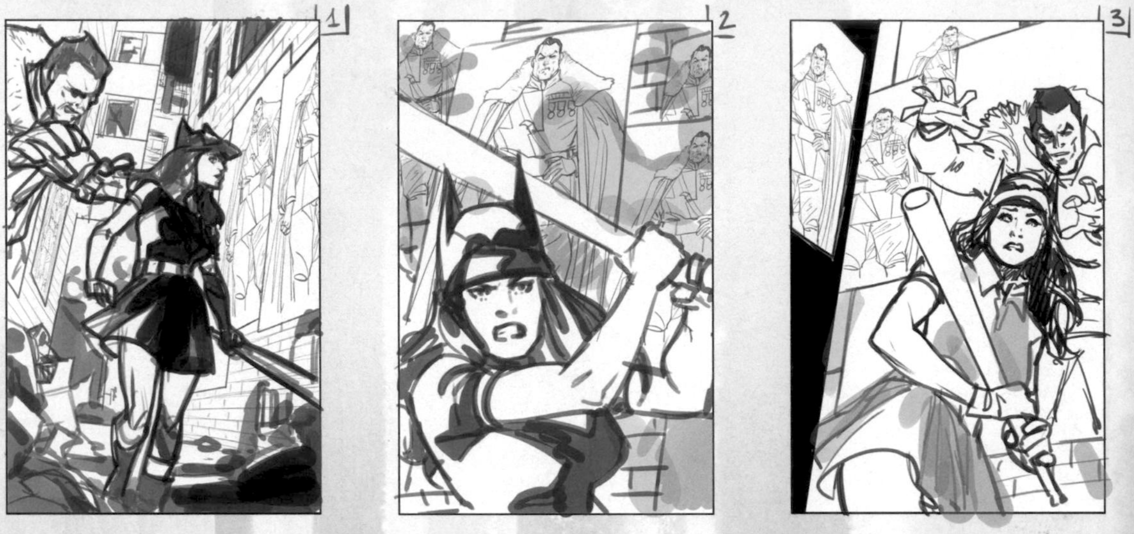
1
2
3

BOMBSHELLS: UNITED #8 cover sketches by TERRY DODSON

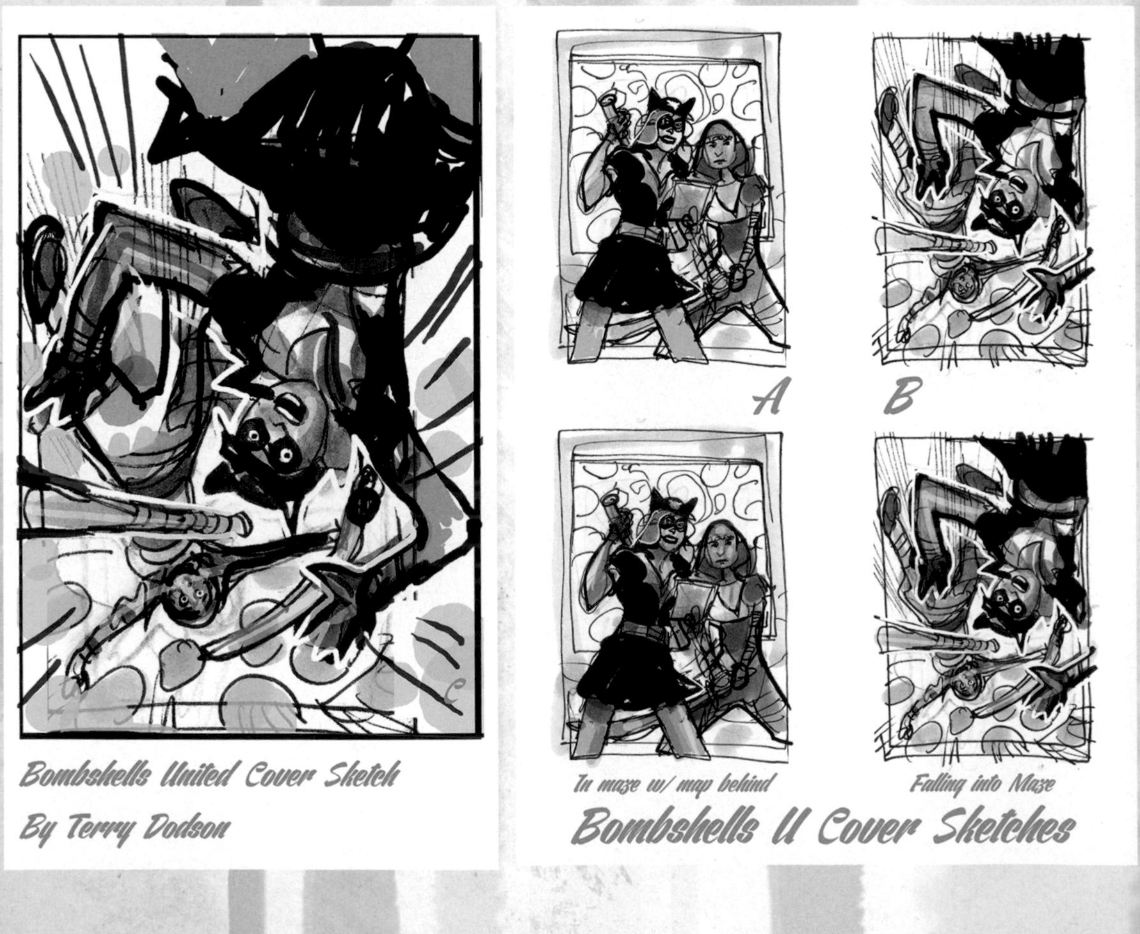
Bombshells United Cover Sketch
By Terry Dodson
A
B
In maze w/ map behind
Falling into Maze
Bombshells U Cover Sketches

BOMBSHELLS: UNITED #9 cover sketches by EMANUELA LUPACCHINO

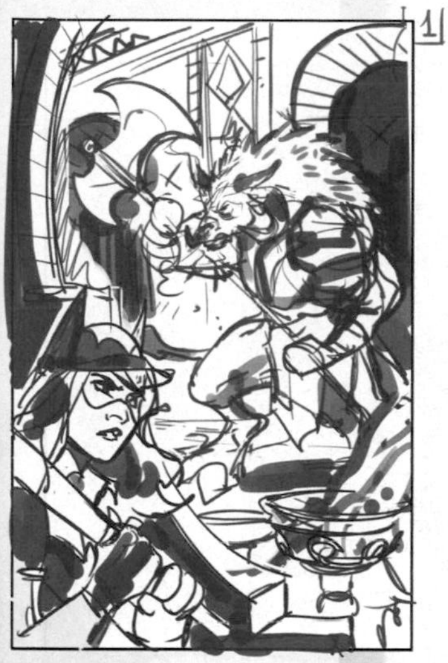
1

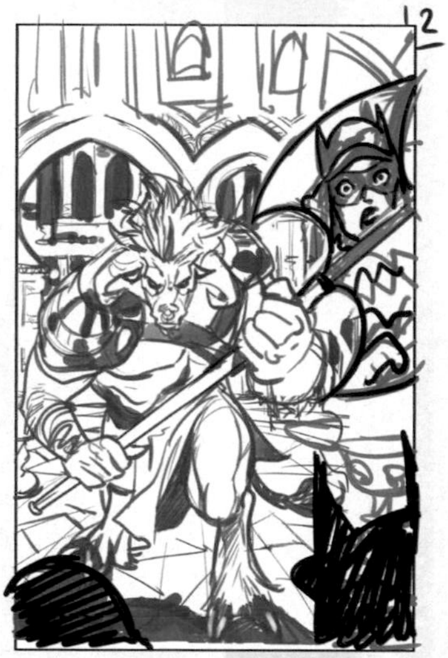
2

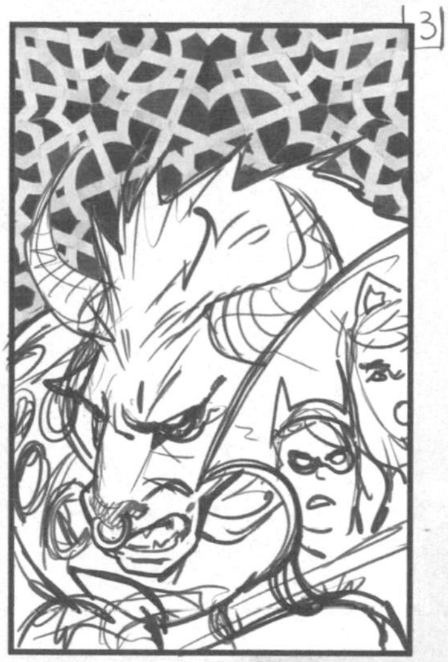
3

BOMBSHELLS: UNITED #10 cover sketches by TERRY DODSON

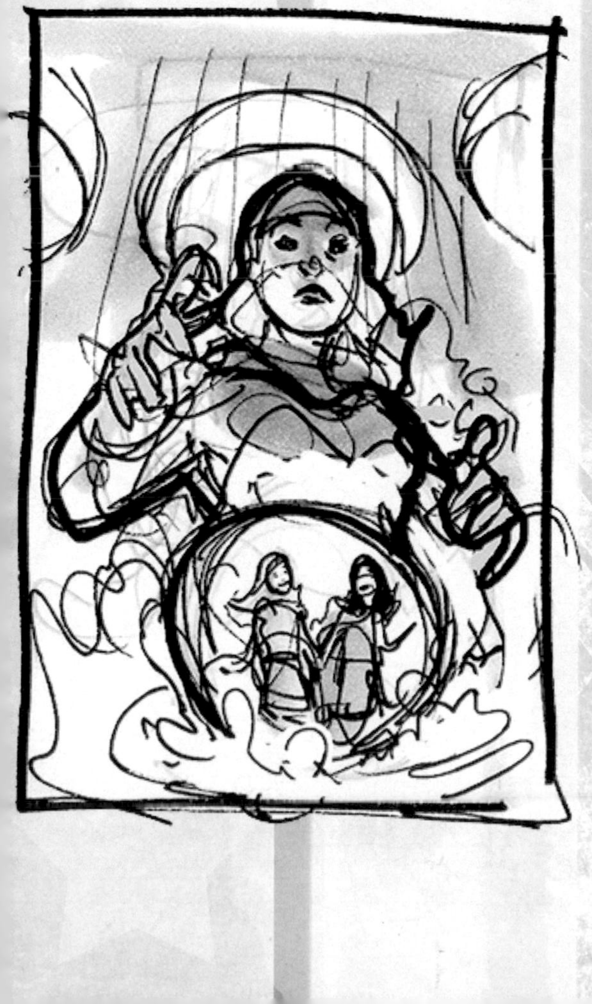

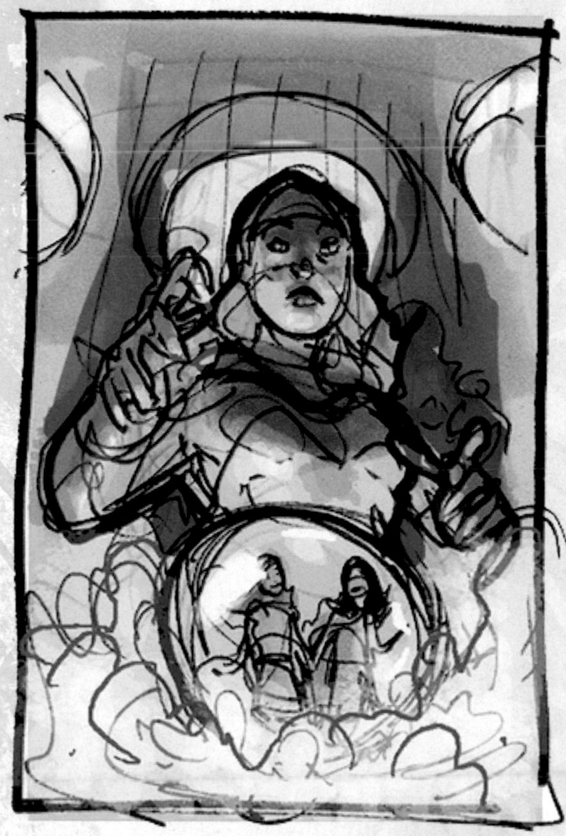

BOMBSHELLS: UNITED #11 cover sketches by TERRY DODSON

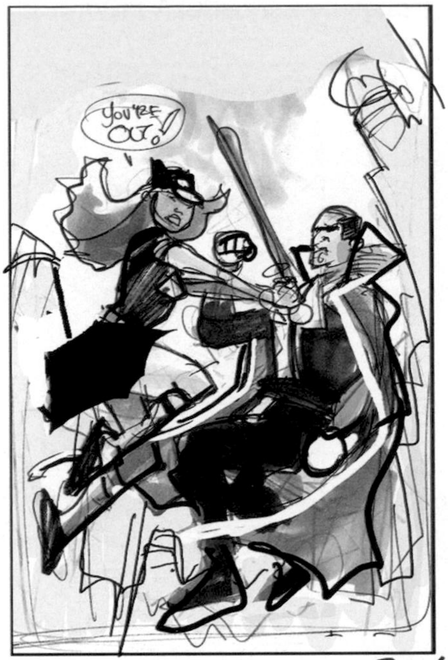
YOU'RE OUT!

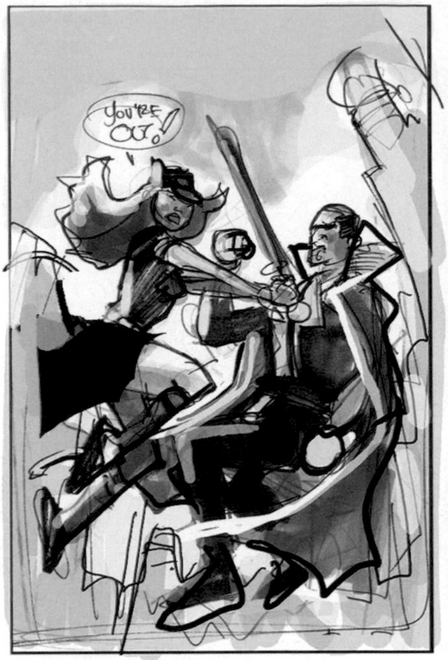
YOU'RE OUT!

Bombshells United Number Eleven

Cover Sketch by Terry Dodson

BOMBSHELLS: UNITED #12 cover sketches by SANDY JARRELL

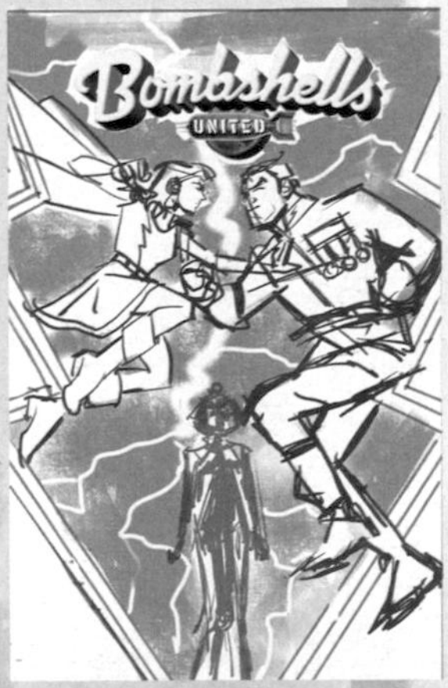
Bombshells
UNITED

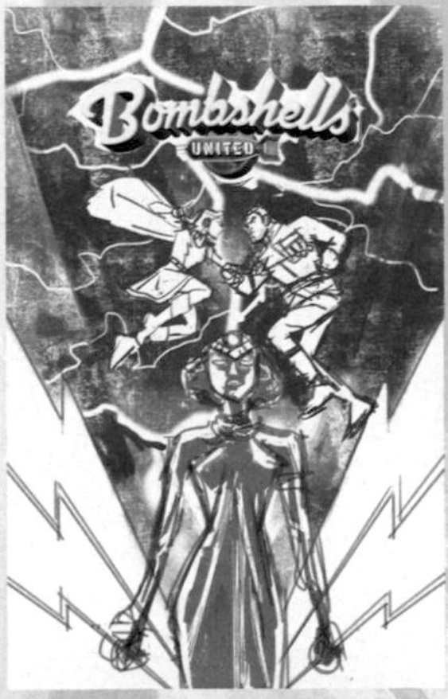
Bombshells
UNITED

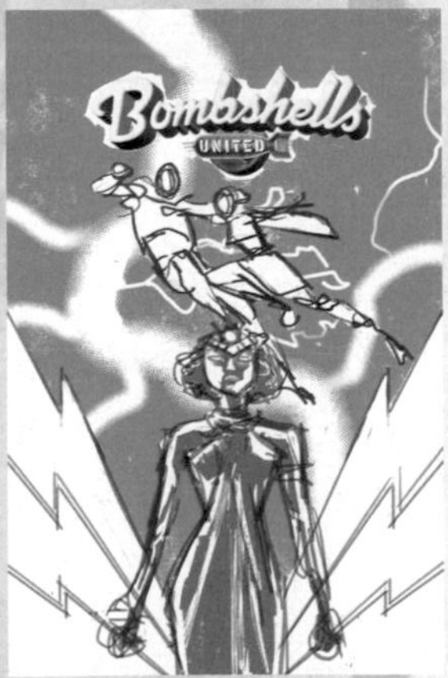
Bombshells
UNITED

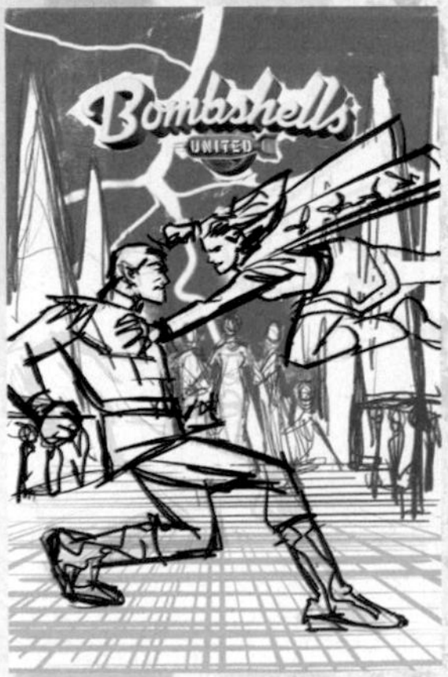
Bombshells
UNITED

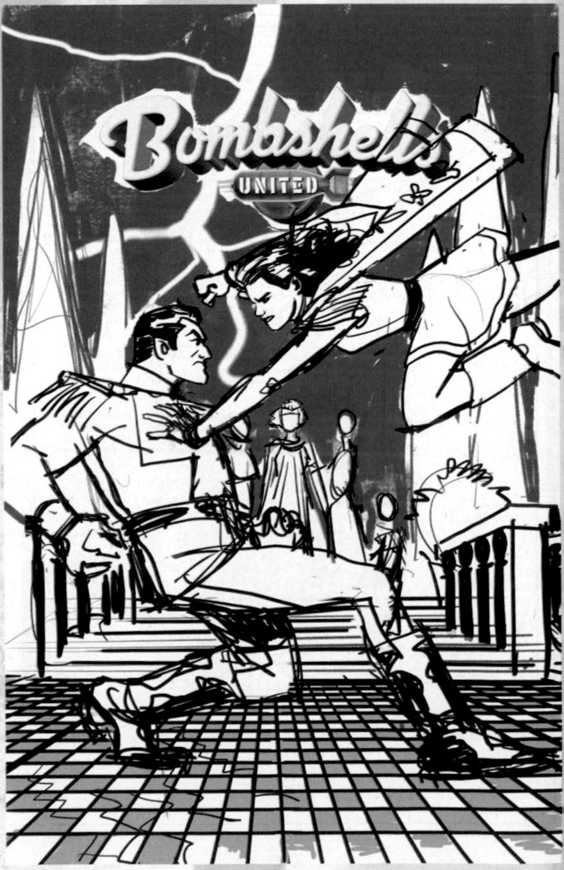
Bombshells
UNITED

BOMBSHELLS: UNITED #8 layouts by MIRKA ANDOLFO

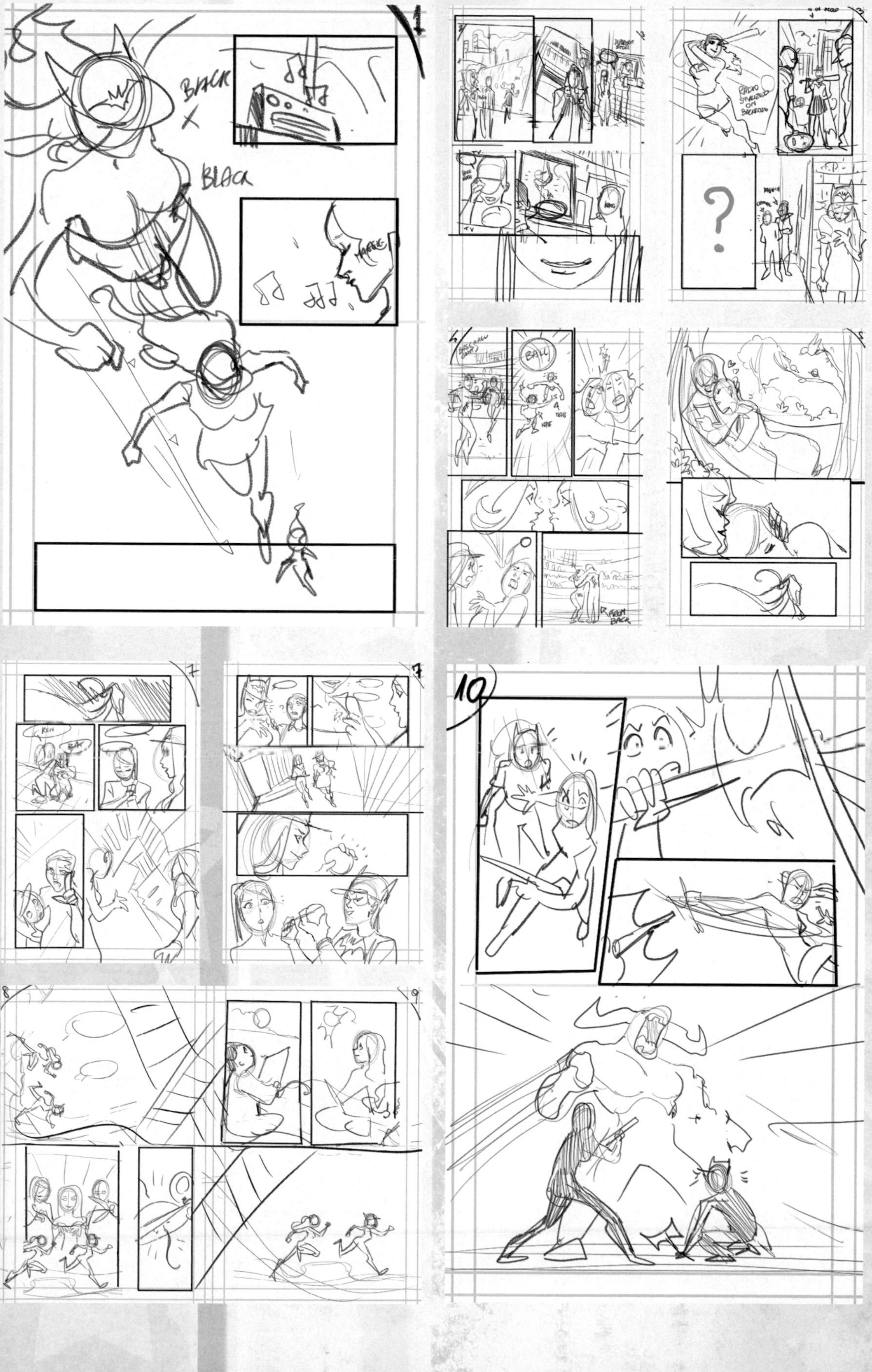
BLACK
BLACK

BOMBSHELLS: UNITED #9 layouts by SIYA OUM

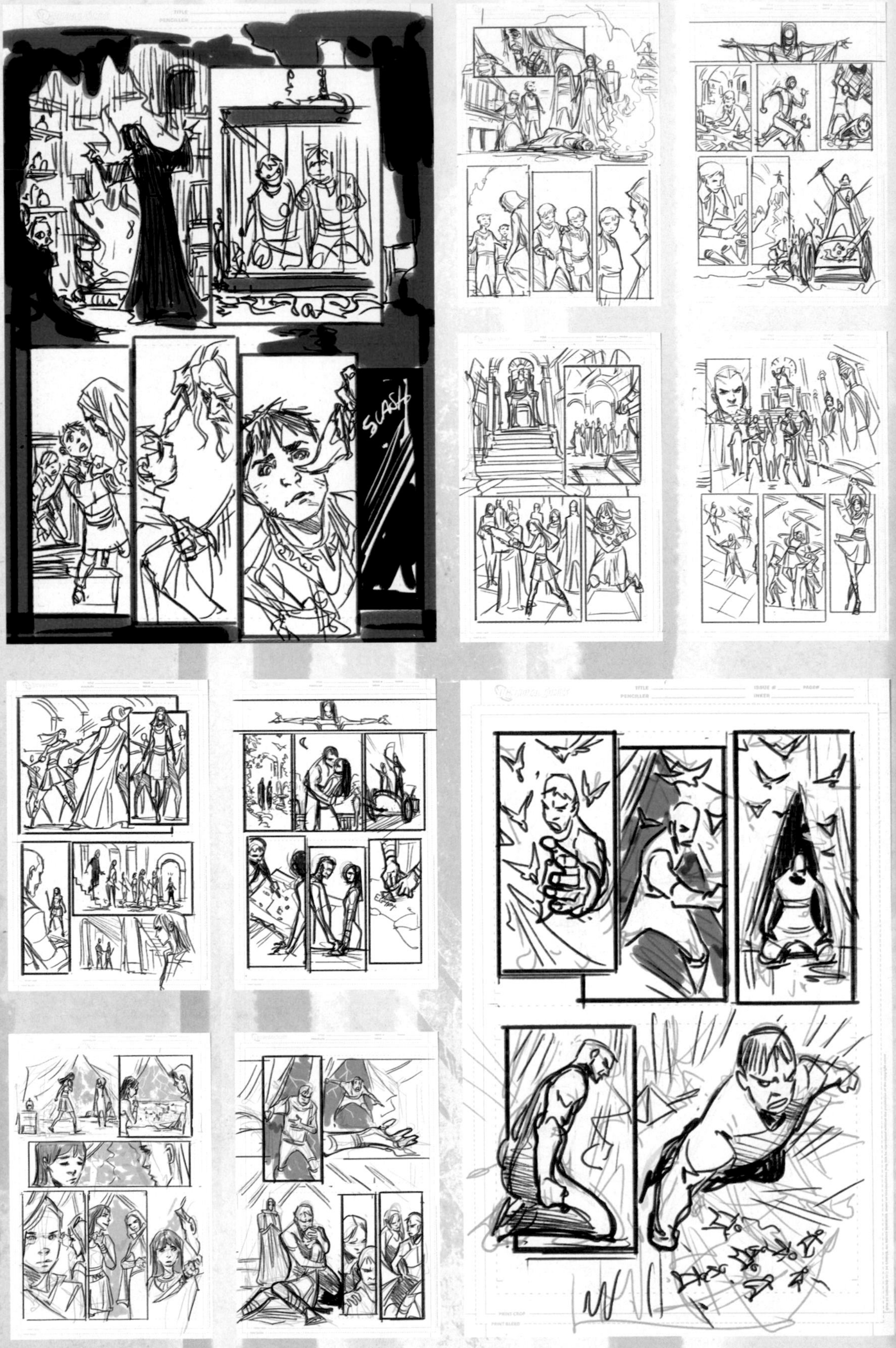
SLASH

BOMBSHELLS: UNITED #10 layouts by DAVID HAHN

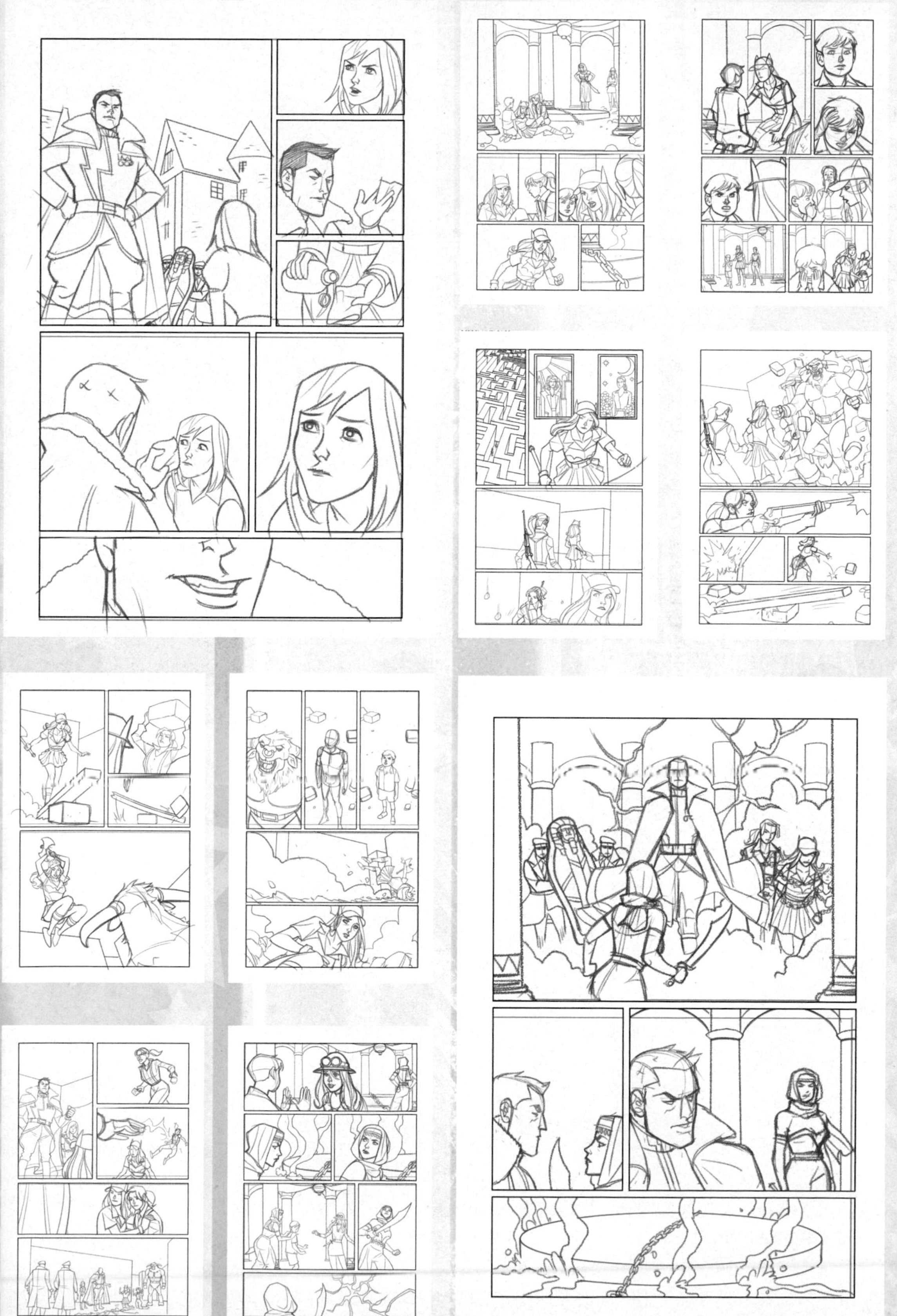

"These are strong, realized women capable of wondrous feats, and Bennett ensures that they remain the heroes of their own stories."
–IGN

"BOMBSHELLS is a win for both female characters and female creators, and that double victory is well worth celebrating."
–NEWSARAMA

DC COMICS
Bombshells
VOLUME 1
ENLISTED
She Can Do It!
Marguerite
BENNETT
Marguerite
SAUVAGE

DC COMICS
BOMBSHELLS
MARGUERITE BENNETT and MARGUERITE SAUVAGE

DC COMICS
Bombshells
Marguerite
BENNETT
Laura
BRAGA
Mirka
ANDOLFO
VOLUME 2
ALLIES

DC COMICS BOMBSHELLS VOL. 2: ALLIES

Marguerite BENNETT Mirka ANDOLFO Laura BRAGA
DC COMICS
Bombshells
VOLUME 3
UPRISING

DC COMICS BOMBSHELLS VOL. 3: UPRISING

READ THE ENTIRE EPIC

DC COMICS BOMBSHEL
VOL. 4: QUEE

DC COMICS BOMBSHEL
VOL. 5: THE DEATH OF ILLUSIO

DC COMICS BOMBSHEL
VOL. 6: WAR STORI

Get more DC graphic novels wherever comics and books are sold!

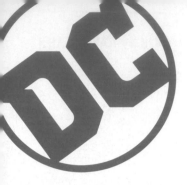

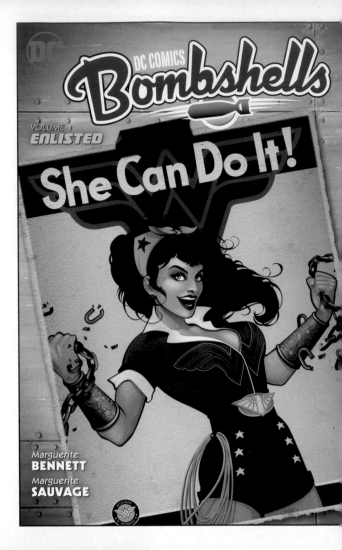

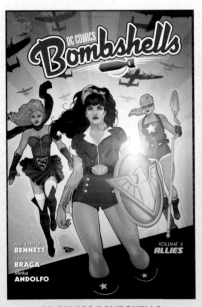

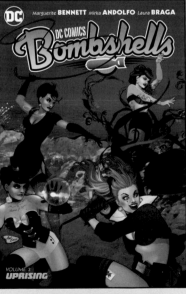